RUNDEL
LIBRARY
FOUNDATION
IN HONOR
OF
Peter Z. Allen

FROM DOLLY GRAY TO SARIE MARAIS

The Boer War in Popular Memory

FROM DOLLY GRAY TO SARIE MARAIS

The Boer War in Popular Memory

Michael Rice

Fischer Press
PO Box 38
Noordhoek
7979

First published 2004

ISBN: 0-620-32160-1
Proof reader: Magdel Palm
Cover design: Julia Raynham
Book design: Sarah-Anne Raynham
Typesetting: Gretel Eastwood
Typeset in Minion 11pt on 13.5pt
Printed by ABC Press, Cape Town

In association with Severn House Publishers
9–15 High Street, Sutton, Surrey SM1 1DF, England.

ISBN: 0 7278 9130 8

CONTENTS

AN IMPERIAL LIGHT HORSE-MAN
A NOVEL
BLORE
823 Blo
PEARSON
A DASH FROM DIAMOND CITY
823 Fen
GREATER BRITAIN
ALFRED H. MILES
FRIEND OR FOE?
BURROW
ONE OF THE FIGHTING SCOUTS
CAPT. F. S. BRERETON
TOMMY CORNSTA
J. H. M. ABBOTT
823 Abb
LONGMANS
With Buller in Natal
823 Hen
G.A.Henty

ACKNOWLEDGEMENTS

This book has been long in the making. I need to thank many people. Stephen Gray who had the idea in the first place. Graham Walker and Tessa de Graaf ex-colleagues at the Johannesburg College of Education, Sheila du Plessis of the Department of History at UNISA and Anton Gouverneur, historian and librarian for their intellectual and technical support. The staff of the Strange Collection, Johannesburg Public Library, the Gubbins Library at the University of the Witwatersrand, the Harold Holmes Library at the Johannesburg College of Education, the Rand Afrikaans University Library and the Transvaal Education Department Library in Pretoria, where in former times Winston Churchill was a guest of the Transvaal Republic for a short time. Lorraine Cox for editing the text. Sarah-Ann Raynham for the design and Julia Raynham for designing the cover. My daughter Gretel for setting the text. Elbert Visser for seeing the final product through production. And, lastly, my patient wife, Ruth.

I wish to express my gratitude to the following copyright holders, publishers and institutions for permission to quote or use illustrations from the works and manuscript collections listed below. Every effort has been made to trace the holder of copyright in works from which substantial quotations appear. Where copyright has been inadvertently infringed, I wish to tender my apologies.

Bancroft, F., *The Veldt Dwellers* (London: Hutchinson, 1912), *Thane Brandon* (London: Hutchinson, 1913) and *The Brandons* (London: Stanley Paul, 1923); Bernstein, Birch, *Tomorrow is Another Day* (Cape Town: Juta, 1951); Blackburn, Douglas, *A Burgher Quixote* (Edinburgh: Blackwood, 1903); Bosman, Herman Charles, *Mafeking Road* ('Mafeking Road', 'The Rooinek') *Unto Dust* ('Peaches Ripening in the Sun', 'The Traitor's Wife', 'The Affair at Ysterspruit', (Cape Town: Human & Rousseau, 1963, 1969); Brandt, Johanna, *The Petticoat Commando* or *Boer Women in Secret Service* (London: Mills &

Boon, 1913); Brecht, Bertolt, *Threepenny Novel* (New York: Grove, 1937); Cathcart, Vera, *Men for Pieces* (London: John Long, 1927); Cloete, Stuart, *Rags of Glory* (New York: Collins 1963); Cossins, George, *A Boer of To-day: A Story of the Transvaal* (London: Allen, 1900); Crisp, Robert, *The Outlanders* (St Albans: Mayflowr Books, 1974); Denton, Kit, *The Breaker* (Sydney: Angus & Robertson, 1973); De Wet, Sampie, *Nine Stories* 'Concentration Camp' (Cape Town: Balkema, 1956); Drummond, Edna, *The Burning Land* (Cape Town: Parnell, 1979); Eden, Dorothy, *Seige in the Sun* (London: Hodder & Stoughton, 1967); Emmanuel, Victor Rousseau, *Derwent's Horse* (London: Metheun, 1901); Galsworthy, John, *In Chancery* (Harmondsworth: Penguin, 1967); Gibbs, Henry, *The Splendour and the Dust* (London: Jarrolds, 1955), *The Winds of Time* (London: Jarrolds, 1956), *Thunder at Dawn* (London: Jarrolds, 1957), *The Tumult and the Shouting* (London: Jarrolds, 1957); Graves, Clothilde Inez Augusta Mary (pseud. Richard Dehan) *The Dop Doctor* (London: Heinemann, 1910); Griffith, George, *Briton or Boer?: A Tale of the Fight for Africa* (London: F.V. White, 1897); Haggard, Henry Rider, *Jess: A Tale of the Transvaal* (London: Smith Elder, 1887); Hemyng, Samuel Bracebridge, *Jack Harkaway in the Transvaal*, or *Fighting for the Flag* (London: E.J. Brett, 1902), *Jack Harkaway's War Scouts among Boer Guerrillas* (London: E.J. Brett, 1902); Henty G. A., *With Buller in Natal* or *A Born Leader* (London: Blackie, 1901); Kipling, Rudyard, *Land and Sea Tales for Scouts and Guides* ('The Way that He Took') (London: Macmillan, 1923), *Traffics and Discoveries* ('The Captive', 'A Sahib's War', 'The Comprehension of Private Copper') (London: Macmillan, 1904) 'Fables for the Staff' ('King Log and King Stork' (24 March 1900), 'The Elephant and the Lark's Nest' (26 March 1900), 'The Persuasive Pom-Pom' (28 March 1900), 'Vain Horses' (29 March 1900), 'Untitled' (30 March 1900), 'Untitled' 31 March 1900) (Bloemfontein: *The Friend*); Laycock, Arthur, *Steve, the Outlander: A Romance of South Africa* (London: Digby Long, 1900); Leipoldt, C. Louis, *Stormwrack* (Cape Town: Philip, 1980); Meade L.T., *A Sister of the Red Cross: A Tale of the South African War* (London: Nelson, 1900); Mitford, Bertram, *Aletta: A Tale of the Boer Invasion* (London: F.V. White: 1900); Moor, Charlotte, *Marina de la Rey* (London: Digby, Long, 1903); Muir, Daphne, A Virtuous Woman (London: Chatto & Windus, 1929); Munnik, G.G., *Major Greville, V.C.: A Tale of the Great Boer War* (Cape Town: Maskew Miller, 1913); Munro, H H., *The Novels and Plays of Saki* ('Alice in Pall Mall') (London: John Lane, 1949); Nash, Thirza, *The Geyer Brood* (London: Cassell, 1946); Nathan, Manfred, *Sarie Marais: A Romance of the Anglo-Boer War* (Johannesburg: Central News Agency, 1938); Nisbet, Hume, *For Right and England: A Story of the South African War* (1899–1900) (London:F.V. White, 1900); Padfield, Peter,

Gold Chains of Empire (London: Hutchinson, 1982); Parker, Gilbert, *The Judgement House* (London: Methuen, 1913); Pearsall, Ronald, *Tides of War* (London: Joseph, 1978) and *The Worm-in-the-Bud* (Harmonsworth: Pelican, 1971); Prance, C.R., *Tante Rebella's Saga* ('Tante Rebella's Saga', 'Between Two Stools', 'A Transvaal Ulysses') (London: Witherby, 1937); Rooke, Daphne, *Mittee* (London, Gollancz, 1951); Rose, F. Horace, *Haidee* (London: Hodder and Stoughton, 1917); Schreiner, Olive, 'Eighteen-Ninety-Nine' in *A Century of South African Short Stories*, Jean Marquard, ed. (Johannesburg: Donker, 1978); Scully, W.C., *The Harrow* (Cape Town, Nasionale Pers, 1921); Seed, Jenny, *The Red Dust Soldiers* (London: Heinemann, 1972); Sinclair, Kathleen, (pseud. Brigid Knight) *Walking the Whirlwind* (London: Cassell, 1940) and *The Sun Climbs Slowly* (London: Cassell, 1942); Smith, Wilbur A., *The Sound of Thunder* (London: Heinemann, 1966); Stables, Gordon, *On War's Red Tide: A Tale of the Boer War* (London: James Nisbet, 1900); Vaughan, Owen, *Old Fireproof: Being the Chaplain's Story* (London: Duckworth, 1906); Viljoen, General Ben, *Under the Vierkleur: A Romance of a Lost Cause* (Boston: Small, Maynard, 1904); Wilhelm, Peter, *L.M. and Other Stories* ('Homecoming') (Johannesburg: Ravan, 1975); Wyllarde, Dolf, *The Story of Eden* (London: Heinemann, 1903); Young, Francis Brett, *Second Mercury Story Book* ('A Message') (London: Longman, 1931)and *The City of Gold* (London: Heinemann, 1939); Arnold, Matthew, *The Poems of Matthew Arnold* (London: [Oxford University Press, 1913); Buchan, John, *Prester John* (London: Nelson, 1961); Chapman, Michael, *A Century of South African Poetry* (Johannesburg: Donker, 1981); Cohen, Morton, *Rudyard Kipling to Rider Haggard* (London: Hutchinson, 1965); Hughes, Thomas, *Tom Brown's School Days* (London: Dent, 1875); Kipling, Rudyard, *Rudyard Kipling's Verse* (London: Hodder & Stoughton 1912.); Melville, Herman, *Billy Budd, Sailor and Other Stories* (Harmondsworth: Penguin, 1976); Monsarrat, Nicholas, *The Cruel Sea* (Cadet ed.) London: Cassell, 1953); Newbolt, Henry, *The Book of the Long Trail* (London: Longmans, 1922); Schreiner, Olive, *The Story of an African Farm* (London: Collins, 1965); Tennyson, Alfred Lord, *The Complete Works of Alfred, Lord Tennyson* (London: Macmillan, 1900); Wilde, Oscar, *The Importance of Being Earnest* (Harmondsworth: Penguin, 1963); Anderson, Rachel, *The Purple Heart Throbs: The Sub-literature of Love* (London: Hodder & Stoughton, 1974); Buchanan-Gould, Vera, *Not Without Honour: The Life and Writings of Olive Schreiner* (London: Hutchinson, 1948); *English in Africa*, Grahamstown, Vol. 5 No. 1 (March 1978) and Vol. 6 No. 1 (March 1979); *FAK-Volksbundel vir Suid-Afrika* saamgestel deur Dr Hugo Gutsche, W.J. du P. Erlank, S.H. Eyssen, (Pretoria: De Bussey, 1938) for the words to 'Sarie Marais';

Fussell, Paul, *The Great War and Modern Memory* (London: University Press, 1975); Gardner, Susan, 'From Murder to Martyr: The Legend of 'Breaker Morant' *Critical Arts Monograph*, No. 1, Johannesburg (July 1981); Gray, Stephen, *Southern African Literature: An Introduction* (Cape Town: Philip, 1979); Hammond, Dorothy and Jablow, Alta, *The Africa That Never Was* (New York: Twayne, 1970); Howarth, Patrick, *Play Up and Play the Game: The Heroes of Popular Fiction* (London: Eyre Metheun, 1973); James, Louis, *Fiction for the Working Man* (1830–1850) (Harmondsworth: Penguin, 1974); Rutherford, Andrew, *The Literature of War* (London: Macmillan, 1978); Schreiner, S. C. Cronwright (ed) *The Letters of Olive Schreiner* (London: Fisher Unwin, 1924); Van Wyk Smith, M., Drummer Hodge: *The Poetry of the Anglo-Boer War* (1899–1902) (Oxford: Clarendon Press, 1978); Bidwell, Maude, 'Sulk or Duty' (pamphlet), *Pen Pictures of the Past*, ed. Karel Scoeman (Cape Town: Human & Rousseau, 1986); Brady Rev. J.E., *Trekking for Souls* (Cedra Missionary Association of Mary Immaculate, St Joseph's Scholasticate, 1952); Buchan, John, *Memory Holds the Door* (London: Hodder & Stoughton, 1941); Doyle, A. Conan, *The War in South Africa* (London: Smith, Elder, 1902); Farwell, Byron, *Queen Victoria's Little Wars* (London: Allen Lane, 1973) and *The Great Boer War* (London: Allen Lane, 1977); Haggard, Henry, Rider, *The Last Boer War* (London: Kegan Paul, 1900); Koss, Stephen (ed.) *The Pro-Boers* (Chicago: University of Chicago Press, 1973); Kruger, Rayne, *Goodbye, Dolly Gray* (London: Mentor, 1967); Marais, Eugene, N., unpublished letter dated 22 February 1897 (National English Literary Museum and Documentation Centre, Grahamstown); Midgely, J.F., *Petticoat in Mafeking: The letters of Ada Cook* (Kommetjie: J.F. Midgely, 1974); Pakenham Thomas, *The Boer War* (Johannesburg: Jonathan Ball, 1979) and *The Scramble for Africa* (Johannesburg: Jonathan Ball, 1991); Pearsall, Ronald, *The Worm in the Bud* (Harmondsworth: Pelican, 1971); Ralph, Julian, *War's Brighter Side* (London: Pearson, 1901); Reitz, Deneys, *Commando* (London: Faber & Faber, 1935); Sandison, Alan, *The Wheel of Empire* (New York: Macmillan, 1967); Sandys, Celia, *Wanted, Dead or Alive* (London: Harper Collins, 1999); and *My Early Life* (London: Harper Collins, 1999); Schreiner, Olive, *Thoughts on South Africa* (London: Allen & Unwin, 1923); Stead, W.T., *Shall I Slay My Brother Boer?* (London: Review of Reviews, 1897); Streak, Michael, *The Afrikaner as Viewed by the English* (1795–1854) (Cape Town: Struik,1974); Tuchman, Barbara, *The Proud Tower* (London: Hamilton, 1966).

A Sister of the Red Cross
A Story of Ladysmith
by L.T. Meade

AN IMPERIAL LIGHT HORSEMAN
HAROLD BLORE

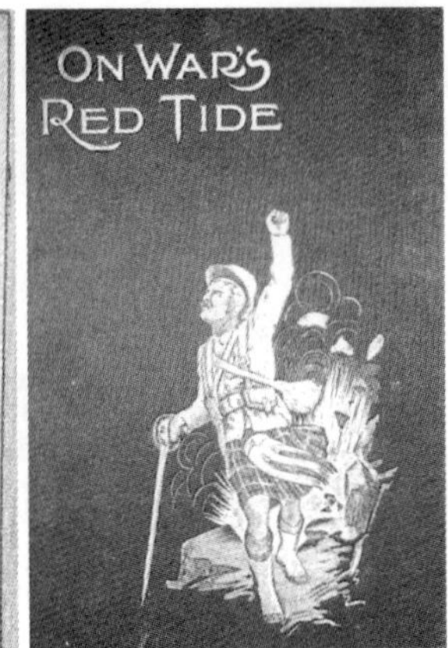
ON WAR'S RED TIDE

Charge!
or Briton and Boer
By G. MANVILLE FENN

ONE OF THE FIGHTING SCOUTS
CAPT F.S. BRERETON

Dick Dale
TOM BEVAN

On The Heels Of De Wet.

EDGAR WALLACE
UNOFFICIAL DISPATCHES
of the Anglo-Boer War

With Buller in Natal
G·A·Henty

INTRODUCTION

As Tommy Atkins[1] left England and embarked for South Africa in 1899, he sang to the girl he left behind:

> Goodbye Dolly I must leave you,
> Though it breaks my heart to go,
> Something tells me I am needed
> At the front to fight the foe.

But the 'call of empire' and the sights and sounds of men marching off to war had their own attractions:

> See, the soldier boys are marching,
> And I can no longer stay –
> Hark! I hear the bugle calling,
> Goodbye Dolly Gray.[2]

Few of those joining up realised they were bidding farewell to more than just their sweethearts. The Second Anglo-Boer War of 1899–1902 was a major turning point in history heralding the end of a reign, a century, and a way of life. It also kicked off the twentieth century with some of what would become all too familiar horrors and metaphors in literature: the concentration camp and guerrilla warfare.

The Queen's Silver Jubilee a few years earlier had given vent to fervent and widespread patriotism. Beatrice Webb wrote in her diary: 'Imperialism is in the air, all classes [are] drunk with sightseeing and hysterical with loyalty.'[3] Yet, for all the revelling in imperial pomp and power, a feeling of unease was festering beneath the complacent surface of Victorian life. Nor does one have to look further than the newspapers, music hall songs, and popular literature to find that behind the façade of smug self-confidence, a more sombre mood was brooding.

Retired generals grumbled in *The Times* about the rise of socialism. Young women were agitating for the vote and for admission to the universities. Oscar Wilde's trial had lifted the lid briefly on things it was best not to think about. In the colonies the natives were becoming increasingly restive. First the Zulus at Isandhlwana and then the Matabeles in the Chartered Territory had the temerity to challenge British rule. Moreover, closer to home England's economic domination was being seriously threatened by America and Germany. The old order was changing. To many patriotic Englishmen, it appeared unlikely to change for the better.

Towards the end of the century, many of England's sons rose to the task of defending their country, not least among whom were a whole host of writers who appealed to the newly literate. Thanks to a century of increasing literacy, the 'penny horrible'[4] shaped mass opinion on a scale matched only by the popular press. The tone was convinced, patronising, and yet strangely ambivalent.

Popular songs also caught the mood. This was an age that took itself seriously; duty before pleasure. The 'assumption of empire' was not taken lightly. Dolly Gray articulated the soldier's regret at having to part from his girl. But, the bugle called and reminded him of Britain's responsibilities and the need to defend the Pax Britannica.

On the other hand, Sarie Marais[5] embodied the nostalgia of the Boer on commando for the girl with whom he identified his 'volk en vaderland' (nation and fatherland).

My Sarie Marais is so ver van my hart,
Maar'k hoop om haar weer te sien.
Sy het in die wyk van die Mooirivier gewoon,
Nog voor die oorlog het begin.
O bring my terug na die ou Transvaal,
Daar waar my Sarie woon.
Daar onder in die mielies by die groen doringboom,
Daar woon my Sarie Marais.

My Sarie Marais is so far from my heart,
But I hope to see her again.
She lived in the area of the Mooi River,

Just before the war had begun.
Oh take me back to the old Transvaal,
There where my Sarie lives.
There by the mealies at the green thorn tree,
There's where my Sarie Marais lives.

Sarie and the Transvaal Republic are inseparable, but there is more to the song than that. Sarie Marais was written after the Boers' defeat by the British in 1902, and appeared in its present form only in 1919. It is essentially a song about a lost cause. Its function was to remind the 'volk' of everything they had lost, and was an appeal to keep that memory – the memory of the 'khakis' and the POW camps on St Helena and Ceylon – alive in Afrikaner mythology.

In important – if unstated – ways, 'Dolly Gray' and 'Sarie Marais' did what popular songs and popular literature have always done: they captured and expressed the popular mood, the spirit of the times, what people were thinking or feeling – or were supposed to be thinking or feeling – in any given era.

This book is about such popular literature (the equivalent perhaps of our airport paperbacks today) and the insights such literature gives about the world beyond its pages.

The role of popular fiction

Like most modern wars, the conflicts between the Boers and British between 1880 and 1902 spawned their own brand of escapist fiction. A considerable body of largely unrecognised and mostly forgotten fiction about these conflicts has accumulated over the last hundred years. In these stories, writers have revealed (sometimes blatantly, sometimes unconsciously) their ideological positions on war, their social and racial prejudices. Boer War fiction represents a rich source of information for those interested not only in the literary and cultural history of early 20th century South Africa, but also in the eroding traditions of the British Empire. 'Honour' and 'patriotic idealism' ('my country, right or wrong'), which were to be seriously undermined by the Great War of 1914–18, were already beginning to be questioned and challenged during the Anglo-Boer War of 1899–1902.

Because meaning in popular literature tends to be more important than form, the meanings that lie beneath the surface of popular fiction, tend to be much more accessible, more naïve, and less concerned with complexity than the literature associated with so-called high culture. The writers of popular novels are often less self-conscious and less critical of the appearance of things than the authors of what is known as 'serious literature'. The visions of the popular novelists tend to be ones in which good and evil, and right and wrong, are easily identified. Values tend to be fixed and immutable, with little room for ambiguity. Moreover, the authors of 'light romance', adventure stories, and escapist fiction often reveal their attitudes unconsciously. This fiction then can be regarded more or less as a reliable mirror of the feelings and values of the vast mass of ordinary people who read and identified with the stories.

As might be expected, attitudes to the Anglo-Boer conflict have changed with the passage of time. Writing about these attitudes has been as much subject to historical fashion – not to say prejudice – as any other war. These fashions are particularly revealing of the widely held and changing public perceptions of the conflict. For, books directed at the mass market must confirm – not contradict – popular perceptions, if they are going to have wide appeal and achieve sales.

A century of South African literature

Although most of the novels about the Anglo-Boer wars in South Africa fall into the realm of popular escapist fiction, their form and style conformed to the general development of South African literature as a whole. South African literature in general, and Boer War fiction in particular, can be divided into roughly three phases: the imperial phase before World War I; the literature produced between the two world wars; and that written after World War II – the era of apartheid. Each of these phases is characterised by the different ideological preoccupations of the writers.

During the period prior to World War I, the experience of the Empire and a sense that great social, economic and historical changes were pending were the issues that informed South African English fiction. As early as 1883, Olive Schreiner's novel, *The Story of an African Farm* reflected many of the tensions confronting those who struggled to make sense of life, as the 19th century drew to a close. Schreiner's novel is all the more remarkable for the way in which it explored those concerns within the unlikely context of remote farm life in the Karoo.

After World War I, the ideological emphasis shifted from a concentration on matters imperial to the emergent imperatives of the building of a Union of South Africa. Sarah Gertrude Millin's *God's Step-children* (1924) was probably as influential as any in suggesting the direction of English South African fiction for the next two decades. Millin's obsession with the so-called horrors of miscegenation coincided with the ideological preoccupation of many English-speaking authors of the time, who were committed to the notion of the Union of South Africa. Most of them saw this union exclusively in terms of the white population. Two notable exceptions to this view were William Plomer's *Turbott Wolfe* (1926), and Laurens van der Post's *In a Province* (1934).

After World War II and with the assumption of power by Dr Malan's Nationalist Party in 1948, Alan Paton's *Cry, the Beloved Country* (1948) charted the direction that has been followed by the majority of English-speaking South African writers since then.

Boer War fiction has followed a similar course to South African fiction in general, though the first or imperial phase includes World War I. The second phase extends roughly from 1920 to 1946, while the third phase embraces the literature written since 1948. Each phase reflects a change not only in the way the conflict was perceived, but also in the wider cultural and political preoccupations of the time in which it was written.

The imperial phase: writers rally to the cause

As might be expected, the vast majority of novels and short stories that were written about the Anglo-Boer War were published around the time of the conflict. Some of the titles published then give a fairly accurate impression of the patriotic fervour that found its way into print: B. Ronan, *The Passing of the Boer* (1899); E. Ames, *The Tremendous Twins*, or *How the Boers were Beaten* (1900); C.D. Haskins, *For the Queen in South Africa* (1900); F. Russell, *The Boer's Blunder* (1900); H. Nisbet, *For Right and England* (1900) and *The Empire Makers* (1900). If nothing else, the dates of publication indicate the optimism of these writers that the war would be over as soon as Pretoria was captured; at the very latest by Christmas 1899.

Obviously, Boer War fiction did not represent British imperial fiction in its entirety. Splendid young men kept the Union Jack flying throughout the length and breadth of the literature of Empire. But this fiction gave the literature of imperialism a powerful impulse and a focal point. Imperialism was popular and with it went jingoism.

But, as Alan Sandison has pointed out:[6] 'A wide indulgence in frenetic jingoism is not the symbol of an unworried nation.' Global British power may have been at its zenith in the 1890s, but for all its apparent glory, there was a deep feeling of anxiety about the future. Social change was in the air and the continental powers, especially Germany, appeared to be challenging Britain's position both in Europe and Africa. The British confidently expected the Anglo-Boer War to be a minor skirmish. It was a profound shock to the ordinary person who saw the British army, supposedly the finest in the world, suffering defeat after humiliating defeat at the hands of an enemy of mostly uneducated peasant farmers who were not even dressed in proper uniforms.

The inability of the Commander-in-chief, Lord Kitchener, to bring the war to a satisfactory close; Emily Hobhouse's reports on the concentration camps; the agitation of the pro-Boers in Britain; and President Kruger's wide popularity (he attracted vast crowds of admirers in Europe), all had a negative impact on British self-esteem.

Patriotic writers of such established (if not enduring) reputations as: G.A. Henty, Bertram Mitford, George Griffith, Bracebridge Hemyng, G.M. Fenn, Ernest Glanville, Marie Corelli and Hume Nisbet, rose to the occasion. They set about the task of praising the manly and necessary joys and justice of fighting for the Empire against the Boers.

Among the more notable literary figures of the day who were closely associated with the events of the Anglo-Boer conflict were two future Nobel Prize winners for literature. Rudyard Kipling

(1865–1936), the poet and novelist famous for *The Jungle Book* (1894), *Stalky & Co.* (1899), *Kim* (1901) and the *Just So Stories* (1902) received the Nobel Prize for Literature in 1907. Winston Churchill (1874–1965), – while not remembered for his novels – also received the Nobel Prize in 1953.[7]

Other notable literary figures in Britain who saw service in South Africa included H. Rider Haggard (1856–1925), famous for *King Solomon's Mines* (1885), *She* (1887), and *Alan Quatermain* (1887); Sir Arthur Conan Doyle (1859–1930) the creator of *Sherlock Holmes*; Sir Percy Fitzpatrick (1862–1931), author of *Jock of the Bushveld* (1907); Edgar Wallace (1875–1932), the master of detective fiction; and John Buchan (1875–1940), whose novels include *The Thirty-nine Steps* (1915) and *Greenmantle* (1916). Indeed, none of these writers were lacking in patriotic fervour.

It was Rider Haggard who ran up the Union Jack in Church Square, Pretoria, when Sir Theophilus Shepstone annexed the Transvaal in 1877. In 1900, Haggard published *The Last Boer War* 'so that any who are interested in the matter may read and find in the tale of 1881 the true causes of the war of 1899'.[8] His novel *Jess* (1887), is set in the first Anglo-Boer War. Ironically, when the man on whom it was said he modelled his hero, Alan Quatermain (the hunter F.C. Selous), later revealed himself as pro-Boer, Haggard attacked Selous in *The Times* for what he regarded as his shameful lack of British patriotism. In the ensuing exchange of letters, Selous wrote:[9]

> I have been an appreciative reader of Mr Rider Haggard's works, though I have always thought that the personal humiliation he endured at the time of the retrocession of the Transvaal to the Boers in 1881 had somewhat warped his judgement concerning that people.

Conan Doyle came out to South Africa as a doctor attached to Lord Robert's forces during the Second Anglo-Boer War. Conan Doyle saw service particularly in Bloemfontein, where he played a major role in improving hospital facilities for the troops. A staunch imperialist, he did not write any fiction about the war. He published a number of non-fictional accounts of it in which he purported to place the true facts before the world: *The Great Boer War* (1900) and, subsequently, *The War in South Africa* (1902), when it was discovered that the war had not ended with the capture of Pretoria in June, 1900.

Percy Fitzpatrick, the South African born director of *Rand Mines Limited*, was one of the original conspirators of the Reform Committee implicated in the Jameson Raid of 1896. While in gaol awaiting trial for his part in the conspiracy, Fitzpatrick began *The Transvaal from Within* (1896), in which he vigorously articulated the 'Uitlander' grievances against Kruger's administration. After the war, Fitzpatrick played an important part in the creation of the Union of South Africa.

Edgar Wallace came to South Africa in 1899 and subsequently became the first editor of the now defunct *Rand Daily Mail*. He produced no work of fiction on the war but his *Unofficial Dispatches* (1901), a collection of factual pieces, recorded his experiences of the war as a journalist.

Kipling wrote five short stories about the Second Anglo-Boer War: 'The Way that He Took', which appeared in *Land and Sea Tales for Scouts and Guides* (1923); 'The Captive', 'A Sahib's War', and 'The Comprehension of Private Copper', which are included in *Traffics and Discoveries* (1904), and 'A Burgher of the Free State'. He also helped edit, and contributed to *The Friend* in Bloemfontein during March and April 1900. At a banquet given for Lords Milner and Roberts, Kipling proposed an ironic toast to Kruger, 'who taught the British Empire its responsibilities, and the rest of the world its power, who has filled the seas with the transports and the earth with the tramp of armed men'.[10] For Kipling, as for many of his contemporaries, war was an adventure, an extension of English public-school playing fields.

Churchill – 'He has a reputation for being bumptious'[11] Chamberlain wrote to Milner – covered the war for *The Morning Post*. The event that linked Churchill's name most dramatically to the war was his capture and subsequent escape from the Staatsmodel School in Pretoria, where he had been held prisoner. The reward for his recapture, dead or alive, was £25. He recorded these incidents and others in several autobiographical pieces.

Although the racial theme was present in South African literature at the turn-of-the-century, fiction dealing with the Anglo-Boer Wars (with one notable exception) all but ignored the existence of black people. Only one novelist who wrote about the war at the time, George Cossins in *A Boer of To-day* (1900), admitted to a black-white problem. On the other hand, some writers who were not concerned with the conflict such as Percival Gibbon in his novel *Margaret Harding* (1911), saw the racial issue as the central problem confronting South Africa. His *Souls in Bondage* (1904) describes the supposedly rootless existence of the 'coloureds'. In this he anticipated Sarah Gertrude Millin.

The second phase: between the World Wars

The second phase, from approximately the end of World War I to the end of World War II, saw an interesting ideological shift take place on two fronts. Firstly, the dominant feature of the fiction written at this time was an implicit ideological commitment to the Union of South Africa. There was no longer the certitude about the momentum of historical progress that had typified the earlier fiction. World War I had destroyed all that. In place of confidence, there was now an anxiety about the future; an anxiety given all the more emphasis by the new problems: the 'poor white'; the 1914 rebellion; the 1922 strike and, ultimately, the Depression. The union of the two white groups was seen as the solution to South Africa's problems.

The conflict was depicted essentially as a civil war in which members of the same family had fought on opposite sides but now, for their common good, had to make peace. This was an attitude already anticipated by Francis Bancroft (pseudonym for Francis Carey Slater) in her early novels *The Veldt Dwellers* (1912) and *Thane Brandon* (1913). It was also the major theme in Daphne Muir's *A Virtuous Woman* (1929), Norman McKoewn's *The Ridge of White Waters* (1934), F.A.M. Webster's *African Cavalcade* (1936), as well as Kathleen Sinclair's saga which includes *Walking the Whirlwind* (1940), *The Sun Climbs Slowly* (1942), and *The Covenant* (1944).

The racial theme had to a large extent lain dormant in Boer War fiction during the imperial phase. Now it began to assert itself. Between the wars there was a growing awareness of the specific nature of the racial issue which was destined to become the dominant theme in South African life and literature.

From the 1930s there was a diminishing concern about depicting the causes and consequences of the Anglo-Boer War as dogmatic assertions to be attacked or defended. Coincidentally, there was a tendency to depict the struggle from the Boer point of view, as in W.C. Scully's *The Harrow* (1921), Daphne Muir's *A Virtuous Woman* (1929), and Manfred Nathan's *Sarie Marais* (1938). The emphasis shifted to a focus on individuals caught up by events they did not understand, trying to work out their personal destinies against a backdrop of cataclysmic events. English-speaking writers had fewer axes to grind.

The third phase: the Apartheid era

From 1948, the call for unity between Afrikaner and English remained, but the race issue became increasingly focal. Certainly, race relations are a major preoccupation in Henry Gibbs' four-book saga: *The Splendour and the Dust* (1955), *The Winds of Time* (1956), *Thunder at Dawn* (1957) and *The Tumult and the Shouting* (1957). The same can be said of Daphne Rooke's *Mittee* (1951).

But most writers after 1948 – with some notable exceptions – treated the war largely as the backdrop for historical 'romance' in which ideological issues are avoided as far as possible, while 'good' and 'bad' characters are evenly divided among both sets of protagonists. Such self-conscious even-handedness is to be found particularly in the novels of Sam Manion, *The Great Hunger* (1964); Dorothy Eden, *Siege in the Sun* (1967); Josephine Edgar, *Time of Dreaming* (1968); Diane Pearson, *The Marigold Field* (1970); Jenny Seed, *The Red Dust Soldiers* (1972); Desiree Meyler, *The Gods Are Just* (1973); and Ronald Pearsall, *Tides of War* (1978). At the same time there was a greater interest in addressing such vexed issues as the concentration camps, the effects of martial law, the 'Handsuppers' and the results of the scorched earth policy. It is worth noting that fiction written about the Anglo-Boer War became – apart from the likes of Stuart Cloete and Wilbur Smith – almost completely the preserve of female writers.

The Anglo-Boer War has continued to be a popular subject for escapist fiction, though not nearly to the same extent that it was at the time of the conflict. Whereas the writers at the height of the British

Empire were overwhelmingly British, with the decline of imperialism, the field was dominated by English-speaking South African writers. It is they, more than anyone else, who had an interest in keeping the Anglo-Boer issue alive.

History vs fiction

Whereas the Anglo-Boer War has always provided writers with the opportunity to tell a tale of high adventure in an exotic setting, the distinction between history and fiction was not always as clear-cut as might be imagined. Birch Bernstein states in the foreword to *Tomorrow is Another Day* (1951), sub-titled *An Historical Romance of South Africa – 1652 to the Present Day*, that his 'main object was to recapture the pageant of the years for which the 'romance' was merely a vehicle'. This saga concerns the history of the Wentzel family from shortly after 1652, when the first ancestor arrived in South Africa, and follows the family fortunes up until 1951. It is a monumental work that traces, through the Wentzels, the history of white South Africa.

The American writer of blockbuster sagas, James Michener (*The Covenant*, 1980), was even more ambitious. His story begins 15 000 years ago, and embraces what is meant to be the totality of South African history. Michener used three families to trace and dramatise this: the Nxumalos, the Saltwoods and the Van Doorns, whose ambitions, worldviews and hostilities provide the gist of the story. The tripartite structure of the novel registers an ideological shift that has taken place since 1951, which acknowledges that the white view is not the only view or necessarily the definitive view of South Africa's past.

Robert Crisp's *The Outlanders* (1964), which is less ambitious in scope, merely purported to be 'the true story of the alien invasion of South Africa'. This claim of authenticity did not inhibit the author from inventing conversations between actual historical characters. He also changed accepted historical facts for dramatic convenience, notwithstanding his protestations to the contrary. It is a generally accepted fact that the discovery of gold is ascribed to George Harrison and not to George Walker. Crisp's explanation for the so-called liberties he has taken is worth noting:

> As far as I am concerned everything that happens in these pages, did happen. The men and women who move through them moved through life. If the conversations they had seem unfamiliar to the historian it is, perhaps, because they have hitherto been unrecorded … . There are other instances where my variation of history does not coincide exactly with the accepted version. This has not been done for convenience or to serve a better dramatic effect. The reader may emerge at the end of it feeling that the truth is far from absolute; that it is subject, like so many of the verities, to interpretation.[12]

The divide, then, between history and fiction may not always be clear-cut. As we shall see during the course of this book, no one has a monopoly on the 'truth'. At best, truth remains subjective. However, some interpretations of the 'truth' are more revealing than their authors would admit.

Realism and 'romance'

Above all, Boer War fiction is a species of 'romance' in which the war is depicted as an adventure in a world where 'love' has the final victory. Complex ideological differences are reduced to simple confrontations between good and evil, while political issues are often equated with questions of moral rectitude.

The realm of 'romance', in this context, has been vividly described in a newsletter put out by no less an authority than the Romantic Novelists' Association:[13]

> Romantic novels are novels which deal with love rather than sex, with courage rather than cowardice, with clean living rather than crime, with decent people rather than degenerates, with questions of right conduct rather than social problems, with eternal verities rather than fashionable psychological theories; are written with humour that does not depend on impropriety, in traditional English

> rather than imitation American; and because of these disadvantages, are seldom reviewed, though read by a vast and respectable section of the community.

Given these criteria, there is no doubt that the most consistent response to the Anglo-Boer conflict in fiction comes from the tradition of historical/war 'romance'. With the passage of time, the commitment to a political stance, or even to 'putting the record straight' has diminished. Romantic drama against the backdrop of war on the African veld, in which the lovers win each other and a nation is brought to birth, is the substance of most English fiction about the Anglo-Boer conflict in recent years.

The basic distinction between 'romance' and realism in South African literature was made over a hundred years ago by Olive Schreiner in her preface to *The Story of an African Farm*:[14]

> It has been suggested by a kind critic that he 'would better have liked the little book if it had been a history of wild adventure; of cattle driven to inaccessible 'krantzes' by bushmen'; 'of encounters with ravening lions, and hairbreadth escapes'. This could not be. Such works are best written in Piccadilly or the Strand: there the gifts of the creative imagination, untrammelled by contact with any fact, may spread their wings.
>
> But, should one sit down to paint the scenes among which he has grown, he will find that the facts creep upon him. Those brilliant phrases and shapes which the imagination sees in far-off lands are not for him to portray. Sadly he must squeeze the colour from his brush, and dip it into the grey pigments around him. He must paint what lies before him.

In the realist tradition, Schreiner continues:

> Nothing can be prophesied … . Men appear, act, and react upon each other, and pass away. When the crisis comes the man who would fit does not return. When the curtain

> falls, no one is ready. When the footlights are brightest they are blown out; and what the name of the play is, no one knows. If there sits a spectator who knows, he sits so high that the players in the gaslight cannot hear his breathing.

Schreiner's vision, like Joseph Conrad's, is of an inimical and indifferent universe. According to this view, realism is thinly served by the bulk of Boer War fiction. However, Peter Wilhelm's short story 'Homecoming' is an exception. His protagonist inhabits the indifferent universe of the realists. He returns to the farm to learn of his parents' death and his sister's madness:[15]

> The War had taught him that when men were caught in a machine they become machine-like, implacable, un-human. But there was a kind of logic in that: the history of his people, told to him by his father, was steeped in blood and movement, machine states. He had understood what he was in. These unheralded deaths and displacements (those of his family) were like lightening from a clear sky. They had no logic; they intimated a senseless universe.

Satire's scorn

South Africa has long attracted the scorn of satirists, both within and without the country. Its tortured history; its isolation from the so-called civilising influences of Europe; its multiplicity of languages and peoples have proved ample fare for satire from Andrew Geddes Bain's *Kaatje Kekkelbek* (1838), through Stephen Blackpool's *Love and the Hyphen* (1908), Roy Campbell's 'The Wayzgoose' (1928), and more recently, in Afrikaans, the writings of Etienne le Roux, Breyten Breytenbach and Pieter Dirk Uys.

Some of the most interesting names associated with satirising the Anglo-Boer conflicts include H.H. Munro 'Saki' in *Alice in Pall Mall*,(1900); G.K. Chesterton, *The Napoleon of Nottinghill* (1904);

Hilaire Belloc, *Mr Clutterbuck's Election* (1908) and Kipling's 'Fables for the Staff', published in *The Friend* in 1900, in which he lampooned the incompetence of the British General Staff. Unfortunately, their satire is so heavy-handed and exclusively focused on a particular set of circumstances and particular personalities that it is of little interest today. This is not true of Douglas Blackburn's *A Burgher Quixote* (1903), which must be one of the most undervalued works in South African English literature. *A Burgher Quixote* is part of Blackburn's Sarel Erasmus trilogy, including *Prinsloo of Prinsloosdorp* (1899) and *I Came and Saw* (1908), in which the author satirised the efforts of the rural Boer population coming to terms with the demands imposed upon it by urban-based capitalist invaders from Britain.

Books for boys

For many late Victorian and Edwardian writers, not least among them, Rudyard Kipling, war was regarded as a game. As long as war was seen from the perspective of the middle and upper classes in which disinterested leadership and self-sacrifice were the prevailing values (values that were nurtured by the British public-school system), the game's ethic could be transferred from the school playing field to the field of battle.

> There's a breathless hush in the Close tonight –
> Ten to make and the match to win –
> A bumping pitch and a blinding light,
> An hour to play and the last man in.
> And it's not for the sake of a ribboned coat,
> Or the selfish hope of a season's fame,
> But his Captain's hand on his shoulder smote –
> Play up! Play up! and Play the game!'[16]

The most important points of etiquette were playing by the rules, accepting defeat gracefully, and being gallant in victory. That the game could and often did result in death was readily acknowledged. However, more often than not, death was regarded within the context of 'muscular' Christianity, simply as a literary device, or as a release from 'this mortal coil' and entry to a better world. Whatever the outcome, the emphasis was on the spectacle in which everyone on the British side, at least, was expected to play by the rules and be as 'cheerful' in defeat as they were 'gracious' in victory. But, as World War I was to show unequivocally, there is a huge disparity between losing a game on the playing field, and losing your life, or witnessing the suffering and death of others in the battlefield.

The 19th century saw the publication of an enormous amount of fiction aimed specifically at children. Most of it set out quite unabashedly to 'improve' the young mind. Captain Marryat (1792–1848), R.M. Ballantyne (1825–94) and Captain Mayne-Reid (1818–83), told a rattling good and morally uplifting yarn interspersed with information about natural history and geography. The writers of English fiction exploited the wars of the Empire to tell exciting and patriotic tales. These tales were set in exotic far-off lands brought under the benign and necessary influence of the Pax Britannica. In *The Bush Boys* (n.d.), Captain Mayne-Reid recounted how he acquired his first lessons in African zoology and his reasons for passing on the information to his young readers:[17]

> Believing, boy reader, that they [his first lessons in African zoology] might also instruct and interest you, I lay them before you. You are not to regard them as merely fanciful. The descriptions of the wild creatures that play their parts in this little history, as well as the acts, habits and young instincts assigned to them, you may regard as true to Nature. Young Van Bloom [his informant] was a student of Nature, and you may depend upon the fidelity of his descriptions.

These remarks highlight two devices used by all writers for the young: the direct address to the youthful reader and the use of authorities to reinforce the notion of authenticity. It is within this tradition that the Rev. H.C. Adams, *Perils in the Transvaal and Zululand* (1887) and Gordon Stables, *On War's Red Tide* (1900), wrote. Although both writers give the impression of extensive knowledge of the country, as we shall see in a later chapter, they never once visited South Africa.

Major-General Ernest Swinton used the same sort of technique in his manual for training junior officers in the arts of war: *The Defence of Duffer's Drift: A Few Experiences in Field Defence for Detached Posts, which May Prove Useful in Our Next War* (1904). While the author wrote short fictional pieces about the Anglo-Boer War, he used the opportunity to pose tactical and logistical problems that young officers in the field might encounter. Many of these same young officers would have recently left school, where they would have had a full diet of 'improving fiction'. Many of them survived the Anglo-Boer War, and assumed positions of significant command in World War I.

Swinton was highly regarded by the military tacticians of his day, and his work was translated into several European languages, including German. Kaiser Wilhelm prescribed his manual on the tactics of war, as essential reading for all his officers, many of whom were to confront their British counterparts in the trenches in Normandy, ten years later. Ironically, Swinton's contribution to the teaching of military science was all but ignored by the British. The lessons of the Anglo-Boer War did not play a significant part in preparing the British for the war in Europe between 1914 and 1918. Swinton was ultimately credited with the invention of the tank that played a decisive part in bringing the Great War to an end.

The glory fades

The war of 1914–18 has had a significant impact on how writers have responded to the subject of war since then. The Anglo-Boer War prepared the ground. Paul Fussell[18] makes the point that while it was still possible to write about 'glory' at the turn of the century, the extent of the horror experienced between 1914 and 1918 meant the subject could no longer be regarded in a 'romantic' light. Rachel Anderson[19] goes so far as to say that the reaction to the Great War was such that: 'Much of the romantic fiction written during the war years avoids the subject altogether, preferring to take refuge in the old themes of love in society life, or marital complications.'[20] Even Arthur Newbolt, who had thrilled patriotic readers for generations with poetry and tales about the 'glory' and 'honour' of defending the Empire, found that in 1922, he could no longer write of 'The sweep and splendour of England's war'. In the introduction to *The Book of the Long Trail* (1922) he lamented the effects of war:[21]

> ... it shows them leaving everything they love best in the world, facing dangers and enduring hardships, matching their courage and skill against those of the other side, overcoming difficulties by land or sea, and all of this for an idea, the love of their country and that for which their country is fighting, the honour and welfare of mankind. But unfortunately this is not all war does: it also shows men at their worst .... I am speaking of certain things done by both sides and quite fair according to the rules of war, in fact unavoidable if you are to fight under modern conditions: millions of men killed or mutilated, millions of homes made desolate, houses and churches, roads and bridges, orchards, pastures and plough-lands turned to mud and dust heaps – in a word, the life of the world made hideous for years, with the survivors glaring at each other across the ruins.

For Newbolt, it was still feasible to harken back to a time when it seemed possible to regard war as, if not exactly good clean fun, at least as 'character-building'. Nonetheless, the 'romantic' view of war that predominated during the imperial phase was a long time a-dying.

Perhaps the most vivid statement indicating the orthodoxy of the romantic position at the turn of the century, now so tarnished especially in the aftermath of Passchendaele and Verdun, was made by Colonel Ian Hamilton, a veteran of Majuba and certainly no stranger to the battlefield. His description of 'the clash of sword and hollow reverberating clang of brazen buckler, the storm and wild joy of battle',[22] was widely accepted both in and out of literature before 1914. It is also a salutary reminder that men do not necessarily learn anything from experience.

It could be argued that earlier writers were constrained to conform to the 'romantic' position as that was what their readers expected. In fact, the 'romantic' view of war was so tenacious, that as late as 1928, more than ten years after the horrors of the Somme, theatre managements in the West End doubted the audience appeal of R.C. Sherriff's grimly naturalistic play about life in the trenches, *Journey's End*. Despite the managers' doubts, however, it was a box-office hit for several years. Times had changed and some writers at least had changed with them, reflecting more accurately than commercial interests an aspect of popular feeling. It would be satisfying if we could leave it at that. But social change is always more complex than it appears at first. In fact, just as surely as there was a general revulsion against war in the twenties and thirties, the 'romantic' image was kept alive and fostered by such mass-appeal publications as the *Boys' Own Paper* and the *Hotspur* which nurtured another generation of youngsters who would go off to fight Hitler. This ambivalence is reflected in the Boer War fiction written between the two world wars.

One of the most popular novels about World War II, Nicholas Monsarrat's *The Cruel Sea* (1953), gives an indication of just how tenacious the romantic view of war was. The foreword to the 'cadet' edition (and therefore intended for children), reveals a complex of responses during the aftermath of World War II, indicative of some of the anxieties born of a sense that Britain's finest hour was past:[23]

> This story of heroism, grit and endurance should be read by every boy and girl in Britain. They will discover at what price our country was protected and delivered from the menace of Nazism. Some people decry the spirit of contemporary Britain. I would ask these gloomy pessimists to remember that Britain's qualities of heroism which this book describes are still latent in our country. Many Ericsons and Lockharts are still to be found in our land.

Just as the Boer War fiction of fifty years previously appears to have been written as to bolster flagging faith in British imperialism, so too, much of the popular fiction about World War II seems to have been written in the same spirit. Margaret Thatcher's speeches, at the time of the Falkland's War were no less fired with a 'romantic' harkening for the 'glories' of Empire.

The pro-Boers

The Second Anglo-Boer War had the effect of splitting the community of writers into two broad camps: those for the war and those against it. The imperialists were in the majority and could count on heavyweights such as A.C. Swinburne, Kipling, Buchan, Conan Doyle and Haggard, among a host of lesser and now mostly forgotten figures. The pro-Boers could number in their ranks: William Morris, George Meredith, George Moore, W.B. Yeats, Sidney and Beatrice Webb, Ouida, Hilaire Belloc, G.K. Chesterton and W.T. Stead. In Stead's 'Shall I Slay My Brother Boer?' (1897), Stead drew an unequivocal parallel between the way Britain appeared to be manoeuvring the Transvaal into a war, and the Dreyfus case in France:[24]

> Dreyfus, like the Boer, belonged to an unpopular race … . Like the Transvaal, he was tried by a tribunal strongly prejudiced against him, and his conviction was obtained by the same unblushing appeals to national passion and self-interest which are relied upon in our press for hounding this nation into war.
>
> In Mr Chamberlain we have the General Mercier of the situation.
>
> The verdict at Rennes condemned an innocent individual to save the honour of the French army.
>
> If we go to war with the Transvaal, we condemn to death a State, to save the prestige of the Jingoes who degrade the cause of British imperialism by their savage determination to avenge Majuba.

Beatrice Webb was no less sure than Stead where to lay the blame for the war: [25]

> The Boers are, man for man, our superiors in dignity, devotion and capacity – yes, in capacity. That, to a ruling race, is the hardest hit of all. It may be that the war was inevitable: I am inclined to think it was. But that it should come about through muddy intrigues and capitalist

> pressure and that we should prove so incapable alike in statesmanship and generalship is humiliating.

Chesterton was proud to be called a pro-Boer:[26]

> I was called a Pro-Boer and unlike some Pro-Boers, I was very proud of the title … . I thought that their (the Transvaal and Orange Free State) farmers were perfectly entitled to take horse and rifle in defence of their farms and little farming commonwealth when it was invaded by a more cosmopolitan empire at the command of very cosmopolitan financiers.

For the pro-Boers there were wider issues at stake than merely the independence of two rural republics and British paramountcy. Jerome K. Jerome, writing to Herbert Samuel in September 1900, said:[27]

> Liberty of thought is to be denounced as treachery to cosmopolitan stockjobbers and their lackeys, who have come to regard England as their own property. The British flag is to be their 'commercial asset'. Our peasants are to be drilled into an armed horde and their blood spent on mere financial exploits for the sole benefit of the rich. And those who prefer the cause of England, her fair name and her prosperity, to the success of the gold mines on the Rand, are denounced by the German Jew Press as unpatriotic.

Many of the pro-Boers (some of whom were members of the Fabian Society), were anti-Semitic. Perhaps this was because one of the main issues upon which they were in agreement was the apparent vested interest of the capitalist financier, in promoting the war, whom they caricatured as the grasping Jew, Hoggenheimer.

It was Olive Schreiner, though, who saw what some of the human implications were. She was under no illusions about the role of the capitalists. The Jameson Raid destroyed whatever hopes she might have had of Rhodes. In a letter she inveighed against Rhodes:[28]

> Rhodes with all his gifts of genius … where below the fascinating surface the worms of falsehood and corruption are creeping … has betrayed all the men who trusted him … Rhodes wants no mental enlightenment, it is the man's heart that is corrupt.

In a similar mood she wrote *Trooper Peter Halket of Mashonaland* (1897), in which she again attacked Rhodes and the *British South African Company*. But her chief concern was for the futile waste of life on both sides. In a letter written shortly after the outbreak of war in 1899 she wrote:[29]

> Oh, this is a wicked, wicked war. When I see our bonny English boys falling and know how many hundreds have yet to fall, and our own brave South African lads dying, while the … who worked up the thing go to their garden parties and lounge about with their cigars and champagne, a bitterness rises in my heart that I never thought could … . It is strange what kindly feeling the Boers have for the soldiers; an old Boer woman said to me the other day with tears, telling me of her sons fighting in the Free State (one of her nephews is already shot), "Ah these poor English soldiers, why should they come out to die? They have nothing against us. Why, why should we have to shoot them? The poor boys." It's all so ghastly that I can't write.

Divided loyalties

The South African conflict was in many respects a civil war. Not only were there many Boers from the Cape, and later the two republics, who joined the National Scouts and fought for the British, but there were many Cape Boers who joined the commandos. This aspect of the war produced some of its finest responses in fiction, for example Herman Charles Bosman's short stories 'The Traitor's Wife' and 'The Affair at Ysterspruit', and Louis C. Leipoldt's novel *Stormwrack* (1980). The question of divided loyalties is a large issue in Boer War fiction, as it has remained in South African life generally. As the war progressed, the number of 'Handsuppers' (those who surrendered) increased, and so did the number of those who joined the British forces and fought against their former compatriots.

After the capture of Pretoria, Kitchener's policy of burning Boer farms and slaughtering livestock to prevent the commandos from re-equipping themselves, and of transporting women and children to concentration camps, was destined to scorch itself into the Afrikaner psyche. Stories spread about the inmates of the camps being fed ground glass. Although they were never substantiated, these stories were given credence by the high mortality rate. Approximately twenty-seven thousand Boer women and children died in the camps. The number of blacks who perished during the war far exceeded the total white fatalities, but as has so often been the case in South African history, the existence of black people was hardly acknowledged until the advent of the ANC government in 1994.

Throughout the Anglo-Boer War, the attitude of the Boers to the camps remained ambivalent. On one hand, they deplored the fact that their wives and children were being herded into insanitary and inefficiently run enclosures. However, they often acknowledged that they would be better looked after there than if they had been left to fend for themselves in the veld, where they would be prey to marauding bands of 'kaffirs'. General Louis Botha actually admitted: 'One is only too thankful nowadays to know that our wives are under English protection.'[30] Nonetheless, the issue of the camps is an emotional one, in which recriminations and vindications of the system have persisted up to the present. It is no small wonder that English-speaking novelists fought shy of the 'scorched earth policy' and the concentration camps, in the early literature.

The Anglo-Boer War in world context

How did the Anglo-Boer War affect Britain and the rest of the world? Hindsight seems to suggest that prior to 1899 the conflict must have appeared inevitable to everyone involved in it. Antagonistic ambitions, conflicting points of view, religious, social, political, economic and racial differences all pointed to some sort of resolution through violent confrontation.

Nor did the conflict end with war. As late as 1980 a successful Australian film, *Breaker Morant*, was based on Kenneth Ross's play and Kit Denton's novel *The Breaker* (1973). The film focuses on Morant's court martial and execution in the Northern Transvaal in 1902. It stirred up controversy among a group of South African critics who had recently discovered the insidious effects of ideology. As one of them put it:[31] '(*Breaker Morant*) is a literal projection and re-enactment of a fantasy about what it means to be Australian and male.' In the Antipodes, it would seem, the site of struggle had shifted from the veld to conflict between the sexes.

By way of contrast, it is instructive to see what effect the Anglo-Boer War had on thinking and attitudes elsewhere. In Europe and America, reactions were as might be expected: somewhat different from those of people more closely involved. These differences in opinion were certainly born out in the fiction written at the time. A number of German, French, Dutch, Portuguese and Scandinavian writers all came out in strong support of the Boers. The Dutch, destined to welcome Kruger into exile, felt a natural affinity for the Boers, on historical grounds. The French, Belgians and Germans – no doubt motivated by envy over Britain's success in Africa – sided with the Boers for a variety of political and sentimental reasons. After Jameson's capture at Doornkop in 1896, the Kaiser's congratulatory telegram to Kruger gives an idea of the anti-British atmosphere prevailing in Europe as the 19th century drew to a close.

Berlin

I express to you my sincere congratulations that without calling on the aid of friendly Powers, you and your people by your own energy against the armed bands which have broken into your country as disturbers of the peace, have succeeded in re-establishing the peace, and defending the independence of the country from those without.

William I.R.

… to which Kruger piously replied:

> I express to your Majesty my deepest gratitude for Your Majesty's congratulations. With God's help we hope to continue to do everything possible for the existence of the Republic.

The French and Germans not only sold arms to Kruger, but approximately one hundred and fifty Frenchmen and seven hundred and fifty Germans served with the Boer commandos. The Comte Villebois Mareuil was described by H.C. Bosman in his short story 'The Affair at Ystersspruit' as: 'The Frenchman who had come all the way from Europe to shoulder a Mauser for the Transvaal Republic. De Villebois, poet and romantic, last ditch champion of the forlorn hope and the heroic lost cause'.[32] The Comte was promoted to the rank of general in the Boer forces shortly before he was killed near Boshof in the Orange Free State. In 1903 when Edward VII visited Paris to patch up old quarrels, his welcome was far from warm. The crowds were still shouting 'Vivent les Boers!'

Motivated by centuries of antagonism for the British, the Irish Brigade that came to South Africa in 1899 to fight on the side of the Boers, consisted at one time of close on five hundred men. The best known was John MacBride, who later married Maude Gonne. The Scandinavian Commando numbered one hundred and seventy-five at the Battle of Magersfontein. The Russians, Dutch and French sent Red Cross teams to South Africa. In *Commando* (1935), Deneys Reitz recorded General Joubert's reaction to the Russian offer, before the war, to equip an ambulance for the Boer forces:[33]

> I was astonished to hear him say that he had refused the gift. He said, "You see, my boy, we Boers don't hold with these newfangled ideas; our herbal remedies (bossies-middels) are good enough."

Officers and men

The British generals were also resistant to newfangled ideas. It took the disasters of Bronkhorstspruit and Majuba in 1881 to convince the

British War Office that scarlet tunics and the carrying of regimental colours into battle were not only anachronistic but suicidal in the era of the Maxim gun.

At the beginning of the Second Anglo-Boer War in 1899 there was no General Staff in the British Army. Strategy was based on experience in the Crimea, some forty years earlier, and consisted almost entirely of close-formation frontal assaults and firing in volleys. Opposing the British in South Africa was an enemy whose tactics were based on mobility and camouflage. Nothing in the training of either the British officers or men prepared them for an enemy who refused to stand and make a 'fair' fight of it, preferring to take cover. When the fighting became too hot, the Boers 'ran away' to return and fight another day. There was no precedent for the ingenious innovation of trenches and barbed wire at Magersfontein. The symbols and strategies of World War I were being forged some fourteen years earlier on the dusty plains of the Karoo.

As Byron Farwell says, the war that started in 1899 was the first 'in which brains and skill on the part of the generals were more important than bravery and endurance on the part of the soldiers and junior officers'.[34] While Barbara Tuchman remarks: 'Military service in one of the elite regiments of Guards or Hussars or Lancers was [an] accepted role for men of wealth and rank, although it tended to attract the weaker minds'.[35]

Training of the British troops consisted of ten months of spit and polish and two months learning formation drill and manoeuvres, of which only three hours was spent on musketry practice. The result was that the ordinary soldiers often had no idea of how to set the sights of their rifles. Kipling made this point in his short story, 'The Comprehension of Private Copper'. In fact, Kipling was so incensed by the inefficiency he discovered in the British army, that he used each of the short stories he wrote about the South African War, as well as his 'Fables for the Staff' in *The Friend*, as vehicles to criticise the British conduct in the war. He was particularly critical of the bureaucratic nature of the army, which tended to ignore new ideas and suppressed initiative. In poems like 'Stellenbosch', he castigated the Generals for their timidity and lack of imagination:[36]

The General 'eard the firin' on the flank,
An' 'e sent a mounted man to bring 'im back
The silly, pushin' person's name an' rank
'Oo'd dared to answer Brother Boer's attack:
For there might 'ave been a serious engagement,
An' 'e might 'ave wasted 'alf a dozen men;
So 'e ordered 'im to stop 'is operations round the kopjes
An' 'e told 'im off before the Staff at ten!

And it all goes into the laundry,
But it never comes out in the wash,
'Ow we'er sugared about by the old men
('Eavy-sterned amateur old men!)
That 'amper an' 'inder an' scold men
For fear o' Stellenbosch!

Not only was the general command lacking in initiative, but the sword, lance and bayonet were proved obsolete against an enemy who refused to stand still. In the Battle of Poplar Grove (1900), the British cavalry failed against De Wet's rearguard action. Thomas Pakenham pointed out: 'The Mauser had made conventional cavalry tactics obsolete.' The 'white arm' had become a 'white elephant'.[37] Nonetheless, when Colonel Douglas Haig who was to control the destinies of British Tommies in Flanders between 1914 and 1918 testified before the Committee of Imperial Defence in 1902 on the lessons for the British of the Second Anglo-Boer War, he deplored the abolition of the lance and reaffirmed his faith in the cavalry sabre.

What of 'our peasants drilled into an armed horde'? The Second Anglo-Boer War saw the end of what was known as the 'Long Peace'. Seldom has an era been less accurately described. In the sixty-four years of Queen Victoria's reign, from 1837 to 1901, British soldiers saw action in no less than two hundred and thirty-two engagements of one sort or another. Until Kipling started publishing his *Barrack-Room Ballads*, little if anything was known of the common soldier who fought and died for the Empire. Andrew Rutherford has pointed out:[38]

In Victorian England 'Tommy Atkins', and to a lesser extent

> his officers, were sociologically unfamiliar breeds; and literature had done little to illuminate their ways of life.

As early as 1892, Lionel Johnson remarked in a review of *Barrack-Room Ballads*:[39]

> It is a curious reflection that the British Army at large, and the British soldier in particular, have received so little attention in literature of any excellence. We have plenty of heroic poems … but of the British Army, as a daily way of life, as composed of individual men, as full of marked personal characteristics and peculiarities, our poets great and small have had little conception. What Smollett in prose, and Dibdin in verse did for the Navy, no one has yet done for the Army.

The Second Anglo-Boer War saw the gradual recognition of the common soldier by the society he served. Tommy Atkins and Drummer Hodge were very different common soldiers from their great-grandfathers who fought at Waterloo. For one thing, they could read and write. The early and middle 19th century saw an unprecedented increase in the publication of books, pamphlets, magazines and newspapers, a general trend to which the whole of Boer War fiction answers. In addition to this, the age had seen the public and often acrimonious debate of such issues as evolution, socialism, the Reform Acts, rights for women and, inevitably, the rights of Empire.

The acquisition of an Empire, as much as anything else, changed the world view of the future Tommy Atkins, who was to lie in the blistering sun at Magersfontein, or sit, shivering and bored, in a corrugated iron blockhouse guarding the railway line between Renoster Kop and Nelspoort during the winter of 1901:[40]

> Few, forgotten and lonely,
> Where the empty metals shine –
> No, not combatants – only
> Details guarding the line.

The 'old order' changeth

Change was in the air in Victorian England, and with it a sense of vulnerability and uncertainty about the future. Accepted positions of privilege and traditional political and social institutions were being questioned. According to the new socialists, led by the Webbs and George Bernard Shaw, they were in urgent need of reform. Not even the Astronomer Royal could make up his mind whether century ended in 1899 or 1900. He finally decided on 1900. Within this climate of uncertainty, the Anglo-Boer War cast serious doubts on the extent and morality of Britain's power.

These uncertainties were given vivid expression in *The Dop Doctor* (1910), a particularly celebrated Boer War novel by Richard Dehan (Clothilde Graves). The hero has returned to London after the relief of Mafeking to a world that, by rights, should have been familiar and comforting, but which had changed for the worse. The Queen is dying and the war continues, a festering sore:[41]

> Yes! The big black opulent city was greatly changed. But the change in the people, affecting all ranks and every class, was even greater. There were compensations, if you could balance against the decay of good manners the improvements in sanitation, or set against the crop of evil sown by the dissemination of the vilest literature in the cheapest printed forms, the attainability, by the poorest, of the noblest productions of literary genius. Or, if in congratulating yourself upon the marvellous progress of Scientific Inventions, hailing from the keen-brained West, you could condone the degradation of the English language in the mouths of Shakespeare's countrymen and countrywomen by the use of American slang phrases, common, vulgar, coarse, alternating with choice expressions culled from the vocabulary of the East-End costermonger.
>
> Privacy and reticence had become unfashionable, impossible in this, the era of the guinea-hunting Press-Interviewer. The barriers of social exclusiveness had

> given way before the push of the plutocrat. The Rubicon between good Society and bad Society had become invisible. Racial suicide and sexual licence most hideously prevailed, spreading like some vile disease from rank to rank, and class to class. Woman had become less womanly, men more effeminate. Home was a word that had no longer any meaning. Religion had decayed; the fear of God was forgotten. But Socialism was springing up, a rank and lusty weed, in crude neglected soil that might have been tilled to good purpose; and a cheap and rowdy form of patriotism was in a very healthy state, although the Union Jack had not yet replaced the Bible in the Board Schools.
>
> Yes, things had changed; and not for the better! … Things had changed, and in the midst of all these changes, the last sands of the Great Victorian Age were running out of the glass.
>
> That wonderful life was drawing to its simple, peaceful, noble, profoundly touching close, this January of 1901, and its ending had been hastened by the war.

Graves was no social democrat. These were not the thoughts and feelings of someone who was immune to the challenges confronting a changing society, but rather a tacit admission that although the class war may not be over, only a rearguard action was possible by those in traditional positions of power and privilege. The basic assumption underlying this rejection of change and nostalgia for the past, is the Tory conviction that increased democracy could lead only to a decline in the quality of life, and the reduction to political insignificance and ultimately the extinction of the very classes that had contributed so much to Britain's greatness and prosperity in the past.

There is no doubt in the author's mind about the relative merits of 'good manners' and 'improvements in sanitation', and she is at pains to present her case so that there should be no doubt in the minds of her readers either. She employs all the shibboleths in her appeal to the conservative and prescriptive values of her readers: class, race and sex.

Notions about the 'purity' of language are tied to concepts of class and national superiority. Religion, the bulwark of civilisation and morality, has decayed and its place has been taken by the anti-Christ: Socialism, 'a rank and lusty weed'. With racial suicide and sexual licence on the increase, women less womanly, men more effeminate and 'home', a meaningless word, the advantages of improved sanitation and cheaply printed classics for the masses seem small compensation in a world dominated by American slang and the guinea-hunting Press-Interviewer.

Graves knew her audience. If the popularity of this novel is anything to go by, it was reprinted twenty-eight times, the probability is that she was expressing the vaguely felt and unarticulated thoughts and fears of many people in Britain.

Many British imperialist writers dramatised what every educated Englishman well knew: that empires rise and fall. The poets of the age had warned that none of man's aspirations or institutions were safe from corruption and change.

For Matthew Arnold:[42]

> … the world, which seems
> To lie before us like a land of dreams,
> So various, so beautiful, so new,
> Hath really neither joy, nor love, nor light,
> Nor certitude, nor peace, nor help for pain …

While Alfred, Lord Tennyson had reassuringly voiced the view that the very fact of change in an imperfect world was evidence of a divine plan:[43]

> The old order changeth, yielding place to new.
> And God fulfils Himself in many ways
> Lest one good custom should corrupt the world.

But, it was left to Kipling to remind Englishmen in the year of Queen Victoria's Diamond Jubilee of their imperfections:[44]

> If, drunk with sight of power, we loose
> Wild tongues that have not Thee in awe,

Such boastings as the Gentiles use,
Or lesser breeds without the Law –
Lord God of Hosts, be with us yet,
Lest we forget – lest we forget!

Evidence seemed to suggest to many writers like Graves that internal and external forces were gathering to confront the Empire with the fate suffered by empires before it. Many writers saw the rise of socialism, which to the ruling classes meant the time when: 'the rich would pay all the taxes and the poor would make all the laws',[45] bringing about the separation of power and responsibility, and therefore the collapse of all social order.

It was in such a paradoxically insecure world that people would turn to Boer War fiction, and to 'romance' in particular, for reassurance, excitement and vicarious entertainment. The turn-of-the-century warring adventure in Africa presented a ready subject, while the continent itself, teeming with herds of game, ferocious tribes, vast deserts and dark, deep forests, was remote and exotic enough to provide a safely distant and mysterious setting for the most stirring of events. The knowledge that southern Africa contained the richest gold and diamond deposits in the world made it appear even more mythical and worthy the winning.

Endnotes

1 Tommy Atkins is a generic name for the ordinary British soldier.
2 'Goodbye Dolly Gray' is the title of a popular song at the time of the Boer War.
3 Beatrice Webb and her husband, Sidney, were leaders of economic and social reform in England at the turn of the 19th century. Both were prominent members of the Fabian Society.
4 The 'Penny dreadfuls' were cheap popular boys' weekly comics or papers. *Hotspur* and *Dandy* are examples.
5 'Sarie Marais' is the title of a popular Afrikaans song by the sisters Bezuidenhout and B de Wet.
6 Sandison 1967: 19.
7 The Nobel Prize for Literature was won in 1953 by Winston Churchill for his *History of the Second World War*.
8 Haggard *The Last Boer War* 1900: vi.
9 Exchange of letters between F.C. Selous and Rider Haggard, printed in *The Times*, London (1899).
10 Kipling's toast to Kruger at a banquet of Lords Milner and Roberts (Bloemfontein, April 1900).
11 Sandys 1999: 16.
12 Crisp 1974: 7.
13 The Romantic Novelists Association, newsletter quoted in Anderson 1974: 273–4.
14 Schreiner 1965: 15–16.
15 Wilhelm 1975: 98.
16 Newbolt, Arthur, 'Vita Lampada' in *The Book of the Long Trail*
17 Mayne-Reid n.d: 5–6.
18 Fussell 1975: 21.
19 Anderson 1974: 174.
20 Newbolt quoted in Howorth 1973: 9.
21 Newbolt 1922: v–vi.
22 Hamilton, Colonel I, quoted in Rayne Kruger's *Goodbye Dolly Gray*, 1967: 84.
23 Monsarrat, N, *The Cruel Sea* 1953: 11.
24 Stead 1897: 6.

25 Webb quoted in Koss 1974: 58.

26 Chesterton, G.K., *The Napoleon of Nottinghill* quoted in Arthur Davy, *The British Pro-Boers* (1877–1902) 1978: 159.

27 Jerome, J.K., letter to Samuel Herbert, September 1900, quoted in Koss, page 149.

28 Schreiner, O., quoted in Buchanan-Gould 1948: 157.

29 Schreiner, O., letter to Adela Villiers, 10 December 1899.

30 Botha, General Louis, quoted in Pakenham, page 569.

31 Gardner, Susan, critique of the film *Breaker Morant*, in *Critical Arts Monograph* (1981).

32 Bosman 1963: 78.

33 Reitz 1935: 17.

34 Farwell 1973: 341.

35 Tuchman 1962: 13.

36 Kipling, R., 'Stellenbosch', *Rudyard Kipling's Verse* 1912.

37 Pakenham 1979: 375.

38 Rutherford 1978: 12.

39 Johnson, L., Review of *Barrack-Room Ballads*, quoted in Green (ed) 1971: 98.

40 Kipling, Rudyard, 'Bridge Guard in the Karroo'.

41 Graves 1910: 552–3.

42 Arnold, M., 'Dover Beach' in *The Poems of Matthew Arnold* 1913.

43 Tennyson, Alfred Lord, 'Morte d'Arthur' in *The Complete Works of Alfred, Lord Tennyson* 1900.

44 Kipling, R., 'Recessional' in *Rudyard Kipling's Verse* 1912.

45 Lord Salisbury, quoted in Tuchman, page 18.

The Staatsmodel School in Pretoria where Churchill was held captive, later the Transvaal Education Department Library.

CHAPTER ONE

CAUSES OF THE CONFLICT: 'Gods of the Jingo'

Drunken with lust of power and pelf
They held nor man nor God in awe
And care for nought but only Self
And cent-per-cent's their only law
These are their lords, and they are rotten
They have forgotten – they have forgotten.

F.W. Reitz, 'Gods of the Jingo'[1]

Variously known as the Second Anglo-Boer War, the South African War, Die Tweede Vryheidsoorlog, the Boer War, Milner's War or alternatively Kruger's War, and the last of the gentlemen's wars, the war of 1899–1902 is the central watershed of the South African experience. This is perhaps more obvious as far as the white population, especially the Afrikaners, is concerned, but it is no less the case for black South Africans. The question of the franchise for the black population was a central issue at the Treaty of Vereeniging in 1902, where it was decided that the franchise could not be settled until representative government for the whites had been introduced.

The relationship between Afrikaner and Briton was by no means simple and straightforward. It has been bedevilled since the first British occupation of the Cape by misconceptions, prejudice, arrogance, ignorance, ethnocentricity and different world views. Given the differences between the British and Boer populations, their proximity and conflicting aspirations in southern Africa, a confrontation ending in the defeat of one and victory for the other, was probably inevitable. The unresolved clash of 1881 with the British humiliation at Majuba, merely served to confirm that a full-scale conflict must come sooner or later. The discovery of gold towards the end of the century ensured that it would be sooner.

The Anglo-Boer War, then, stands at the crossroads of South African history, between pastoral Old Testament values and 20th century cynicism.

It had long been the ambition of imperialists (even before Rhodes) to weld South Africa into a federation and extend the British sphere of influence in Africa in the face of competition from Germany, France and Portugal. The economic position of the Transvaal Republic under President Burgers provided the British with the pretext they needed. The Boers, like the citizens of any country, resented taxes and tried to avoid paying them. In a country where an individual's independence and freedom were prized above social or communal responsibility; where taking in the harvest took precedence over military duties, it is no small wonder that a government and laws that did not bring immediate benefits were treated with scorn. By 1875 the Transvaal was teetering on the brink of bankruptcy, and the Postmaster General was forced to pay himself in postage stamps.

The curtain raiser

Sir Theophilus Shepstone arrived in Pretoria in January 1877, ostensibly to help the Republic to regularise its finances and reduce its financial difficulties. After some months of negotiations, Shepstone annexed the Transvaal in the name of the British Crown. Instead of resolving the problems of the former republic, annexation made them worse, as nationalistic opposition to British rule grew under the leadership of Kruger and Joubert. A meeting was held at Paardekraal near Krugersdorp in 1880 which reaffirmed the Boer determination to remain independent.

The first shots of the First Anglo-Boer War were fired in Potchefstroom, where a British garrison was attacked by Cronje; the same Cronje who would command the Boers at another famous victory twenty years later at Magersfontein. It was Cronje, too, who was destined to surrender to Lord Roberts at Paardeberg on the nineteenth anniversary of the Battle of Majuba. Following the Boer victory at Majuba, independence was reclaimed by the Transvaal, with the British proviso that the Transvaal remain under the Queen's suzerainty.

One of the key clauses in the agreement to restore independence was that all adult European males in the Transvaal were to have equal rights. This clause was to have serious repercussions later in the mid-1890s, when the Uitlanders demanded a say in the administration of the country. It also had further implications for the black population, which only achieved equality more than one hundred years later.

The annexation of the Transvaal and the War of Independence served to unite Afrikaners throughout South Africa and gave them the beginnings of a national consciousness. It also gave the Transvaalers a special sense of achievement. Had they not taken on the greatest power of the age and won? The euphoria of 1881 was destined to linger and convince the Boers that if they had triumphed once, they could do it again.

The land of Ophir

After the Battle of Majuba, imperialist plans for a federation were shelved for the time being. The South African Republic, as the Transvaal became known, might have continued to exist indefinitely in peace, poverty and obscurity, but for the discovery of gold on the Witwatersrand in 1886. This discovery was complicated by Rhodes' efforts to expand British influence to the north of the Limpopo River.

The South African Republic was psychologically and administratively incapable of dealing with the thousands of Uitlanders attracted by the prospect of quick and easy riches. The Uitlanders, most of whom were English speaking, were not interested in the Boers or in understanding the Boer point of view. In 1886, the Rand promised riches and progress, and the Boers wanted none of it. Within ten years, there was a city of hard-drinking, gambling, aggressive speculators and hangers-on where there had once been bare veld. These speculators had little or no time for the Old Testament principles upon which the Boer Republic was founded and governed. What was worse, the local Boer population was soon thought to be outnumbered by what appeared to them to be a godless horde of foreigners. The Uitlanders had come to destroy their idyllic pastoral way of life that had been won with such hardship, fortitude and sacrifice.

By the mid-1890s, the Uitlander 'grievances' as they had come to be known, were concerned basically with nationalisation and the franchise. The Uitlanders reasoned that if they paid most of the taxes, they should have some say in how the state's revenue was spent. Kruger was prepared to give them certain limited political rights if they gave up their British citizenship and became Transvaal nationals. However, by 1892, Kruger was worried that if he allowed the Uitlanders burger and franchise rights, they would outnumber and swamp the Boer population. Indeed, he believed they did already outnumber them. Thus, by giving away burger and franchise rights, he would in effect be giving his country away to foreigners.

British imperialist writers made much of the Uitlander grievances and Kruger's reluctance to relieve them. However, except for a small minority who formed the Reform Committee and plotted with Rhodes and Jameson, most Uitlanders appear to have been too busy making money to have been concerned about Kruger's corrupt administration or their own lack of political power. Kruger argued that if the Uitlanders did not like conditions in the Transvaal they could always leave. As they stayed, it was obvious the compensations outweighed the grievances. Nonetheless, a situation arose whereby the Transvaal could be and was manipulated chiefly by Rhodes, Milner and Chamberlain, to deprive it of its independence and incorporate it into the British Empire.

The Bloemfontein Conference of June 1899, called to resolve differences between Kruger's administration and the Uitlanders, ended in stalemate. Kruger turned to Lord Milner with tears in his eyes and said: 'It is my country you want!' Kruger was right. The Transvaal possessed all the qualities that made it an ideal colonial acquisition. Its strong geographical position gave it access to central Africa. It had a healthy climate. Above all, it possessed the richest gold fields in the world, richer by far than anything in myth or legend. Here indeed was the fabled land of Ophir, for which the colonial powers had been searching with little success since Europeans first rounded the Cape in 1498.

No doubt, the Uitlanders did have grievances. No doubt Kruger's government was corrupt; but by the end of the Bloemfontein Conference, Milner and Chamberlain had manoeuvred a tiny nation into a corner from which it could not escape. However, they did not reckon on the Boers' determination to resist any force that attempted to destroy their existence as a people. For, an important aspect of their self-image, was their belief in themselves as 'God's chosen people'. When they had trekked like the Israelites into the wilderness, had they not taken His Word as their inspiration and His Law as their law? Had He not delivered them from their enemies and given them a land of their own?

British imperialist motives: greed vs idealism

From the British point of view, two contradictory but curiously complementary factors led to the Anglo-Boer War: greed and idealism. The Anglo-Boer War is not the only example in history of human beings being moved to action by the most gross and sublime motives, simultaneously. The watchwords of the 'scramble for Africa' were 'Christianity', 'civilisation' and 'commerce': David Livingstone's 'three Cs'. The fact that commercial interests commonly used the missions and the ideals of European 'civilisation' as covers for ruthless economic exploitation did not mean that all the colonialists' motives were irredeemably corrupt. But certainly, as Joseph Conrad showed so vividly in *Heart of Darkness*, for all King Leopold's professed idealism, the brutal and cynical reality of the trading stations in the Congo contradicted what the philanthropists in Europe fondly imagined was the 'civilising mission' of exploration. In the case of southern Africa, the Witwatersrand was the prize that glittered.

The ideals of imperialism were complex. Notwithstanding all that has been levelled at it, 19th century British imperialism was not as completely imbued with venal ambition as its critics would have us believe. Francis Younghusband, explorer and mystic, summed up the ambivalent attitude of many imperialists to the Empire in a letter to the poet Arthur Newbolt:[2]

> If we can, besides looking after our own particular rights and interests, draw up with us to a higher level, these hundreds of millions dependent on us, we shall have done a nobler work in the world than has been accomplished by any nation yet.

The high priest of imperialism, Cecil John Rhodes, drew contradictory reactions from admirers and critics alike. W. T. Stead, who was to become one of Rhodes' fiercest critics, had once called him the 'Abraham Lincoln of South Africa'.[3]

On the other hand, Mark Twain, who was in South Africa just after the Jameson Raid, observed:[4]

> [Rhodes] tricks the Reformers into immense trouble with his Raid, but most of them believe he meant well. He weeps over the harshly-taxed Johannesburgers and makes them his friends; at the same time he taxes his Charter settlers 50 per cent, and so wins their affection and their confidence, that they are squelched with despair at every rumour that the Charter is to be annulled. He raids and robs and enslaves the Matabele and gets worlds of Charter-Christian applause for it. He had beguiled England into buying Charter waste-paper for Bank of England notes, ton for ton, and the ravished still burn incense to him as the Eventual God of Plenty. He has done everything he could think of to pull himself down to the ground. He has done more than enough to pull sixteen common-run great men down; yet there he stands, to this day, upon his dizzy summit under the dome of the sky, an apparent permanency, the marvel of the time, the mystery of the age, an Archangel with wings to half the world, Satan with a tail to the other half.
>
> I admire him, I frankly confess it; and when his time comes I shall buy a piece of the rope for a keepsake.

To many, Rhodes was the symbol of scheming British capitalism. He believed that the Anglo-Saxon race was the highest evolved in a divine plan, and that world peace and civilisation in general depended on the spread of British civilisation. Rhodes' inspired vision convinced W.T. Stead that in the conflict with the Transvaal Republic:[5]

> He is the foremost representative of the great struggle for the federal principle on the part of States, organized on the basis of freedom, religion, liberty, and progress, against a State which has slavery as its chief corner-stone, and which uses the powers of a corrupt Oligarchy in order to render South African union impossible.

John Buchan, another convinced imperialist, looking back nearly half-a-century later during the dark days of 1941, recalled:[6]

> I dreamed of a world-wide brotherhood with the background of a common race and creed, consecrated to the service of peace; Britain encircling the rest of her culture and traditions, and the spirit of the Dominions like a strong wind freshening out the stuffiness of the old lands. I saw in the Empire a means of giving to the congested masses at home, open country instead of a blind alley. I saw hope for a new afflatus in art and literature and thought. Our creed was not based on antagonism to any other people. It was humanitarian and international; we believed we were laying the basis of a federation of the world. As for the native races under our rule, we had a high conscientiousness; Milner and Rhodes had a farsighted native policy. The whiteman's burden is now an almost meaningless phrase; then it involved a new philosophy of politics, an ethical standard, serious and surely not ignoble.

Given the times in which Buchan was writing, such a harkening back is understandable. Many men and women supported the ideals of the British Empire for altruistic reasons; that their altruism was founded on rampant self-interest was a complication more often than not overlooked.

Polemics

Ideology then, is an important factor in assessing the role of imperialism in southern Africa. This is no less true within Boer War fiction than out of it. Many writers have stated their position quite blatantly and have left the reader in no doubt about their prejudices. In a strangely prophetic novel written some three years before hostilities, George Griffith asked in the preface to his novel *Briton or Boer?: A Tale of the Fight for Africa*: 'Is the Briton or the Boer … going to rule South Africa?' He was in no doubt about Britain's 'right' to rule over 'lesser breeds' and from this unflinching perspective, he tried hard to 'set the South African matter right', once and for all. As in all polemical Boer War fiction the writer's intention is crucial in determining how the conflict is presented, regardless of which voice the writer uses.

Some writers chose to present the case of the Briton versus the Boer as a debate between characters. This was a favourite device when 'romance' was in the air. In such fiction, the result is almost always a foregone conclusion: the English partner wins over the Boer. However, the later the novels were written after the war, the greater were the attempts at objectivity, and 'love' does not always succeed as it used to. Attempts were made in the 1930s, to write novels entirely from a Boer point of view. Gradually the accent moved away from taking sides to perceiving the conflict as a civil war. C. Louis Leipoldt's *Stormwrack*, and more recently, Wilbur Smith's *The Sound of Thunder*, and Kit Denton's *The Breaker*, entirely ignore the issues that led up to the Boer War.

The prefaces or introductions of many of the early novels, such as Griffith's *Briton or Boer*, Hume Nisbet's *For Right and England*, Bertram Mitford's *Aletta: A Tale of the Boer Invasion*, J.Q. Dixon's *Genevieve de Brabant* and G.G. Munnik's *Major Greville, V.C.*, have prefaces or introductions in which political issues; the 'rights and wrongs', as perceived by the writers are discussed, and the writers' intentions are spelled out. Griffith's novel is particularly noteworthy, appearing as it did in Queen Victoria's Diamond Jubilee Year, just after the Jameson Raid. In his preface, he says that his concern was to warn his fellow countrymen of the dangers ahead lest they be blinded by the show of imperial power during the Jubilee celebrations. Griffith was obsessed and outraged (as were many of his contemporaries) by Britain's humiliation at the Battle of Majuba. According to Griffith, Majuba had made:[7]

> … a so-called Paramount Power … the laughing stock of a mostly hostile world by apologising to the insolent and triumphant Boers … . Let the Empire show by her acts that she is in earnest when her responsible ministers say that at all costs her supremacy in South Africa will be maintained.

W.T. Stead saw the situation differently. In his pamphlet 'Shall I Slay My Brother Boer?' (1899) he wrote:[8]

> If we go to war with the Transvaal we condemn to death a State to save the prestige of the Jingoes who degrade the cause of British Imperialism by their savage determination to avenge Majuba.

Few writers were more forthright than Hume Nisbet. In the preface to his *For Right and England* he laid the blame for the war, as did Griffith, squarely at the feet of Gladstone's administration. According to him, it merely surrendered, after the defeat at Majuba. The present government, under Lord Salisbury, he claimed, found itself at a disadvantage when dealing with Kruger because they were: 'Handicapped by the tactics of their cowardly predecessors, and hampered by the living enemies of Empire', namely the Little Englanders of whom the most vocal was W.T. Stead. By this time, Stead who had once been an ardent Rhodes' supporter, had become one of his most virulent critics.

Nisbet was not shy about proclaiming the justice of England's cause: 'to repel slave-driving invaders from our territories'. It was common cause among many earlier British writers, including Livingstone, that the Boers kept slaves. Thus, all right-thinking imperialists held that it was part of Britain's civilising mission in Africa to eliminate slavery. Livingstone, Stanley and a whole host of earnest nineteenth-century explorers financed their journeys through Africa – to say nothing of promoting European commercial interests – in the name of eliminating slavery from the continent.

Although slavery did not officially exist in the Transvaal and Orange Free State republics, the British often protested that the Boer practice of indenturing black labour was merely a disguised form of slavery. (The practice of indenturing black labour survived the Anglo-Boer War and was destined to be exposed for what it was in the 1950s by *Drum Magazine*, which published a series of articles describing labour practices on the potato farms in the eastern Transvaal.)

Like many jingoes, Nisbet waxed righteously indignant about the fact that it was the Boers who invaded British territory in Natal on 10 October 1899. In response to Stead's 'Shall I Slay My Brother Boer?' Nisbet poured forth the following diatribe:[9]

> We do not call murdering bushrangers 'brothers'. Society repudiates such pests, and regards them as vermin to be exterminated. Those who support and act as advocates and decoys for these outlaws are also punished when discovered. The Transvaalers ceased to be members of civilization over two centuries ago. We trust that our liberty-making Empire pilots may hold firm to their purposes and never relax their present efforts, in spite of all criticism, until these bushranger Boerlands have ceased to exist as States, and the Boers have been forced to become law-abiding Colonists. This end accomplished, none of us will count the cost, for we have done our duty to God, our Country, and Humanity at large. This is a Holy War, and we speak without prejudice.

For Right and England is a startling example of one of the uses of fiction.

Notwithstanding Britain's long history of conflict with the Boers in southern Africa, imperial pride blinkered all but the most hardened cynics. That the Boers should have had any justification for mistrusting British intentions appears to have remained a mystery to most early writers.

Fair play

There were other avenues open to authors who *post-facto* chose to deal with the causes and aims of the Anglo-Boer War. In the interests of 'British even-handedness', many writers tried to present both sides of the story as they perceived it. Whether they chose to hold up the narrative with heavy doses of histrico-politico editorialising or whether they allowed their characters to debate the pros and cons, their arguments are usually stacked in favour of the British position.

Bertram Mitford is one of the earliest popular writers who tried to give a more-or-less balanced picture. But then he had been a farmer and later a journalist in the Cape and was well able to appreciate the Boers' side of the story. For all that, when it came to the push, Mitford remained and revealed himself as a convinced imperialist. In his *Aletta: A Tale of the Boer Invasion* (1900) (the title should serve as a warning) the villain of the piece, Andries Botma, addresses a gathering of Cape Boers, hoping to convince them to rise in rebellion and join their republican brothers. Mitford used Botma's fanatical outpouring to discredit the Boer point of view, while at the same time reinforcing the apparent reasonableness of the British position. Ironically, Mitford came perilously close to doing the opposite. He knew South Africa too well. Many of the arguments he put into Botma's mouth about past British treachery were close to the bone. Botma begins his harangue claiming that:[10]

> A horde of English Bloodsuckers had poured in [to the Transvaal] fevered by the lust of gold, and still more and more until the land was overrun by them, as the land of Pharaoh under the plague of locusts. And not only that, but they brought with them every life and soul destroying vice, which Satan and his hell-

> kingdom, Europe, could bring to bear to contaminate and utterly corrupt a God-fearing people … .
>
> "Brothers, I have been in England; I have seen her millions of people, her splendour, and her enormous wealth. But I have seen more. I have seen her weakness. I have seen her large cities, and their vice and squalor. I have seen the frivolous luxury of her rich, and the hideous misery and want and desperation of her poor; and I tell you that for all her outward strength she is a weak nation, a rotten nation, with all her best blood poisoned by disease, and her common blood turned to water by foul air and hunger and drunkenness. And this is the nation which is greedy for our land, is ravening to steal the gold which it contains." Then raising his voice to a thunder pitch: "Brothers, shall this go on? Now, nay, it shall not, I tell you. All is in readiness. For years we have been in readiness, increasing our armed might, and now we are ready to strike – to strike with a force and terror that shall amaze the whole world. Be in readiness, too, brave burghers, patriots all; and to deliver this message to you am I here tonight. God does not will that this rotten, frivolous, and enfeebled nation shall rule over you any longer. Be ready, for the day is at hand 'Africa for the Afrikanders!' is our watchword."

This extract is interesting chiefly for the part it played in Mitford's overall strategy. In the introduction to his novel he claims that current British stereotypes of the Boers are a gross misrepresentation. There are Boers, he is eager to reassure us, who are not ignorant and bigoted, and who do wash regularly. Yet when it comes to his story, all those who oppose the British are portrayed as unwashed fanatics. The basis of their treachery is in their lack of hygiene and religious intolerance.

An attempt at a more balanced picture of the Boers is provided in Arthur Laycock's *Steve, the Outlander* (1900). A bellicose group of Uitlanders in a Johannesburg public house, discuss the causes of the approaching war:[11]

> "Drop negotiations and pick up bullets and drop them in the right place and we'll soon settle matters."
> "That's what I say, Nat. Have you signed the petition, Max?"
> "Yes, signed it half a dozen times. Is that enough?"
> "Just enough for you, old man. Max is good at that game."
> "Is he as good at handling a gun as a pen?" asked Sellars.
> "Not so good as you, old man. Here, you'll have to put your fist to this petition, Sellars."
> "So I will; I'll put both fists to it, and to the Boer's nose as soon as I feel he oppresses me."
> "Why, bosh! What's the use of talking like that? We're not oppressed of course, but we must work some racket up to get this country from the Boers."
> "But look here, Sellars," chimed in another, "we pay all the taxes and we get no representation. How's that for square? Call yourself a democrat too."
> "Paul [Kruger] would have given the franchise but for that brilliant Raid."
> "Would have given us Pretoria, say, at once, or would have given us his own hog's head; just as likely. We know those promises of Paul's."

Such cynicism is not often encountered in Boer War fiction. Later, (p. 298) Laycock hints at whom he believes is responsible for the war: 'the fat financiers of the Golden city … the peaceful, pushful Jews … [who] fought Kruger with their mouths': the British Uitlanders and foreign adventurers, 'Irish-Americans, the Germans and the Hollanders', who with an eye to the main chance allied themselves with the Boers.

Owen Vaughan presented a much more serious and complex examination of the Boers in *Old Fireproof* (1906). The narrator, a rather ingenuous and naïve Anglican chaplain, is forced to reconsider the implications of waging war against the Boer republics. It is to Vaughan's credit that he manages to make the point as strongly as he does without touching on any of the usual arguments. The chaplain is consumed by doubts:[12]

> These men wore no uniform, and the thing seemed to cry out upon me, all accusation, that they were peaceful men snatching up weapons to defend themselves from wanton attack. If a nation puts its men in uniform, and drills them to text-book exercises, it may well look to be attacked by war, since, by wearing war's trappings and dabbling in war's formulas, it has recognised war and thus given war a right of operation against it. But this nation, against which we brought such vast armies, had worn no uniform, practised no drill, privileged no military caste, harkened none after the maxims of this modern Caesar or that – surely all that was proof that it had never contemplated war as being possible, and proof, too, that we must be in the wrong.
>
> A nation which made none of the preparations for war would surely have agreed to anything in reason rather than let things come to war. Surely our demands must have gone beyond the extreme when unprepared men would face even war with the greatest empire in the world rather than yield. We must have asked that which men could not give and yet live on, facing their living thoughts. Like the voice of the prophet of old, suspicion cried these thoughts upon me as I looked at this man.

Old Fireproof can be read as a story about youth losing its illusions. As such it might be regarded as an allegory of British imperial idealism. The chaplain is compelled by experience to reconsider all his naïve and facile views about himself, war, other people, God, sex, and the world in general. He discovers that opinions formed in the abstract, away from life's lived experience are seldom of any help when confronted with actuality. The author, Owen Vaughan, did not try to explain the war in terms of the political or social issues of the day. He is one of the first writers who depicted it from the point of view of the individual's crises of conscience rather than from the point of view of politics. In this he anticipated writers of the next generation who lost their innocence in the trenches at Verdun and the Somme.

The decline and fall

It seemed evident to many writers at the turn of the 19th century, such as Griffith, Nisbet and Mitford, that internal and external forces were gathering to confront the Empire with the same sort of fate suffered by those who had been crushed in the path of its expansion. One way of tackling the issue of this threat while simultaneously avoiding it, was to put criticism of the British way of life into the mouths of the enemy. If a character accused England of being rotten and rapacious, such as Botma in Mitford's *Aletta*, the reader was free to dismiss such criticism as being typical of perceived Boer prejudice and hypocrisy. Whether in the mouths of the enemy or not, however, such claims have a way of backfiring. They reveal the deep disquiet and insecurity that inspired these writers to take up the pen in defence of the Empire.

There was also a conviction that Britain needed to reassert its position in the world. At home there was growing evidence of inevitable and irresistible social change. Abroad, there were fresh challenges, especially from an ambitious and belligerent Germany. The Kaiser's telegram to Kruger after the Jameson Raid caused an uproar. The potential German threat became almost an obsession with many British writers of Boer War fiction.

For all the outward show of British wealth and power at the Queen's Jubilee Celebrations, there was a sense of tension, vulnerability and uncertainty about the future. There was a need to bolster self-esteem, reassert values and to support the justice of Britain's cause. This helps to explain the intensity of the passion that the British pro-Boer writers managed to stir up at home. The pro-Boers were seen not so much as supporting the Boer republics, but as being defiantly and dangerously anti-British; as standing up for everything that would sweep away traditional British values.

In 1897, when Eugene Marais was studying law at the Inner

Temple, he recorded his impressions of London, in an unpublished letter:[13]

> But under all this pride and pomp of wealth and power there are not signs wanting which would gladden your heart could you be here to see and note them. I have arrived at a fortunate time, for I shall see the first stages in the decay and dissolution of a great Empire. History has taught you the symptoms and they are here. They meet you at every turn and corner. It is the body of a giant attacked by internal cancer and the invisible suppuration showing faintly through this apparently healthy skin. The symptoms which you see in their church are no longer invisible in their politics. As the Church of England is only Roman and water – an assumption of power and glory outwardly, which this poor dead spirit within does not warrant and cannot support, so this nation speaks of itself with a great flourish of trumpets and a burning of incense, and behold it is sick, – sick unto death; and we, Pienaar, you and I, shall live to see it in the throes. We shall live to see retribution [extirpating?] the Destroyer of Liberty, and maybe we shall be able to strike a blow at the falling harlot and remember the blood of our people which she has poured out like water. Yes, we shall live to see the day of the Small Nations, when they arise to pay back their just debts into the treasury of wrath, with compound interest. The time is near at hand, – nearer than you dream of. Do not therefore let an opportunity pass by of teaching our people to hate and loathe the oppressor, the Thief and Liar, who has crawled over the earth like a tarantula and laid up for itself great store of hate among many nations. Her troubled times are visible upon the horizon like clouds, dark and ominous on the inside and shining like pillars of fire upon the pathways of the little nations.

> In the Temple one comes into contact with the youth of the upper and middle classes, the men to whom the destinies of this nation will be entrusted; and if you could see them your heart would sing with joy. You see these young men, with spirits burning dimly in the sockets – oppressed by tedium vitae and incapable of being roused to interest in anything outside themselves. As to fair and just views, they are incapable of forming them on any subject under the sun. They are the heirs of centuries of power and wealth and vice and their ugly faces tell you they are as impotent as they are unworthy of holding the reins of power which chance has placed in their feeble hands. Like the church, the nation has still the outward crust of greatness, and within, it is a mass of putrefying suppuration. Truly this is another vindication of Nature's eternal laws. It is as true of a nation as it is of an individual that as one sows so shall one surely reap.
>
> [I?] find all this has not wearied you – but I feel deeply on what I have discovered and I am solemnly convinced that my deductions are not false. If I hear from you in reply I shall continue these impressions from time to time if they interest you at all.
>
> Truly yours
> Eugene Marais

Marais was not an objective observer. In fact, there is little to choose between his invective and that of the Jingoes. Marais, like Hume Nisbet, succumbed to the sound of his own voice. The difference is, of course, his letter was never intended for public consumption.

It is difficult to say precisely what the causes of the war of 1899–1902 were. Authors writing at the time were obviously too close to the events they were describing. Those writing later had the advantage of hindsight and historical research, but were still confronted with the problems of selection and emphasis.

Nevertheless, certain possible causes stand out more clearly than others, for example: British imperial ambitions, Uitlander grievances, the gold on the Rand and Kruger's intractable attitudes. All these were given greater or lesser emphasis according to the prejudices and fashions of the time. There were other factors – perhaps not as easily identified – but they exerted definite pressures, nonetheless. War is often used by politicians as a means to distract people from domestic tensions and to impress foreign competitors. Boer War fiction indicated there was a general need for British politicians to do both.

My country, 'right' or 'wrong'?

Ambivalence about the age was easier to express in fiction than ambivalence about the justice of Britain's cause. Patriotic calls, especially in times of war, inevitably stir up a conflict of emotions. Passionate expression often disguises ambivalent misgivings. Such was the passion of the novelist and poet W.C. Scully.

Few writers at the turn of the 19th century could escape being passionate about the Anglo-Boer War, and Scully was no exception. In 1904, he was commissioned to gather evidence about the losses suffered by the civilian population and to recommend reparations. The stories he listened to of Boer suffering under British martial law, and the Cape Government's later refusal to honour its commitment to pay reasonable reparations to the Boers, inspired him to write *The Harrow* (1921).

Scully was one of the first British writers to put the blame for the war squarely at the feet of the capitalists. According to him they manipulated public opinion through the press, which they controlled, spread lies about Kruger, exaggerated every little incident which touched on the Uitlander grievances and generally promoted fearful propaganda about the 'Great Afrikaner Conspiracy'. *The Harrow*, written in 1904, was published only later, in 1921. Initially, publication was delayed because the author felt his book was too controversial. Yet, it remains a mystery why he chose to publish when he did.

Both 1904 and 1921 were times of severe depression in South Africa, in which labour (the poor, white, mainly Afrikaans-speaking workers) came into head-on conflict with their capitalist bosses. In the main, these bosses were the same capitalists who, in Scully's view, had been responsible for the Anglo-Boer War in the first place. The capitalist industrialists were able to dictate to the government on matters affecting economic policy. Mining costs rose and wholesale retrenchments seemed to be the only way to reduce costs. But the government relied on the white miners' vote to remain in power. Matters came to a head in December 1921, when white miners' wages were unilaterally reduced. The following month saw the 1922 strike, during which General Smuts, a hero of the Anglo-Boer War, was forced to suppress the miners with arms in the interests of the mining magnates.

It is in this context that Scully revised his novel. Perhaps the 1904 depression and his experiences as a commissioner prompted him to write *The Harrow*. Perhaps the troubles of 1921 convinced him that the time was ripe to reveal the extent of capitalist power over South Africa:[14]

> The magnates of the Rand, having amassed enormous fortunes, became megalomaniacs. It was not enough for these men, who had nearly all arisen from obscurity, that they had acquired more money than they could make use of. They sickened with desire to possess all, to enmesh the state in a golden chain, the links of which would soon be riveted over the whole of South Africa.
>
> A platform was necessary from whence to operate. They had with characteristic astuteness, gauged the gullibility of an England drunken with the poison-wine of spurious imperialism, so they chose the platform of loyalty to the British flag. How these cosmopolitan punters must have winked at each other behind the curtain … .
>
> When the 'League', which was the progenitor of the Progressive Party of a few years later, was defeated at the polls in 1898, the circumstance was truly read as a sign that the people of the Cape Colony were determined to make a stand against capitalism. It was then that war was decided upon, by the Randlords and their dupes.

For all his vehemence, Scully was not as single-minded as one might suppose. Later,[15] having poured out pages of scorn on British methods and motives, rather disappointingly he revealed the extent of his own ambivalence:

> When all is said and done, I do not suppose that any one of us – bitterly as we are opposed to England's South Africa policy – would ever dream of wishing to live under another flag.

Whereas many writers had been obsessed with Britain's power and prestige, Scully was one of the first to realise the importance of economics in the conflict. This does not mean that earlier writers were unaware of the role of gold, but they tended to see it in symbolic rather than economic terms. That is, they saw it as something that was dug out of the ground, largely by British efforts, and a just reward for their ingenuity. They did not represent gold as being a vital factor in the economic development of South Africa. They did not see gold as affecting its labour relations and economic balance, and ultimately the distribution of power within the body politic.

Salve for wounds

Many of the English novels about the Anglo-Boer War written in the 1920s and '30s showed a desire to heal past wounds and promote unity between the two white groups in the interests of the Union of South Africa. However, whereas in the English fiction, the emphasis was on the healing of disagreements and old wounds, many novels in Afrikaans, for example T.C. Pienaar's *'n Merk vir die Eeue* (1939) and Van Bruggen's *Bittereinders* (1935), seem intent on keeping the old contentious issues alive. But it must be remembered this was a period of intense Afrikaner nationalism often accompanied by strong anti-English feelings. The 'poor white problem' was largely an Afrikaner problem. In the main, those who suffered most in the 1929 Depression, and in the perennial drought, belonged to the same group who had lost the war.

That English-speaking writers did not always achieve the objectivity they were aiming for is not to be wondered at. In fact, all too often they were patronising and paternalistic as they tried to gloss over past differences. At the same time, a number of English novels began to appear that depicted the war from a Boer point of view. One of the earliest of these was Daphne Muir's *A Virtuous Woman* (1929). For Daphne Muir the causes of the War were the 'unfortunate discovery of gold and diamonds' and the doomed hope of the Boers that they would found 'a nation which [would] be able to maintain South Africa for the Afrikaners – and by Afrikaners they mean the white men of their blood, speaking Afrikaans'.[16]

A Virtuous Woman is devoted entirely, and with compassion, to the saga of the Boer women, yet there is some evidence of resentment of Afrikaner exclusivity. Nonetheless, Muir tried to be even-handed, apportioning blame to both sides.

Norman McKoewn's *The Ridge of White Waters* published a few years later (in 1934), also explored the war from the Boer point of view. In his efforts to be fair, McKoewn attempted to have the best of all possible worlds. His story is told largely from the point of view of a young English girl who married into a Boer family. Deborah is torn between her loyalties to the land of her birth and to her husband Gideon. He too is conflicted:[17]

> "It is not all the fault of the English," he said, gentle with her, "nor is it altogether Paul Kruger who is to blame." A sudden anger seized him and he raised his fists in anathema above his head. "It is the Ridge!" he burst out. "The Ridge of White Waters, stained with mud and gold, and now to run red with the blood of good men. God was not kind to his people when He put such temptation in their way. We should have run from it as our fathers did from the English. It is a worse enemy! They would only hold our bodies, but this has taken our souls as well."
>
> It was her turn to be gentle now and her arms went around him, and her soft lips soothed his sore heart. Their tears mingled in the pillow, while outside

> the tears of God poured down and the grass for the horses began to grow.

Whether it's Gods will or the rain's, Boer and Briton are depicted here as victims of circumstances beyond their control.

In a novel written shortly before World War II, when the whole issue of unity between the two white groups was assuming a greater urgency for English-speaking South Africans than hitherto, Manfred Nathan began his *Sarie Marais* (1938), by examining the South African conflict in terms of global issues. Nathan presented a case in which the Anglo-Boer War was a relatively minor conflict, which was part of, and an expression of the worldwide tensions and anxieties of the day: international trade and power rivalries, the insecurities of social and technological change and the rise of the finance capitalist. Because of the so-called blessing of universal education, whole populations could easily be persuaded to support corrupt politicians. When it came to discussing the causes of the war, though, the best Nathan could do was to provide his heroine with the emotive but weak argument that the British presence in South Africa was merely to prevent the Boers from ruling themselves. Everything for Sarie hinges on 'freedom':[18]

> "Perhaps, if this were our own country." she said, "we might have more things of our own – to remind us of where our people come from."
>
> "But this is your own country," the Lieutenant replied.
>
> "How is that?" inquired Sarie. "England took the country from the Dutch."
>
> Lieutenant Playfair was inwardly amused at the trend of the conversation. He had no intention of discussing politics with the girl, but he could not help the rejoinder: "The Dutch have full say in the affairs of this country. Why, you have a Dutch – a South African – government ruling the Cape Colony now."
>
> "It's not the same thing as having your own flag," said Sarie. "In the Transvaal we have our own Republic and are perfectly free."

There is much to comment on here, from the Lieutenant's name, his patronising chauvinism, to the rights of conquest, and if the English took the country from the Dutch, who did the Dutch take it from?

Nathan set out to tell the story from the point of view of 'Sarie Marais, the national heroine of the Boer people'. One suspects though, that Nathan's intention was not so much to promote understanding and tolerance, as to contribute to the political programme of encouraging the two white groups to bury the past in the interest of facing the future together. This is born out when the villain of the piece turns out to be not a Boer, or even a renegade Englishman, but a German secret agent. In this novel, as in so many novels, the Kaiser's telegram is interpreted as misleading the Boers and giving them a false sense of their own security. But as far as Nathan was concerned, Munich had come and gone. The South African government was split between Hertzog and Smuts; between those who wanted to remain outside of any war that might erupt in Europe and those who felt that their loyalty lay with the British Empire. The approaching war clouds in the Northern hemisphere gave writers a definite excuse for introducing anti-German sentiments into their novels.

The German threat was seen as a major factor in Kathleen Sinclair's *The Covenant* (1944). The hero, Stephan, is discussing the possibility of war with his Afrikaner wife:[19]

> "There are many old scores to settle. But there is a worthier reason. Every Englishman will have to fight if British power is to survive in South Africa. Kruger has openly boasted of having Germany's friendship, and the German influence in the Republics is already strong, and growing daily."

After World War II, the German threat diminished in importance. In *The Geyer Brood* (1946), Thirza Nash commented on the antagonists as they sized each other up at the Bloemfontein Conference of 1899:[20]

> Behind Milner was the might of the British Empire, and behind Kruger the determination of the Boers and, alas, the grisly hope of 'Foreign Intervention' –

> from Germany – which was nothing but a myth, and vanished into thin air.

In these novels of the 30s and 40s, intermarriage between Afrikaner and Briton tended to contribute to a more balanced view of the conflict. It was a short step from describing the war in terms of divided family loyalties to understanding it as a civil war. The most powerful statement in this regard came from Louis Leipoldt in his novel *Stormwrack*, written in the 1930s but long forgotten until it was discovered and published in 1980. It is one of the few works, along with Bosman's short stories, that is readable in its own right today.

Stormwrack is set in the Clan William district of the Western Province. The narrative depicts the village gradually awakening to the gathering tensions of the approaching war. Major issues are debated by every shade of opinion, from the League of Loyal Women to rabid Afrikaner nationalists without suggesting an easy solution. Nor do his characters cling to their convictions. They are forced to reconsider what they have taken for granted, again and again. Matters come to a head when a Boer commando invades the district, and martial law is imposed by the British Army. Many families have relatives fighting on both sides. The village pastor's main concern is that his wounded son may have been shot by 'someone of his own kin'.[21]

From the 1950s onwards, less and less attention was given in novels to the causes of the Anglo-Boer War. Perhaps because political commitment is lacking in these later books, the conflict was treated as little more than an excuse for 'light romance' against an exciting and credible background. In Robin Collins' *The Four Coloured Flag* (1958), Henry Gibbs' *The Tumult and the Shouting* (1958), Wilbur Smith's *The Sound of Thunder* (1966) and Kit Denton's *The Breaker* (1973), for example, there is no sense of a political point of view. In 1963 when Stuart Cloete's *Rags of Glory* appeared, the background of the story is important only in so far as it provided Cloete with an opportunity to dwell on Victorian decadence; a subject he was later to make the theme of a full length novel. For Cloete, the years immediately before war broke out were 'the time of black and white, of wrong and right. Few people could see grey or recognise finer shades of opinion'.[22]

In his introduction Cloete declared his position:[23]

> The Anglo-Boer War combined some of the features of both the American Revolution and the Civil War. As in America, it was a war of cultures. In Africa it was England with her colonies of the Cape and Natal fighting two little republics of the north. A civil war in which brother was against brother, in which, as in America, an industrialized people attempted to force a material and alien culture upon farmers who were fighting for a way of life.

What this analysis ignores is more important than the points that it makes. Cloete air-brushes out the economic imperatives driving imperial aggression. He begs the question as to how Boer and Brit might be described as brothers; though one is left with the nagging doubt that it is simply because they are both 'white men'. In other words, his understanding of the conflict is based on racial prejudice and little more. The indigenous black inhabitants could not be described as brothers and therefore equals of either of the antagonists. They certainly have no role to play in the drama as he sees it. Nor is there any serious attempt to explore the nature of the 'war of cultures'. So much for recognising 'finer shades of opinion'.

As a rule, the ways in which the writers of popular literature presented the issues that precipitated the Second Anglo-Boer War were determined by their own ideological positions. Time lends different perspectives, and the causes of the conflict as perceived in popular literature were and are often a product of the writers' preoccupations.

Endnotes

1 Reitz, F.W., 'Gods of the Jingo' in Chapman, M. (ed.) *A Century of South African Poetry*.

2 Letter from Francis Younghusband to Arthur Newbolt quoted in Howarth 1973: 8.

3 W. T. Stead quoted by Hume Nisbet, *For Right and England* 1900: viii.

4 Mark Twain, 'Diamonds' in *Writers' Territory*, ed. Stephen Gray Cape Town: Longman, 1973: 38.

5 Stead 1899: 6.

6 Buchan 1941: 125.

7 Griffith 1897: vii.

8 Stead 1899: 6.

9 Hume Nisbet, *For Right and England* 1900: ix.

10 Mitford 1900: 6–8.

11 Laycock 1900: 289.

12 Vaughan 1906: 35–6.

13 Eugene Marais, 22 February1897. Unpublished letter discovered by Stephen Gray.

14 Scully 1921: 48–9.

15 Ibid.

16 Muir 1929: 139.

17 McKoewn 1939: 268.

18 Nathan 1938: 9.

19 Sinclair 1944: 148.

20 Nash 1946: 184.

21 Leipoldt 1980: 232.

22 Cloete 1963: 80.

23 Ibid.

Storm clouds rise over the Transvaal.

CHAPTER TWO

THE SOUTH AFRICAN LANDSCAPE: 'Amazing, ablazing, aglow'

> 'land of rivers without water, women without beauty,
> flowers without smell.'
>
> Samuel B. Hemyng, *Jack Harkaway in the Transvaal*[1]

As the British Empire expanded during the 19th century, the heroes of African exploration – Burton, Livingstone and Speke – thrilled a patriotic British public with accounts of strange and 'savage' peoples in distant lands, filled with vast deserts, equatorial jungles, mighty lakes, rivers, and waterfalls. It was an age of exploration and discovery, of cartography, of collecting and cataloguing. Palms, proteas and orchids bloomed for the public at Kew Gardens. Agapanthus, gladioli and pelagonias from the Cape began to make their appearance in private conservatories in Britain.

Geography and natural history became all the rage. As early as 1795, the British Royal Society had been interested in acquiring the posthumous botanical papers and drawings of Colonel Robert Jacob Gordon, commanding officer at the Cape and naturalist. The going price for this collection was £1 200, a considerable sum for those days.

Romantic adventure stories set in far-flung parts of the Empire were extremely popular, especially those for the young imperialist. These stories had the dual function of imbuing patriotic fervour and educating the reader in the wonders of nature.

Many early writers, following in the wake of R.M. Ballantyne, *Coral Island* (1857), *Martin Rattler* (1858) and Captain Marryat, *Mr Midshipman Easy* (1836) exploited the settings the Empire supplied to pad their stories with history, geography and natural science for the edification of the young. They and their contemporaries set out quite self-consciously (and confidently) to 'improve' the young mind while entertaining it. Thomas Hughes pronounced the creed of these writers in his preface to *Tom Brown's School Days* (1857): 'I can't see that a man has any business to write at all unless he has something which he thoroughly believes and wants to preach about.'[2]

The motive was moral. This approach to juvenile fiction had its origins in Rousseau's *Emile* (1762). Two of Rousseau's ideas on education were to become (via Wordsworth's poetry) especially influential in English children's fiction during the 19th century. The first of these was that children should be brought up in close harmony with nature, so that through constant exposure to what was perceived as the moral basis of creation, they would develop a natural morality. The second idea was that the key to developing the child's intellect was through stimulating his curiosity, or, as Coleridge put it:[3]

> ... to give the charm of novelty of things of every day,
> and to excite a feeling analogous to the supernatural,
> by awakening the mind's attention from the lethargy
> of custom, and directing it to the loveliness and
> wonders of the world before us.

In Britain, the reading public was expanding rapidly. Although education would have to wait till 1880 before it became compulsory, there was a wide-spread thirst for knowledge. Subscription libraries were extremely popular, and the burgeoning trade-union movement encouraged the establishment of reading rooms in its working men's clubs. 'High-minded' Victorians saw literature as a powerful means to stimulate and improve the young mind. Boer War fiction for the young was no exception. Apart from providing a rattling good yarn, the war in South Africa gave writers a means of educating the budding imperialist, and an opportunity for what today would be seen as crude propaganda in the defence of the Empire.

Attitudes to children and literature have changed a great deal since the Boer War. While writers of children's fiction still recognise and cater for the need for a fast-moving and suspenseful story, there is little or no attempt today to preach or impart 'moral' information disguised as fact. Geography or history lessons are not given with moral overtones. There has been a move away from overt didacticism. Instead, there is an emphasis on providing a safe context in which children can experience vicariously various developmental, emotional and psychological states. Where religion has declined, its place has been taken by psychology. Nevertheless, the motivation is no less Rousseauian than that of 19th century British writers. Only now, instead of coming away from the literary experience a 'better' person, the young reader is assumed to become a more 'balanced' and 'integrated' one. The focus has shifted from the soul to the *id*.

It is useful to compare Boer War juvenile fiction with a popular example of juvenile war fiction from the second half of the 20th century. Ann Holm's *I am David* (1969), for example, is a story about a young Jewish orphan boy's flight across Nazi-occupied Europe. Part of the writer's purpose was to enable the reader vicariously to come to grips with and confront such states of mind as fear, isolation and rejection. Of course, there is also a moral dimension, but it is essentially an ideological one. David finds himself in a chaotic world in which he can trust no one. He has to rely on his own resources. There is no one he can turn to for support; certainly no adult. Adults are responsible for the war. As far as David is concerned, adults have lost their moral authority.

In nearly all 19th century juvenile fiction, though, adult authority is respected. There is usually at least one strong adult figure on whom the young hero can rely, who provides a moral touch stone, and at least one point of stability in an unpredictable world. Even Huckleberry Finn has his Jim. However, since World War II, the adult world in children's fiction has become treacherous. Adults are not only untrustworthy but often weak. The child protagonist is forced to rely on his own resources. These changes in style not only reflect changed attitudes to children and childhood, but also reflect a loss of faith in the traditional nuclear family decimated by divorce; and a loss of faith in Church and state institutions.

Perils in the Transvaal and Zululand (1887) by the Rev. H.C. Adams, which covers the Zulu wars and the First Anglo-Boer War, is typical of the kind of fiction written at that time for a juvenile audience. The author's disclaimer is notable:[4]

> It is a plain unvarnished tale, and I trust historically true, because I have studied the reports of all good London newspapers. I trust, moreover, that it is true to scenery, true to nature, true to life, because it is a story of soldiering and sailoring.

The story begins in a British public school, as so many of these stories do, but quickly moves through a series of adventures at sea to South Africa, where the hero, George Rivers, is shipwrecked off the coast of Natal. George and his friend Reginald are fortunate in meeting one of the English settlers who takes them under his wing. Lessons in history, describing the settling of Natal (and not all of it uncritical of British colonial policy), the rise of 'the black Napoleon' Shaka, and Dingaan, and the conflict between the Zulus and the Voortrekkers. The South African setting not only provides Adams with an exotic backdrop to his 'history', but also enables him to provide scenic interludes between adventures.

A journey through the Natal uplands gives the author the opportunity to describe the landscape. He has to make up with imaginative detail and literary convention what he lacks in direct experience.[5]

> The ground was still soft from heavy rain in some places, but a few hours' hot sun dried it. The air was fresh and balmy … . Aromatic shrubs, graceful sugar bushes, wild flowers of every imaginable colour, such as in England would be accounted the rare beauties of the conservatory, grew in profusion on either side of the track they followed. The air was rich with a thousand fragrant scents. In the middle distance kaffir hovels or white-gabled farmhouses occasionally

> presented themselves, each surrounded by orange or palm groves; and white peaked mountains, set in their frame of the richest blue, formed a perfect background to a lovely picture … . The track he pursued led through a country wilder than any George had yet seen. It ran for miles along the banks of a small but most picturesque stream, the banks of which were clothed with trees of every variety. The mimosa predominated, but it was intermingled with date-trees and kaffir plums and huge cacti, with their sword-like leaves, and acacias already coming into flower. Overhead hoopoes and parrots kept up a never-ending chorus, while countless tribes of monkeys and squirrels leaped and chattered among the branches.

The first thing that strikes one about this passage is the density of the description. The Natal uplands are visualised in essentially English terms. The author is familiar with the variety and compactness of the English countryside and has conceived of Natal in the same way. The failure of Adams' description, for all the detail, is one of scale. His mountains, unlike Olive Schreiner's, are not characterised by:[6]

> … a certain colossal plenitude, a certain large freedom in all its natural proportions … . If Nature here wishes to make a mountain, she runs up a range for five hundred miles; if a plain, she levels eighty; if a rock she tilts five thousand feet of strata on end … . There is nothing small or petty in South Africa.

By the time Gordon Stables (another author given to welding history, geography and literature together for the edification of the young) wrote *On War's Red Tide* (1900), there had been a shift in the emphasis given to setting and the strategies used by writers to win their readers' confidence. The geography lesson is still there, only now the presumptions underlying it are more pronounced and perhaps more urgent. Above all, it appears that the young reader must be 'wooed':[7]

> And now, reader, I have a favour to ask you – if you mean to follow me to the war … . For your peace of mind as well as your author's, I wish you to look at a good map. I desire you to know a little about the lay of the land and the water, and the relative position of the more important towns, villages and forts that figure in the fighting. You must not look at an overcrowded map. I myself hate an overcrowded map. To put it mildly, such a map is confoundedly confusing.
>
> But really it isn't half bad fun looking at a map of the war, if it be a skeleton map, and if the fellow who built it isn't a champion jackass.
>
> Well, at the left hand or west side of the map you'll easily find Cape Town … .

And so on, around the coast with suitable nautical interjections: '… clap on more canvas … . 'Bout ships now, and under a crowd of canvas we skirt the coast once more … .' The tour of South Africa is concluded with an imaginary train journey through Natal to Pretoria with parenthetical lessons on the pronunciation of local Zulu names:

> Tugela (Be careful how you pronounce this word please, so as not to offend anyone who 'knows a thing or two') … Ingane (pronounce In-gah-nay, and I shall feel exceedingly grateful) … .

The lesson is rounded off with:

> If the reader, then, has followed the routes I have pointed out, he will have learnt all he needs to know concerning the topography of the seat of war; and I am vain enough to credit myself with a far funnier, and ten times more useful, way of teaching geography than that which obtains at schools.

Compulsory education had taken its toll. Learning is no longer exciting, but a bore. Overriding Stables' patronising and hearty comradeship is his need to convince the young reader that acquiring knowledge is not only easy but also fun; the youthful mind should not be put off by an apparent welter of detail. All that is needed are a few easily understood general truths. Nor was this attitude limited to Stables. An examination of the children's literature of the time reveals that it was wide spread. It was associated with the notion that the swot who did well at school was inferior to the lad who was good at sport and a natural leader. This attitude was not limited to fiction. Several generations of young imperialists went out to the colonies and administered thousands of square miles under the same illusion. These same young men arrived with preconceived ideas of what to expect of the continent and its inhabitants, derived from the plethora of popular writing about Africa. Without doubt, the most influential of which was H. Rider Haggard's *King Solomon's Mines* (1886).

'I WAS THERE, AND THIS IS WHAT IT WAS LIKE'

From the 1880s onwards, increasing numbers of Britons were attracted to Africa as tourists, fortune seekers, settlers, administrators and hunters. It was a literary age. Everyone wrote. Everyone read. Letters, diaries, articles, pamphlets and books recording experiences and impressions proliferated. In fact, many British writers had had some experience of South Africa at one time or another; nor were they slow to exploit their local knowledge. The Jameson Raid and the second Anglo-Boer War were well-covered by English, American and Continental journalists. But of necessity, the journalists were more focused on the action than on the countryside. For example, Doornkop, the site of Dr Jameson's surrender to Cronje in 1896, was widely known, to judge from the British newspapers. However, few readers in England could have had anything but the haziest notion of what the veld around Doornkop looked like, to say nothing of the country the raiders had travelled through since leaving Pitsani in Bechuanaland. Earlier in the century, the British 1820 Settlers had disembarked in Algoa Bay in a similar though much more disastrous state of ignorance.

The writers of Boer War fiction, then, had the problem of creating a literary landscape about a country that was unfamiliar to the vast majority of their British readers. Douglas Blackburn who was trying to write an indigenous South African novel in the 1890s, was highly critical of those local 'colourists' who decorated their novels with nothing more than the trappings of authenticity and:[8]

> [the] undiscriminating English public [who] take it for granted that any man who has spent sufficient time in the country to be able to mis-spell a few stock native names and phrases is worth listening to as an oracle on any South African subject from the Scab Act to the quality of veldschoons in use in a particular district.

These remarks appeared in an article attacking Rider Haggard for talking 'frothy nonsense' and 'drivel' at the South African Writers' Dinner in July 1896. Haggard had enraged Blackburn for expressing his imperialist view that there was a 'need' to impose British rule on the Transvaal. Nonetheless, many early popular writers who had direct experience of the country, such as Bertram Mitford, Ernest Glanville and Haggard were not slow to realise and exploit the rich potential the country offered to writers for high adventure in exotic settings.

Haggard's *Jess* (1887) was one of the earliest Boer War novels written by someone who had first hand experience of South Africa. *Jess* was enormously popular and remained so for decades, going into at least twenty-seven editions. It was translated into French the year it was published and into Urdu nearly forty years later, in 1923. Between 1911 and 1916, over 64 000 English copies were sold.

Jess is set largely in the Wakkerstroom District in the Transvaal. It was to this district that Haggard brought his wife in 1880. The farm Hilldrop, in Natal near Newcastle, was their first home. Hilldrop became Mooifontein in *Jess*, although moved across the border into the Transvaal, more or less midway between Wakkerstroom and present-day Lothair. Haggard's feel for the country is evident in the opening paragraphs:[9]

> The day had been hot even for the Transvaal, where the days still know how to be hot in autumn, although the

> neck of summer is broken – especially when the thunder storms hold off for a week or two, as they do occasionally. Even the succulent blue lilies – a variety of agapanthus which is so familiar to us in English greenhouses – hung their long trumpet flowers and looked oppressed and miserable, beneath the burning breath of the hot wind which had been blowing for hours like the draught from a volcano. The grass too, near the wide roadway that stretched in a feeble and indeterminate fashion across the veldt, forking, branching, and reuniting like the veins on a lady's arm, was completely covered over with a thick layer of red dust. But the hot wind was going down now, as it always does towards sunset. Indeed, all that remained of it were a few strictly local and miniature whirlwinds, which would suddenly spring up on the road itself, and twist and twirl fiercely round, raising up a mighty column of dust fifty feet or more into the air, where it hung long after the wind had passed, and then slowly dissolved as its particles floated to the earth.

The Boer War apart, *Jess* is essentially a love story about sexual passion and mental breakdown. Haggard used the natural setting to symbolise, allegorise and mythologise the action. Descriptions of the veld convey covert suggestions of sexual passion. Hills, predictably described as swelling bosoms, appear on the horizon whenever the emotional temperature is about to rise. Love is associated with mountains, with all the concomitant allusions to perilous paths, crevasses, lofty peaks, yawning precipices, and so on.

Paradise Lost

The popular 19th century literary image of Africa was of an unspoiled Eden. As the century progressed, this image changed. Writers with literary pretensions increasingly used the metaphor, the Dark Continent, to describe Africa. Popular writers began to give Africa sinister attributes, and now inferred or stated openly that although Africa may have been an Eden, it was an Eden after the Fall, in which snakes and other horrors abounded, culminating in such unspeakable visions as those in Conrad's *Heart of Darkness*.

Africa appears in *Jess*, as it does in *She* and *King Solomon's Mines*, as a corrupt Eden. It is an image that served Haggard well. For instance, in developing the relationship between his hero, Captain Niel and Jess's sister Bessie, Haggard slipped from realism into parable and back again. Captain Niel tries to persuade Bessie to go for a walk with him in a blue-gum plantation. Bessie is already more than half in love with him, but like all virtuous girls in Victorian fiction, cannot declare herself to her man. What girl could resist a man who has risked life and limb to rescue her from a rogue ostrich? (The St George motif is established early and elaborated in a variety of guises, with a villainous Boer taking the role of the dragon.)

The myth of Africa as the corrupt Eden is evident in Bessie's observations. She 'looked through the open kitchen door at the lights and shadows that chased each other across the swelling bosom of the hill behind the house'.[10] The plantation is crawling with puff-adders. She hesitates, but after Niel reassures her, they go for a walk, which confirms Bessie in her feelings for Niel, who unwittingly leads her to believe he is not indifferent to her. Unfortunately, Bessie confesses all to her sister, Jess, who is herself secretly in love with Niel. The rest of the novel, with a variety of complicating factors, such as the First Anglo-Boer War, is concerned with Jess's efforts to disguise her feelings and sacrifice herself for Bessie's happiness.

Jess is probably the most complex female character Haggard ever created. She, too, lives in a corrupt Eden, an inner world of the mind and spirit, in which the enemy is not a real live puff-adder (no matter how symbolic), but a deep and unresolved inner conflict, for which Africa stands as the metaphor. Early in the novel, when she has begun to realise the extent of her feelings for Niel, she walks alone in the kranzes far from the farm-house. Her conflicting moods are reflected in the description of the surroundings:[11]

> It was one of those glorious afternoons that
> sometimes come in the African spring, although it was

> so intensely still. Everywhere appeared the proofs and evidences of life. The winter was over, and now, from the sadness and sterility of its withered age, sprang young and lovely summer clad in sunshine, bediamoned with dew, and fragrant with the breath of flowers. Jess lay back and looked up into the infinite depths above. How blue they were, and how measureless! She could not see the angry clouds that lay like visible omens on the horizon. Look, there, miles above her, was one tiny circling speck. It was a vulture, watching her from his airy heights and descending a little to see if she were dead, or only sleeping.
>
> Involuntarily she shuddered. The bird of death reminded her of Death himself also hanging high up yonder in the blue and waiting his opportunity to fall upon the sleeper. Then her eyes fell upon a bough of the glorious flowering bush under which she rested. It was not more than four feet above her head, but she lay so still and motionless that a jewelled honeysucker came and hovered over the flowers, darting from one to another like a many coloured flash. Thence her glance travelled to a great column of boulders that towered above her, and that seemed to say, "I am very old. I have seen many springs and many winters, and have looked down on many sleeping maids, and where are they now? All dead – all dead," and an old baboon in the rocks with startling suddenness barked out "All dead" in answer.

Pathetic fallacy and image are intermingled. The winter and summer images are of Jess herself whose life, hitherto so bleak and unfulfilled, has just been touched by love. The 'angry clouds', the 'bird of death', the message from the rocks and the old baboon reflect Jess's attitude to life which is at war with her newly awakened emotions and sensuality, symbolised in the flowers, dew and honeysucker.

The essential conflict in the minds of the 'romance' novelists, such as

Haggard and his contemporaries, was between the vastness of the land that seemed to alienate man, and the image of a beautiful country with a perfect climate. But they went further and imposed an allegorical or mystical element in order to establish mood and tone. In *Jess*, for instance, the young struggle to reconcile the stirrings of love and sex with their notions of honour, in a landscape crawling with snakes. In Dolf Wyllarde's *The Story of Eden* (1903) the Serpent is ever ready to strike:[12]

> It is characteristic of civilisation in South Africa, that savage nature is generally to be found on the other side of the hedge. A rich man's carefully cultivated garden will be bounded by a line beyond which is a cheerful prospect of uncultivated land with the appearance of raw veld; a pretty red road, open and harmless in the morning sunlight, will change, suddenly, at the rapid descent of darkness, into a horribly lonely place, with battle, murder, and sudden death, or worse, – lying in wait in the hundred yards or so between one friend's house and another's. But then, the houses stand well away from the road, in their own grounds, as a rule, and people who possess any nerves are haunted by a dread that a call for help would be lost in the space between. Robberies do take place, though not often; but the white women have two bogies they shun, – the Kaffir after dark, and the snake which glides across the soft, red earth and is hardly visible.

Wyllarde's landscape holds definite and immediate terrors. Civilisation is on this side of a comforting hedge, where white women never have to face a fate worse than death. Beyond the carefully cultivated garden is nature, red in tooth and claw: Eden after the Fall, complete with black devils and invisible snakes. This passage reveals much about the author's prejudices. Little wonder that the hero and heroine escape to England at the end of the novel, unlike so many of their contemporaries who remained to settle. For Wyllarde, the country is fit only for Boers and 'Kaffirs'.

From the Queen of Sheba and Cleopatra to *King Solomon's Mines* and *Prester John*, Africa has been filled with mythical treasure troves; from Monomotapa to the land of Ophir. The discovery of the Zimbabwe Ruins and a few gold artefacts beneath its crumbling walls in the 1860s did nothing to lessen the Scramble for Africa. The myth of untold riches became reality with the discovery of diamonds near Kimberley in 1867 and the gold reef on the Witwatersrand in 1886. For centuries, men had been lured to the African continent in search of their fortunes. The discoveries of 1867 and 1886 surpassed their wildest dreams. And certainly, if there had been no gold in the Transvaal there would have been no war.

The view of South Africa as an Eden, corrupt or otherwise, is essentially pastoral. Cities barely figure. But in those 'romances' that portrayed South Africa as a rich prize to be added to the Empire, cities and towns play a more prominent role. Writers of these novels tended to restrict their vision of Africa to the insides of certain hotels and clubs: the Mount Nelson Hotel in Cape Town, the Rand Club in Johannesburg, and the De Beers Club in Kimberley. G.M. Fenn's *A Dash for Diamond City* (1901) is a case in point.

In Arthur Laycock's *Steve, The Outlander* (1900), most of the action takes place in Cape Town and Johannesburg. Laycock was the only writer to dwell at any length on Table Mountain. This seems strange when one considers that for the vast number of travellers, soldiers and writers, Table Mountain must have been their first sight of South Africa. Laycock's mood is inspirational, his hero, despised and rejected in love, spends a night agonising on the side of Table Mountain. The mountain inspires Steve with magnanimity, high ideals and noble purpose:[13]

> That night he slept among the trees at the foot of Table Mountain. It was cool and pleasant out there, and he felt that there was comfort in that mighty mountain which had reared its giant form aloft through the centuries.
>
> "The eternal mountain!" he cried, as he looked up

> the rugged steeps in the bright clear light of morn. "The eternal mountain! Changeless! Changeless! Men may come, men may go; women may be false; hearts may be broken; lives may be cursed; all may be vanity, falseness, but the eternal mountain is changeless!"
>
> Slowly, yet with deliberate steps, he walked into the town, his eyes were ever turning aside to the right and sweeping the broad, serrated face of the giant Table.
>
> "Yes changeless!" he mused. "As I also will be; God witness it! I, too, will be changeless. Though she has been false, though she has riven my heart in twain, I'll be true to her. I'll be changeless as the mountain! Yesterday I cursed her; to-day I say, God forgive her!"

The mountain may be mighty, eternal and changeless, but Steve remains a working-class hero (the only one in the fiction) with aspirations, trapped by his creator's cliches.

'Turkey-carpet' style of writing

The opening pages of Clothilde Graves' *The Dop Doctor* (1910) are written in a similar 'high-flown' style in which (to echo Gertrude in *Hamlet*) too much 'art' is expended on too little matter. In an English tradition extending from Haggard to Wilbur Smith, the novel opens with what is almost an obligatory scene in Boer War fiction: a journey across the veld, inevitably by ox-wagon:[14]

> Upon a day near the end of August, one long, brilliant South African winter, when the old Vierkleur waved over the Transvaal, and what is now the Orange River Colony was the Orange Free State, with the Dutch canton still showing on the staff-head corner of its tribarred flag, two large, heavily-laden waggons rolled over the grass veld, only now thinking of changing from yellow into green.

> Many years previously, the wheels of the old Voortrekkers had passed that way, bringing from the Cape Colony, with the household gods, goods and chattels, language and customs of the Dutch, the slips of pomegranate and peach and orange trees, whose abundant blossoming dressed the orchards of the farms tucked away here and there in the lap of the veld, with bridal white and pink and hung their girdling pomegranate hedges with stars of ruby red. But days and days and nights and nights of billowing, spreading, lonely sky-arched veld intervened between each homestead.
>
> The flat-topped hills were draped and folded in the opal haze of distance; the sky was perfect turquoise; the rounded kopjes shone like pink topaz, unclothed as yet with the young pale green bush. To the south there was a veld fire leaping and dancing, with swirling columns of white smoke edged with flame. But it was many miles away, and the north-west wind blew strongly, driving some puffs of gold before it. Perhaps there would be rain ere long.

Perhaps not. The veld to the south of Mafeking must be one of the most barren and unattractive parts of the country. Not for nothing is it known in Tswana as 'Mafekeng': 'the place of stones'.

For all the details of the veld fire leaping and dancing and rolling wagon wheels, the scene is static, like a vast, lurid canvas imbued with ornate sensuality. The decoration is only matched by the cumbersome sentence construction which often leaves the reader gasping for breath and grasping for the meaning. But then, Graves was nothing if not ambitious. In the dedication to her novel she described her desire to write a book that will 'live':[15]

> What have the long years brought me since first, with pen for pickaxe, I bowed my loins to quarry from the living rock of my world about me, bread and a home where Love should smile beside the hearthplace, and

> chiefly for Love's dear sake, that men should honour you who, above all on earth, I hold most in honour – a name among the writers of books that live?

Francis Brett Young summed up *The Dop Doctor* as follows:[16]

> The Second Anglo-Boer War lent its name to a flamboyant best-seller, *The Dop Doctor*: the crude, violent, intensely sentimental narrative of a woman who called herself Richard Dehan, anticipating in its theatrical presentation of the scene's surface, the cheapness of its emotions, its rhapsodical eroticism and its hysterical adulation of the prepotent male, the novels of other women such as Cynthia Stockley.

Graves was writing well within a vogue that included Ouida and Marie Corelli what *The Morning Post* critics of Marie Corelli's *Vendetta* (1886) described as 'her full-blooded, Turkey-carpet style of writing'.[17]

One of the staple ingredients of South African 'romance' is the thunderstorm which can be rolled across the veld to add pyrotechnics for dramatic effect. Hardly a Boer War novel exists that does not have at least one thunderstorm. The following episode is the sort of anecdote that has become part of South African folklore. For her readers it must have been especially horrifying, and characteristic of an alien continent.[18]

> There was a big rainfall on the third day. It began with the typical South African thunderstorm – deafening, continuous rolls and crashes of heavy artillary, and lightning that blazed and darted without intermission, and ran zigzagging in a horrible, deadly, playful fashion over the veld, as though looking for dishonest folk to shrivel. One terrible flash struck the wheel-oxen, a thin double tongue of blue flame spread flickering from ridge to ridge of the six gaunt backs ... there was a smell of burning hair – a reek of sulphur. The team lay outstretched on the veld, the heavy yolk

> across their patient necks, the long horns curving, the thin starved bodies already beginning to bloat and swell in the swift decomposition that follows death by electric fluid.

It is interesting to compare Graves's description with a similar one written by Fr. Porte, O.M.I., who arrived in Mafeking in 1894, some sixteen years before *The Dop Doctor* was published:[19]

> After visiting the Catholic farmers of the District and having performed the ordinary Sunday duties (it was Jan 8th 1894), I went for the last time to speak to Montsioa, chief of the Baralongs. When returning at 4 o'clock in the afternoon my servants asked me to allow them to cross with the waggon to the other side of the river, which in consequence of the continual rains was fairly high and would not take long to be filled level with the banks. A storm was threatening. I urged the servants to make haste while I went to Baptize some children in the town. It was 5.30 in the evening when suddenly a young girl rushed into the house crying out "Oh! Mother, all Father Porte's oxen are killed". I hastened to the waggon, which was about 300 yards from the town on the bank of the river. Yes, of the 14 oxen which formed my team, twelve were lying on the road stark in death. Only two had escaped, 'France' and 'England'. When I arrived I saw the driver holding the smaller boy in his arms. In a second I had a bottle of arnica out. We pulled his tongue forward to permit breathing and the passage of the arnica. When the doctor arrived the servant was much better. He had not been struck by the lightning, only partly suffocated. However, the lightning struck only two or three yards from him, just between the two front oxen. The fluid ran along the steel chain to which the yolks were attached, killing in its passage seven oxen on the right and five on the left, struck the

> shaft, where it made some grooves, then the axel of the front wheel and there it passed into the ground under the waggon where the soil was horribly ploughed up.
>
> Several sparks tore a piece of wood from the back and struck two steel bars which supported the tent beside the back wheels. There is no doubt, if I had been in the wagon according to my custom, I would have been killed. My heart is full of gratitude towards God, because he has visibly protected both my servants and myself. The driver was absent during the accident, having gone to get water at the river. Certainly I experienced a painful moment when I saw stretched on the ground, this team which had carried me more than 800 miles and which everyone admired along the road. I thought also of the anxiety my telegram would cause your Lordship the next day. But *Pater noster, fiat voluntas tua: Dominus dedit, Dominus abstulit.*

It is not recorded if the good Father had any literary ambitions, but on the strength of this entry he could have taught Graves a thing or two.

Realism

Rudyard Kipling was the most famous literary figure of his time to visit South Africa during the Anglo-Boer War. It may come as a surprise to Kipling's admirers to learn that the 'bard of empire' had never seen war at first hand before he arrived in South Africa in February 1900. He wasn't the first well-known writer to describe the heat of battle without having experienced it. Stephen Crane had never seen a shot fired in anger when he wrote *The Red Badge of Courage* (1895). Kipling enjoyed his war. While in Bloemfontein for two weeks, he helped edit *The Friend*, an experience he was to look back on with delight:[20] 'Never again will there be such a paper. Never again such a staff. Never such fine larks.'

Kipling's first experience of war was at Modder River, itself the scene of heavy fighting some weeks earlier, when he saw the wounded returning from the Battle of Paardeberg, then still in progress. A few months later he saw his first battle at Karree Siding. Soon thereafter, he wrote the short story 'A Sahib's War'.

Kipling recorded the trouble he had getting the background right when he was writing 'The Captive':[21]

> I could not get my lighting into key with the tone of the monologue. The background insisted too much. My Daemon said at last: "Paint the background first once for all, as hard as a public-house sign, and leave it alone." This done, the rest fell into place with the American accent and the outlook of the teller.

The result is a picture of wartime Simon's Town; naval station and transit camp for Boer prisoners, then destined for Ceylon, St Helena and Bermuda:[22]

> The guard-boat lay across the mouth of the bathing-pool, her crew idly spanking the water with the flat of their oars. A red-coated militia-man, rifle in hand, sat at the bows, and a petty officer at the stern. Between the snow-white cutter and the flat-topped, honey-coloured rocks on the beach the green water was troubled with shrimp-pink prisoners-of-war bathing. Behind their orderly tin camp and the electric-light poles rose those stone-dotted spurs that throw heat on Simonstown. Beneath them the little *Baracouta* nodded to the big *Gibralta*, and the old *Penelope*, that in ten years had been a bachelor's club, natural history museum, kindergarten, and prison, rooted and dug at her fixed moorings. Far out, a three-funnelled Atlantic transport with turtle bow and stern waddled in from the sea.
>
> Said the sentry, assured of the visitor's good faith, "Talk to 'em. You can, to any that speak English. You'll find a lot that do."

> Here and there earnest groups gathered round ministers of the Dutch Reformed Church, who doubtless preached conciliation, but the majority preferred their bath. The God who Looks after Small Things had caused the visitor that day to receive two weeks' delayed mails in one from a casual postman, and the whole heavy bundle of newspapers, tied with a strap, he dangled the bait.

Kipling uses the setting to comment with sardonic scepticism on the ways men order or disorder their lives. In the midst of war, Simon's Town is an ironic picture of domestic tranquility. The Boer prisoners are enjoying themselves in the sea while their guards, bored and sweating, rock gently in the cutter. The old *Penelope* has lost her warlike appearance beneath a host of domestic functions. The ministers of God, about whose message there is some doubt, are largely ignored. And above all, there is not a God of Wrath or War or Vengeance or even of Grand Universal Design on the Rhodes model, but a 'God who Looks after Small Things' and sees to it that the mail arrives, albeit two weeks late.

A little-known story by Kipling, 'The Way that He Took' (he claimed it was based entirely on fact), gives ample evidence of the accuracy of his eye and his capacity to create atmosphere through attention to closely observed detail.[23]

> The guns of the Field-Battery were ambushed behind white-thorned mimosas, scarcely taller than their wheels, that marked the line of the dry nullah; and the camp pretended to find shade under a clump of gums planted as an experiment by some Minister of Agriculture. One small hut, reddish stone with a tin roof, stood where the single track of the railway split into a siding. A rolling plain of red earth, speckled with loose stones and sugar bush, ran northwards to the scarps and spurs of a range of little hills – all barren and exaggerated in the heat haze.
>
> Southward, the level lost itself in a tangle of scrub-

> furred hillocks, upheaved without purpose or order, seared and blackened by the strokes of the careless lightning, seamed down their sides with spent water courses, and peppered from base to summit with stones – riven, piled, scattered stones. Far away, to the eastwards, a line of blue-grey mountains, peaked and horned, lifted itself over the huddle of the tortured earth. It was the only thing that held steady through the liquid mirage. The nearer hills detached themselves from the plain, and swam forward like islands in a milky ocean. While the Major stared through puckered eyelids, Leviathan himself walked through the far shadows of it – a black and formless beast.

The story is set in the southern Karoo near Matjiesfontein, overlooked by the Witteberge, a setting Kipling was to use in his fine poem 'Bridge Guard in the Karoo'.[24] The haze and mirage are emblematic of the main theme: nothing is as it seems. This is no despoiled Eden but a grim and uncompromising land where death lurks in the shadows. The twisted, distorted landscape, at once beautiful and deadly, is a constant reminder to those who pass through it to take nothing for granted and to be ever on their guard.

Olive Schreiner's only piece of fiction directly associated with the Anglo-Boer War is her short story 'Eighteen-Ninety-Nine'. It marks an important step in her development as a writer of fiction. It has none of the romanticism or mysticism of *The Story of an African Farm* (1883) or *Trooper Peter Halket of Mashonaland* (1897).[25]

> It was a warm night: the stars shone down through the thick soft air of the Northern Transvaal into the dark earth, where a little daub-and-wattle house of two rooms lay among the long grassy slopes.
>
> A light shone through the small window of the house, though it was past midnight. Presently the upper half of the door opened and then the lower, and the tall figure of a woman stepped out into the

> darkness. She closed the door behind her and walked towards the back of the house where a large round hut stood; beside it lay a pile of stumps and branches quite visible once the eye grew accustomed to the darkness. The woman stooped and broke off twigs till she had her apron full, and then returned slowly, and went into the house.
>
> The room to which she returned was a small, bare room, with brown earthen walls and a mud floor; a naked deal table stood in the centre, and a few dark wooden chairs, home-made, with seats of undressed leather, stood round the walls. In the corner opposite the door was an open fireplace, and on the earthen hearth stood an iron three-foot, on which stood a large black kettle, under which coals were smouldering, though the night was hot and close. Against the wall on the left side of the room hung a gun-rack with three guns upon it, and below it a large hunting-watch hung from two nails by its silver chain.
>
> In the corner by the fireplace was a little table with a coffee-pot upon it and a dish containing cups and saucers covered with water, and above it were a few shelves with crockery and a large Bible; but the dim light of the tallow candle which burnt on the table, with its wick of twisted rag, hardly made the corners visible. Beside the table sat a young woman, her head resting on her folded arms, the light of the tallow candle falling full on her head of pale flaxen hair, a little tumbled, and drawn behind into a large knot.

Schreiner, unlike Graves, does not rely on a whole host of rhetorical devices to bludgeon her reader. At an archetypal level, the unadorned style and stark setting reflect the elemental fate of all such women in peace and war: to bear children and mourn their dead. Their world is based on life's necessities: shelter, fire, water, weapons for hunting and the Bible, while at the political level, the women's plight and the Boer cause are deftly associated with the elemental world they inhabit. This setting is in striking contrast to the decadent, superficial and arrogant world of the imperialist conquerors and 'polite society' in London.

These extracts taken from the early fiction give an accurate picture of the ways in which South Africa appeared to writers and readers of the time. In this respect, Boer War fiction is no different from any other South African fiction written at the time. Purple passages describing the veld have diminished with time, so that since World War II, references to the setting tend to be brief. For example, it is sufficient for Herman Charles Bosman to begin 'The Traitor's Wife' with:[26]

> We did not like the sound of the wind that morning as we cantered over the veld trail that we had made much use of, during the past year, when there were English forces in the neighbourhood.
>
> The wind blew short whisps of yellow grass in quick flurries over the veld and the smoke from the fire in front of a row of kafir huts hung low in the air. From that we knew that the third winter of the Boer War was at hand. Our small group of burghers dismounted at the edge of a clump of camel thorns to rest our horses.

Not only is the stark realism of the setting an integral part of the tale, it is sketched in a way to suggest that Bosman and his reader share a world of common experience. But more than that, the description of the highveld winter needs no elaboration to suggest the hardship of war on commando and the bitterness it engendered. The winter wind, the yellow grass and the camel thorns provide a fitting backdrop to the battlefield.

ENDNOTES

1 Hemyng 1902: 4.
2 Hughes 1857: Preface.
3 Coleridge 1906: 153.
4 Adams 1887: 107–8.
5 Ibid: 296.
6 Schreiner 1923: 50.
7 Stables 1900: 53.
8 Blackburn quoted by Stephen Gray in *English in Africa* (Grahamstown Vol. 5 No. 1 page 11 March 1978.
9 Haggard 1887: 1–2.
10 Ibid: 111.
11 Ibid: 54–5.
12 Wyllarde 1903: 216.
13 Laycock 1900: 238.
14 Graves 1903: 1.
15 Ibid: v.
16 Young, F.B. South African Literature in *The London Mercury* (London Vol. 19 No. 113 March 1929).
17 Bigland, E. 1953: 87 quoted in *The Morning Star* of Marie Corelli.
18 Graves op sit: 23.
19 Porte O.M.I., … quoted by Rev. J. E. Brady, *Trekking for Souls* 1952: 218–9.
20 Kipling, R., quoted by Charles Carrington, 1955: 307.
21 Ibid: 326.
22 Kipling, 'The Captive' in *Traffics and Discoveries* 1904: 6.
23 Kipling, 'The Way That He Took' in *Land and Sea Tales for Scouts and Guides* 1923: 25–6.
24 The blockhouse and iron bridge referred to in Kipling's poem stand next to the main road between Laingsburg and Matjiesfontein, to this very day.
25 Schreiner 1974: 79–80.
26 Bosman 1963: 86.

The white arm at full stretch.

Thunder of hoofs and a bugler's cry,
And down through the veldt came the British horse –
Down with a rush on the burgher ranks
With a whirlwind's sudden force… .

(Anon)

CHAPTER THREE

THE BATTLEFIELD: 'I killed a man at Graspan'

I killed a man at Graspan,
I killed him fair in a fight,
And the Empire's poets and the Empire's priests
Swear blind I acted right,
The Empire's poets and the Empire's priests
Make out my deed was fine,
But they can't stop the eyes of the man I killed
From starin' into mine.

M. Grover, 'I killed a man at Graspan'[1]

Tales of death and glory on the battlefield have enthralled readers from Homer to the present day. The reasons are not hard to find. The battlefield affords an ideal opportunity to dramatise the hero's dash and courage against a panorama of death and destruction. His victory or defeat is a metaphor for the fate of larger forces with which he is identified. Inevitably, in Boer War fiction, at any rate, the whole conflict is allegorised in terms of the small cast in the foreground. For, like the war, the novels end in victory and defeat, with the promise of new beginnings for those who have acted out their personal dramas against a background of a nation coming to birth.

In the main, the fiction reveals two attitudes to war. On the one hand, war is described as a necessary fire through which the protagonists and nations must pass in order to test their mettle and bring them to fulfilment and maturity. More frequently though, war is depicted simply as hell. What is interesting, though, is the language writers mobilise to convince their readers of this truth. Ironically, what often emerges is a highly idealised and 'romanticised' picture, notwithstanding the conventional acknowledgement of the horror. For, it is within the context of the battlefield that the writer most often reveals his own moral stance. The imagery used and the sentiments placed in the mouths of the characters, including the narrator, are often more telling of the writer's own inadvertent feelings than any deliberate authorial interjections.

TRIAL BY FIRE

War as a 'cleansing fire' is illustrated vividly in Owen Vaughan's *Old Fireproof, Being the Chaplain's Story* (1906). Vaughan is atypical. Unlike many writers of escapist fiction he was too skilful to take a dogmatic stand on the heroics or hellishness of war. Instead, he allows his narrator, a naïve and somewhat unimaginative army chaplain, to tell his own story. Each episode in the novel tests the chaplain's preconceived and idealistic notions of war, life, love, honour and responsibility. His attitude to battle is well illustrated early in the story:[2]

> All the noblest as well as the vilest of human movements and aspirations lie to this touch stone of battle. Is a nation great and proud? Bring it to the touch of battle, and, behold! Unless it abide the shock, its glory and its greatness are but an added spoil and a prey to its enemies. Battle wielders are the supreme lords of earth under God. The ultimate measure of a nation's strength and standing in the world is but the measure of its strength in the day of battle. And these men were players of the red game – veterans of no mean record. Should they not, then stand stiff with pride of the flesh, or shine with exaltation of the spirit?

This is the language of 'romantic idealism' at its most exalted. It is also seriously at odds with reality.

Paul Fussell pointed out in *The Great War and Modern Memory* (1975), that much of the diction that typifies popular fiction written before World War I was a consequence of the revival of interest in, and popularisation of, medieval stories and legends from the mid-19th century, by Tennyson, A.C. Swinburne, and the paintings of Burne-Jones and William Morris. Chivalry in love and war became popular themes in literature and art.

It is well known that the language people use to a large extent indicates the way they perceive the world. It can also explain much of their behaviour. The self-conscious literary language that characterises so much fiction, especially popular fiction from the 1880s onwards, created linguistic spectacles that distorted the relationship between language and the world. This language relied on the prestige of French or Latinate words over the supposedly more down-to-earth and direct Anglo-Saxon. In addition, such 'literary language' was believed to be superior to colloquial English, which was thought to be 'tainted' by class markers such as regional dialect, local accent and slang. To be direct was to be crude. Simple, straightforward expression was perceived as plebeian. Language expressed the class divisions of the day, and as literary culture was firmly in the hands of the educated middle-classes the use of 'literary language' expressed their desire to distance themselves from the 'lower orders'.

In popular fiction then, and now, for that matter, the 'officer classes' are always given accentless dialogue. One of the ways used to distinguish the 'lower orders' was to provide them with dialogue that contained some sort of deviant accent; deviant that is from the rounded and polished tones associated with the 'upper classes'. In practice this usually meant dropping h's at the beginnings of words and g's at the ends of words. This practice is exemplified in Kipling's work. Certainly, it is true of G.A. Henty and his imitators, whose novels were devoured voraciously by juvenile readers well into the 20th century. The continued popularity of much of this type of juvenile fiction – well beyond the demise of the world it purported to represent – may account for the longevity of the values it stood for; values that were only seriously challenged by Elvis Presley and *Playboy Magazine* in the 1950s.

Fussell provides an extensive list of ordinary words and their raised equivalents.[3] Many words in his list appear consistently in early Boer War fiction. A horse is a 'charger'; the enemy is the 'foe'; danger is 'peril'; to attack and conquer is to 'assail' and to 'vanquish'; and a special favourite, to be brave, is to have 'pluck'. 'Battle wielders' and 'supreme lords' are good examples of this type of 'raised language'. In Vaughan's novel, the dead are referred to as the 'slain'; a troop of enemy horsemen is a 'host'; a man's chest is his 'breast'; the excitement of battle is the 'battle-light', and the enemy is predictably referred to as 'hordes' or the 'foe'.

Many popular 19th-century hymns, such as 'Onward Christian Soldiers', also provide extensive examples of this kind of language. Muscular Christianity was also drafted into promoting the 'cause of empire'.

What does such language do? The type of language people habitually use shapes the ways in which they perceive the world. The effect of using the kind of 'raised language' described by Fussell is to remove the horror of the war and turn it into a literary convention of waving flags, honour and glory, unsullied by blood and gore. In the modern era, those responsible for directing the course of war, and giving orders to kill the enemies of the state have often used language to disguise and mitigate the full force of their actions. Significantly, the Americans in Vietnam used the chilling expression: 'terminate with extreme prejudice'. What they plainly meant was 'kill'. The same goes for the former South African Defence Force's notorious expression 'remove from society permanently', and, more recently in Iraq 'regime change'.

In this context it is worth remembering what that arch-realist, Falstaff, had to say on the subject of honour on the battlefield:[4]

> Can honour set a leg? No. Or an arm? No. Or take away the grief of a wound? No. Honour hath no skill in surgery then? No. What is honour? A word. What is that word honour? Air. A trim reckoning! – Who hath it? He that died o' Wednesday. Doth he feel it? No. Doth he hear it? No. It is insensible then? Yea, to the dead. But will it not live with the living? No. Detraction will not suffer it: – therefore I'll none of it: Honour is a mere scutcheon, and so ends my catechism.

Owen Vaughan's novel is especially interesting because he consistently exploited the language resources of his day to reveal the hollowness of the values and attitudes they expressed. In many ways, *Old Fireproof* anticipated the anti-war novels of the 1914–18 War. It is certainly not typical of the kind of popular fiction being produced at the time.

Vaughan's protagonist is an ironic portrait of the stock romantic hero. The chaplain is uncritical of his world and unaware of any other possibilities. But he is different from his contemporaries in one important respect. His creator does not identify with his character's values and attitudes. Much of what is worthy about the novel is as a consequence of the ironic tension between the chaplain's perception of the world and the author's exposure of the superficiality of his views.

The chaplain experiences a series of traumatic events in a succession of battles that gradually change the way he regards war, in much the same way that 2nd Lieutenant Raleigh, in R.C. Sherriff's play *Journey's End*, is forced by his experiences to reassess his views of war. Caught up in the frenzy of battle, the chaplain forgets his commitments and joins in the shooting:[5]

> But oh! So few we were – so few men, so few rifles, and those men coming yonder were so many! Fury seized me that we might not stop this mass after all. A flame scorched me, eye and vein and brain, a rage that we might perhaps die like tigers smothered by the hordes of the deer; a rage that frenzied me till in that rage I forgot God, forgot God's ministry, remembered no more the solemn ceremony which had set me aside from sinful passions, consecrating me holy to do the work of Christ, remembering nothing but this crash of battle and the challenge that roared in it.
>
> Like a man demented I raged, the rifle of a wounded man in my hands, shooting and shouting, goading men to kill, my own hands doing the work of killing, …

The most significant event in the chaplain's painful growth occurs when he comes across an old Boer dying from his wounds in the veld. He is forced to see him not as some abstraction, the 'fallen foe', but as another human being, who in his last moments speaks of his wife and children.

A very different kind of hero, in Gilbert Parker's *The Judgement House* (1913), is 'purified' by dying in battle. It was a central belief of the author that the war 'served as a sieve to sift people, and it served as a solvent of many a life-problem'.[6] When death comes for the hero, Byng, it is not a waste. He has been 'cleansed'.[7]

> The War had purged his mind, cleared his vision. When he left England he was immersed in egoism, submerged by his own miseries. He had isolated himself in a lazaretto of self-reproach and resentment … . Because of this obsession of self, he was eager to be done with it all.

This view of war is seldom reflected in the Boer War fiction written after World War I. The effect of the Somme and Verdun and the evidence of political incompetence and the bumbling of the High Command made such idealism less tenable.

'It was hell, I tell you'

The alternative, then, to the view of war as a trial by fire is that war is hell. The fact that a literary convention can quickly degenerate into a cliché, however, makes it no less a truth. As far as this truism is concerned, the interest lies in the various ways writers have gone about persuading their readers that war is, indeed, hell.

The Boer defeat at Paardeberg was a favourite set piece for writers of Boer War fiction, because it was the first major British victory after a series of catastrophic and humiliating defeats, beginning with Magersfontein and culminating in what came to be known as Black Week, in which the British suffered defeats at Talana, Nicholson's Nek and Stormberg.

While Paardeberg saw the capture of Cronje, one of the most famous (if not the most imaginative) Boer generals, the victory was to prove a mixed blessing to the British. The battle was fought beside the

Modder River into which the putrefying carcasses of cattle and horses from Cronje's laager were thrown. It was from lower down this river that the British soldiers took their drinking water. Two weeks later, when Lord Roberts captured Bloemfontein, a typhoid epidemic broke out, virtually immobilising the British army – an epidemic that Dr Arthur Conan Doyle did much to control.

The following passage from *Men For Pieces* (1927) by Vera Fraser Cathcart, describes the aftermath of the battle of Paardeberg:[8]

> Then all was still once more, and the red orb in the west dropped behind the mountains of Paardeberg with sinister calm, like a carnivorous beast replete with human blood, the lingering rays illuminating the prostrate remnants of men; and those writhing in wordless agony, less limbs or bowels, or eyes; and the still white faces of yesterday's glorious youth, with ugly gashes across cheek or brow. The curses of delirious agony mingled with moans from blanching lips that called on softer names, as the glow in the west sank lower, and slowly died. Dark shadows with succour moan like ghosts among them, looking for those who could still articulate.

Cathcart wrote after the Great War – the war to end all wars. It is not surprising therefore that she appeared anxious to depict the effects of war as she did. In her efforts to get her readers to share her own lurid vision, she made use of every literary device she could muster. The result is a dramatic example of 'literary over-kill'. It would be a 'hardened' reader indeed who could resist this sort of manipulation.

Writing some thirty years later, Henry Gibbs, in his novel *The Tumult and the Shouting* (1958), described the aftermath of Paardeberg in the following terms:[9]

> Riding into the laager they found a scene of devastation. Guns facing the pair of steep hills from which the drift gained its name, lay wrecked. Shapeless, twisted wheels canted crazily on their axles, a great wreckage

> strewn among the dead and injured men, ponies and cattle lying disembowelled and limbless, abandoned.
>
> This was the end of hundreds of thousands of pounds which Kruger and his Volksraad had grabbed by taxes from Uitlanders in Johannesburg and paid to armament manufacturers of Germany, this broken cooling useless scrap metal, the guns which had shelled Kimberley. Many wagons were smashed, sun-bleached hoods split and flapped in the breeze, curved hoops exposed like ribs from which sinew and muscle had been ripped away, disselbooms pointing at the overcast sky like gaunt prophetic fingers. Most were of recent construction, only a few old enough to provide a link with days when they sailed like ships over a wilderness that contained only Kaffir kraals and the lairs of wild beasts.
>
> Listless amid this shambles, too stunned to display more than crestfallen bewilderment, were six thousand Boers. Among them stood a small number of distraught, stiff, white-faced women, more fearful of their anticipated fate with the conquerors than the daughters of Persia with the legions of Alexander or Trojan women, whose grandmothers had fought alongside their men against Zulu and Kaffir and perished agonizingly under their lust and assegais.

Gibbs' novel is typical of much Boer War fiction written since World War II. If the Gibbs' extract is compared with Cathcart's, one is struck by the relative sparseness of Gibbs' prose. Unlike Cathcart, Gibbs made little use of either metaphor or pathetic fallacy. Gibbs' second paragraph, however, displays some interesting narrative features, which in their own way, are as revealing as Cathcart's purple prose. Ostensibly, Gibbs' second paragraph forms part of the omniscient author's survey of the devastation after the battle. The effect is to shift the focus from the battle to the short-sighted motives of those prompted by mercenary gain who are responsible for these scenes of carnage: Kruger and the German armament manufacturers. An earlier generation of writers would have been inclined to link Kruger with German-Jewish capitalist interests. For Gibbs, it was enough that World War II is part of recent memory.

In *The Tumult and the Shouting*, and his other novels written within several years of one another, there are constant reminders of what the Boers suffered at the hands of the 'Kaffirs'. If Gibbs' writing is placed in the wider context of South Africa in the mid-1950s, his concern with a black uprising and the possible consequences becomes all the more significant.

The 50s saw the enactment of much of the legislation that was to create the apartheid state. The 50s also saw the first concerted and organised opposition by the African National Congress and the Congress of Democrats to the racist policies of the Nationalist Government in South Africa.

A common cry by white politicians of the time was the need to protect white women from the 'uncontrollable lusts of black men'. It was a heady warning, rewarded in successive general elections. In Gibbs' novel, the reader is never allowed to forget for long that the war might create a situation of which the black tribes could take advantage. Gibbs was exploiting a deep-rooted fear in his presumed white readers of a black uprising, with the added piquancy in the not-too-subtle suggestion that the Boer women awaited the same fate that has befallen the women of conquered armies since time immemorial. Presumably, being raped by an 'assegai-wielding Kaffir' would be worse than the same fate at the hands of a British Tommy. As for an uprising, the Zulus actually did rise up in May 1902, at Holkrantz, where in one night they killed fifty-six Boers.

'It's all in the mind'

An earlier writer who took a more dispassionate view of events, eschewing both the ritual fire and hell versions of war, was Victor Rousseau Emmanuel. Although it is not certain whether this author saw active service in South Africa during the Second Anglo-Boer War, it is known that he had to flee and hide from the Boers. It is perhaps his first-hand experience of being shot at that has leavened his prose with a sense of irony. Most of the episodes in his novel *Derwent's Horse* (1901), are treated in a low-key parodic manner. Very little fighting is described. Agonies suffered by the protagonist are agonies of the imagination.[10]

> And all at once Lowndes became conscious that he was afraid – horribly, madly afraid. His heart was drumming in his ears like a piston. He cowered down in the grass and buried his head in the earth. He put his hands in front to form a screen. He wanted to get up and charge with a bayonet; he would brave a thousand wounds in the mad intoxication of battle. Anything rather than lie there helpless with those horrible bullets hissing and hooting over him. There was little chance of a trifling wound. He would be hit in the head, and his soul would go yelping into eternity before he knew that he had ceased to live.

Neither Emmanuel nor Vaughan 'romanticised' the actual events on the battlefield, though they may have harboured 'romantic' views on the efficacy of violence. They were fully aware of the terrors and waste of war, yet neither succumbed to the temptations of self-indulgence in describing them. The point is, though, that while these writers understood the horrors of war and wrote about them with restraint, they had not yet reached the point where they could throw off the 'romantic notion' that war ultimately brought the best out in men; that it was a cleansing fire. There was little understanding on their part that prolonged exposure to violence brutalises rather than sensitises the sensibility; or even that the logic of war imposes a brutal necessity that in other situations would call forth solutions based on love, as for example Captain Vere learns in Melville's *Billy Budd.*

It took World War I to show that – notwithstanding the fact that men are capable of great acts of self-sacrifice and generosity – if they are exposed for any length of time to the danger of losing their lives, they are most often brutalised or suffer a mental breakdown. This condition was known as 'shell shock'. Today it is known as 'Post Traumatic Stress Syndrome'. It is not for nothing that Stanhope, in *Journey's End,* drinks to anaesthetise himself and that large sections of Thomas Pynchon's *Gravity's Rainbow* and Kurt Vonnegut's *Slaughterhouse 5*, are set in mental homes.

THE REAL THING

Thus, writers who had actual experience of battle tended to write with greater restraint than those who had not. G.G. Munnik, for example, fought in a Boer Commando for much of the war. He was captured and sent to a prisoner-of-war camp in India. After his return to South Africa, he played a role in establishing Union in 1910. Shortly after the Act of Union he wrote *Major Greville, V.C.: A Tale of the Great Boer War* (1913), in which he invested his hero with all the qualities of an English gentleman he had come to admire while he was in captivity.

Although Munnik's novel is clearly an attempt to soothe freshly healed wounds and to promote tolerance between the recent antagonists in the interests of creating a (white) Union of South Africa, the novel derives what strengths it has from the author's direct experience of war. In two terse sentences Munnik creates a sense of the unpredictable, at once destructive and incomprehensible:[11]

> A large jagged splinter struck the speaker's right arm, and left it hanging from the shoulder. He looked at it stupidly for a moment as if not realising what had happened, and then tried to staunch the blood that had squirted from it with the fingers of the other hand.

Munnik's contemporary, Francis Bancroft (*The Veldt Dwellers*, 1912), on the other hand, relies on literary convention, and presents a very different picture of men going into action:[12]

> While they woke and yawned, and grasped for their arms, grim war was upon them with the whiz of bullets, the screams of pain, the cries of vengeance, the hissing of shot, the fearful riving and rending of body

> and limb, the horrible presence of carnage and death strewn over the veldt-world, polluting the air, where but ten minutes since the freshness and fragrance of the awakening day alone had reigned.

In this world, and perhaps only in this world, the hero 'could have laughed aloud for the pure and simple joy of finding himself alive and facing the delight of battle'.[13]

The anti-war novel

Just as the Anglo-Boer War anticipated many of the features that became common-place in the 20th century, so did the early fiction of such writers as Munnik, Emmanuel and Vaughan anticipate the realism that was to be the dominant feature of popular war fiction after 1920. Thus, Leslie A. Fiedler's contention that 'before 1920 the anti-war novel did not exist' must be regarded with some circumspection.[14]

Douglas Blackburn's satire, *Kruger's Secret Service* (1900), is one of the most biting anti-war novels to have emerged from the Boer War. For most writers the general assumption was that there were two opposing factions joined in combat to settle their differences. Blackburn's perceptions were much more complex. Blackburn conceived of the war as a hideous civil conflict in which brothers turn on one another, and it is not always clear who the enemy is. This is an attitude to the war that only generally came to be accepted in the 1930s.

In Blackburn's novel, the battlefield becomes the scene of ironic action. It is little wonder, as the following episode illustrates, that the narrator reflects on 'warfare as something bizarre and even grotesque':[15]

> Well, on this occasion that I mentioned, the battle of Bester's, one of the Natal irregular regiments actually came under fire of another body of irregulars posted on a hill on the other side of the valley. We had no signals with us, and I, with some others, was immediately despatched from the one station to the other to tell the men what they were doing, to assure them that we

> were not Boers, and to beg them to turn their rifles in another direction. I need scarcely say that this job proved anything but acceptable to me. To carry despatches under fire is bad enough, but when you carry despatches you are not approaching the enemy, you merely run the risks that any exposed individual must run upon a battlefield. To carry a message, however, to a body of men which happens to be firing on the very body of men which you have just left, and to cross the intervening space with the horrible suspicion in your mind that they must think you all the time to be an enemy, is a very nerve-harassing experience indeed.

What the narrator describes elsewhere as a 'blunder' is in fact much more complex than that. There is no sense in this episode that he is aware of the irony of what he is describing. For him the issue is simply that he and his comrades might be killed accidentally by their own side. However, this event illustrates the point that armies can have a will independent of the individuals who make up their number; that the organisation of war can be so mismanaged that it can turn armies upon themselves. If the enemy cannot be engaged, an army may create an enemy, even of its own troops, in order to justify its existence.

Guerrilla warfare

The Second Anglo-Boer War was fought in two distinct phases. The first was dominated by set battles and sieges; the second, after the capture of Pretoria in June 1900, by guerrilla action. It was in this latter phase that the British limitations in conducting an irregular war, which called for innovative tactics, were most severely exposed. Of all the British writers active at the time, Kipling was the most consistent in criticising the way the British conducted this phase of the war.

One of Kipling's most vivid descriptions of guerrilla action is in his short story 'The Comprehension of Private Copper'. Relying on what Kipling calls his 'pastoral instincts', that is, his expertise as a poacher in

Sussex, Private Copper becomes aware that the enemy is close at hand. His experience at stalking rabbits comes in handy:[16]

> Private Copper crawled up the side of a bluish rock-strewn hill thinly fringed with brush a-top, and remembering how he had peered at Sussex conies through the edge of furze-clumps, cautiously parted the dry stems before his face. At the foot of the long slope sat three farmers smoking. To his natural lust for tobacco was added personal wrath because spiky plants were pricking his belly, and Private Copper slid the backsight up to fifteen hundred yards … .
>
> "Good evening, khaki. Please don't move," said a voice on his left, and as he jerked his head round he saw entirely down the barrel of a well-kept Lee-Metford protruding from an insignificant tuft of thorn. Very few graven images have moved less than did Private Copper through the next ten seconds.
>
> "It's nearer seventeen hundred than fifteen," said a young man in an obviously ready-made suit of grey tweed, possessing himself of Private Copper's rifle. "Thank you. We've got a post of thirty-seven men out yonder. You've eleven – eh? We don't want to kill 'em. We have no quarrel with poor uneducated khakis, and we do not want prisoners we do not keep. It's demoralising for both sides – eh?"

The Karoo is not Sussex, nor are the Boers rabbits. Although Private Copper is more adept than his mates at reading the signs of the veld and using the cover it provides, he is clearly not as skilled in veldcraft as the Boer who traps him.

Kipling uses this episode to comment on a number of issues. None of them reflects well on the training and tactics adopted by the British. Most obviously there is the fact that the British were ill-equipped to deal with this sort of irregular warfare. They did not have the skills that made the Boers at once so observant, adaptable and dangerous. Following on from this is the serious criticism implied in the Boer's contemptuous remark: 'It's nearer seventeen hundred than fifteen'. One of the chief criticisms levelled at the British training programme after the war was the inordinate amount of time devoted to 'spit and polish' and to marching in formation. Musket practice was given hardly any attention at all. As a consequence, many of the troops who arrived in South Africa were incapable of even setting the sights of their rifles properly.

It was during the guerrilla phase of the war that the Boers abandoned their German Mausers in favour of English Lee-Metfords because of the scarcity of Mauser ammunition. The British troops were, from all accounts, very undisciplined about the way they left ammunition lying about in the veld, thereby providing the Boers with a cheap and ready supply. In fact, the Boers virtually equipped themselves from the British supply columns for the last year of the war. Another point worth commenting on is the obvious class and educational differences between Copper and his captor. The popular image of the Boers in England was of an upstart peasantry of uneducated religious bigots. Clearly, the young Boer in Kipling's story does not conform to the stereotype.

The Boer's remarks about the fate of prisoners points to a problem the Boers faced once they entered the guerrilla phase. There was no doubt that the Boers were incapable of keeping the prisoners they took. And in this, the last of the 'gentleman's wars', there was no question of shooting them out of hand. Alternatively, while it might have been demoralising for the Boers to win engagement after engagement and then have to turn loose the very men they had been fighting it was as demoralising for the British troops to return shamefacedly to camp, usually minus their uniforms, and admit yet another humiliating defeat.

Kipling had a grudging respect for the Boers in the field, which he expressed in a poem entitled 'Piet':[17]

I do not love my Empire's foes,
Nor call 'em angel; still,
What is the sense of 'ating those
'Oom you are paid to kill?
So, barrin' all that foreign lot

Which only joined for spite,
Myself, I'd just as soon as not
Respect the man I fight.
Ah, there, Piet! – 'is trousies to 'is knees,
'Is coat-tails lyin' level in the bullet-sprinkled breeze;
'E does not lose 'is rifle an' 'e does not lose 'is seat,
I've known a lot of people ride a dam' sight worse than
Piet.

Kipling was the first British author to describe the life of the ordinary Tommy, which he celebrated in *Soldiers Three* (1888) and *Barrack-room Ballads* (1892). Kipling's insights into the suffering of common soldiers made him particularly popular with the rank and file, and contributed significantly to the success of the newspaper *The Friend* when he helped edit for a short while after the capture of Bloemfontein. Kipling delighted in showing up the limitations of the military mind and the staff officers. His 'Fables for the Staff' were aimed at exposing the unimaginative and often pompous attitudes of the officers:[18]

> A General, having offered libations to Fortuna, went out to fight a Battle in the course of which his Frontal Attack developed into a Rear Guard action, and his left Flank became a Modulous of varying Elasticity for several hours, owing to his right Flank having wandered towards the Equator.
>
> The Enemy seeing these Inexplicable Evolutions, were so overcome with Amazement that They retired in large Numbers and left the General a complete Victory.
>
> A week later, the General, learning from the Reports of his Staff that he was a Heaven-born Strategist, diligently read a Book and gave Battle upon the lines therein laid down.
>
> After this he was never seen to smile but frequently heard to murmur: "If I had only trusted my bally Luck instead of a bally Book, I should not now be travelling first-class to Stellenbosch."

> MORAL – Invention is a good servant, but the Letter killeth.

Fashions in humour have changed. Kipling's heavy-handed satire has much in common with the laboured captions of contemporary cartoons; but, for all that, the criticism voiced in this fable had a very serious intention. Acknowledged as 'poet of empire' he occupied a privileged position from which he could aim his barbs with impunity. Kipling continued to champion the cause of the common soldier throughout the war, in poetry, short stories and journalistic pieces, while keeping up an unremitting criticism of the high command's lack of initiative and imagination.

Ben Viljoen's account of guerrilla war in his *Under the Vierkleur* (1904) contains authentic detail that is worth reading. He was a successful 'vegtgeneraal' himself, and was only captured some months before the end of the war. As a 'bittereinder' he chose exile after the war rather than submitting to the provisions of the Peace Treaty of Vereeniging.

Viljoen's description of a skirmish has all the immediacy of an event experienced. Danie, his hero, has ordered a mug of coffee from a group of Burghers as they wait for the fighting to begin:[19]

> As he reached the extreme right of his line, the English guns suddenly reopened with terrific rapidity of service. The bursting shells covered the Boer position with smoke and dust. He turned, and ran back towards the centre of the little valley. Right ahead of him, still behind their boulder, the six card-players sat grouped about a new-made fire, engaged in preparing the coffee he had ordered. They were still laughing, and, as he could see, were paying no attention to the renewed shell-fire, apparently with the feeling that, as long as they were not in the fighting line, it concerned them nothing. As he was almost upon them, as he leaned his body to one side to avoid them in his run, he heard a fierce whirl of infinitesimal shortness, – before his very eyes a great mass of fluffy, bright

> yellow cotton evolved from nothing directly above their heads, – it streaked and circled with red, – there was a tremendous crash! For the briefest fraction of a second he had a horrible vision of a world full of doubled and disjointed, of broken and contorted men, of dirt and dust and ashes and flaming brands, all suspended in a horrible golden haze. Then the world went black.
>
> When he woke to consciousness, it seemed to him as if hours had passed. In reality it was but seconds … . Where the fire had burned a great gash was torn in the earth. At the bottom of the ragged hole a naked human fore arm, with shattered bone of the elbow protruding from its upper end, lay amid some few charred sticks of wood, still clasping in its stiffened fingers a twisted iron ladle. Within a radius of twenty paces of the spot, six torn and mangled bodies almost unrecognisable as human earth defiled the grass.

From the other side

It may appear anomalous that Viljoen, like Munnik, chose to write in English. But then it is often forgotten that most of the educated Boers were brought up in a cultural environment where English was taken for granted. Many of the politically influential families such as the Reitzs and the Fischers employed English speaking governesses to bring up their children. Deneys Reitz recorded with pride that his grandfather had met Sir Walter Scott 'to whom he [had taken] a lion skin which the poet Thomas Pringle had sent from Cape Town, and he became intimate with the great writer … and at our home scarcely a night passed without a reading from Burns or Scott'.[20] Afrikaans was yet to be co-opted as a rallying point by the nationalist movement. In fact, many of the most influential Afrikaans literary figures of the first three decades of the 20th century often preferred to write in English. Eugene Marais and C. Louis Leipoldt both wrote extensively in English, sometimes drafting in English what later appeared in Afrikaans. For example,

Leipoldt's Boer War poem 'Oom Gert Vertel' was written originally in English.

One of the most moving and penetratingly ironic accounts of war is to be found in C. Louis Leipoldt's *Stormwrack* (1980). This novel, written originally in English as one of a trilogy, has had a curious history. The unpublished manuscript was lost shortly after Leipoldt's death. It was discovered and finally published in 1980, nearly fifty years after it was written.

The battle at the climax of the novel is fought across the garden that the protagonist, Andrew Quakerley, has spent fifty years cultivating and nurturing. The garden is the central image of the novel. It represents that delicate balance between complexity, diversity and order that rests on reason and tolerance known as 'civilisation':[21]

> Old Andrew, sitting in his study with Joan, could hear the sound of firing quite plainly. It came in regular volleys; that was the defending force. It came in desultory cracks from beyond the river. Once a bullet struck the window, shattering the glass, and repeatedly the thump of a concussion on the woodwork could be heard, or the soft plump of a missile impinging on the thatched roof. The war was very close, unpleasantly intrusive, but the old man had no thought of danger. His one anxiety was now for his garden.
>
> In the dark, drizzling rain that continued to fall throughout the evening, he watched the soldiers taking up their positions in the gardens. They hauled the guns through the hedges, over the flower pots; they chopped down trees to get a clearer view. He felt too anxious to stay and watch what they were doing, and, besides there were definite orders that all civilians should be indoors, all lights extinguished. There was nothing to do but sit in the study, listening to those nearby sounds, and to imagine all sorts of things, none of them pleasant, all disturbing.
>
> He was sensible of his age, his tiredness, his irritability; sensible, above all, of a deep disappointment

> which he could not analyse to his own satisfaction. His garden ... as he thought of it, a wave of strong emotion passed over him, and his fingers involuntarily grasped the arm rest of his chair. Now there was fighting going on in his garden ... men were dragging the gun carriages across the paths, the wheels were making deep ruts in the gravel; but that was nothing – that could be repaired. But the guns would do much more damage, and so would the horses ... what a mess ... what a mess! It surprised him that he could not feel himself indignant, fiercely angry, when he thought of what his garden was suffering – that he could not transfer, as it were, part of that suffering to himself, glorying in it as martyrs for a faith glory in the contumely they suffer for it, yet passionately resenting it as something done to humiliate him. The irregular beat of the rifles outside and the steady drip of the rain falling on the stoep were too depressing to permit of the luxury of self pity.

Stormwrack represents one of the few attempts by a serious writer to give extended attention to the fictional possibilities the Anglo-Boer conflict offers. With few exceptions, the 'romantic notion' of war was, and still is, widely accepted. Nonetheless, in the early fiction, one thing emerges fairly clearly – the existence in embryo of an attitude to war which was generally identified with later English poets and writers of World War I. Malvern van Wyk Smith points out in *Drummer Hodge* (1978), while discussing the emergence of Boer War poetry that:[22]

> The 'development' of war poetry to the heights of World War I depended not only, or even primarily, on the increasing fatality and horror of methods of warfare, but also on wide-ranging Victorian changes in attitudes towards the army, the soldier, the volunteer, and the war itself. These changes were connected, in turn, with the rise in democracy and universal education, and made themselves felt in the radical, socialist

> and humanitarian opposition to war which by 1899 was well-organised, articulate and influential.

The same could be said about the fiction. With the passage of time, the impulse to write poetry about the Boer wars has declined. This is not so of fiction; the Anglo-Boer wars have continued to be a source of interest for many writers. Novels, and to a lesser extent short stories, have continued to be produced at fairly regular intervals. This reasonably consistent production of novels has provided an accurate measure of how attitudes to the conflict and to the notion of warfare have changed with the passage of time. After World War I, conventional views of heroism disappeared fairly quickly, with the emphasis shifting away, during the Dominion period, from the imperial ideal of military conquest, to that of promoting a union between the two white antagonists. Of necessity, such a change in attitude has demanded that writers face some of the realities of war. Since then, that impulse has lost much of its impetus.

The 'new romanticism'

In the post-1948 era, a 'new romanticism' emerged in the works of, for instance, Robin Collins, *The Four Coloured Flag* (1958), Stuart Cloete, *Rags of Glory* (1963), Wilbur Smith, *The Sound of Thunder* (1966), Dorothy Eden, *Siege in the Sun* (1967), and Edna Drummond, *The Burning Land* (1979). In these novels, action is described almost exclusively for its own sake. Lip-service is paid to the horrors of war. Like the sex scene, as we shall see later, the battle scene is merely used to add sensational excitement to the flow of events and keep the pages turning. An episode from Stuart Cloete's *Rags of Glory* illustrates the point:[23]

> The English came on, their bayoneted rifles at the high port. Many fell, dropping under the fire of the Boers poured into them, but they were not checked. Boetie brought two down with two shots, missed another, and went on firing. He heard a cry and saw Jan Beyers go down. Hetta knelt beside him for an instant. Then,

> seeing he was dead, she stood over his body, her legs apart, and poured shot after shot into the advancing troops. Before God that girl could shoot. Her long fair hair was down, streaming behind her in the breeze that had sprung up and blew the dust and smoke reeking hot cordite into their faces.
>
> A bugle call rang out. An officer shouted, "Charge!" raising his arm. Moolman brought him down with a shot in the breast. The English, still closer now just below the crest of the ridge, were for an instant invisible. Then their bayonets and helmets appeared and the fighting became hand to hand. Moolman parried a thrust, drove his Mauser barrel into his opponent's belly, and fired. As the man fell he seized his Lee-Metford and fought bayonet to bayonet with the man who followed him. Hetta Beyers, her yellow mane flying, was holding her rifle by the barrel and laying about her. Boetie, who had dropped back a pace to push another clip of cartridges into his magazine, saw her smash the skull of an English soldier who had lost his helmet. Her eyes blazing, screaming with fury, she flung herself onto another man and went down with a bayonet thrust in her side.

In Cloete's novel, battle follows battle as he attempts to document the entire course of the war. The Boer woman, Hetta, fighting beside her husband has no function in the story outside this episode. Nor has the exalted language, characteristic of so much fiction at the turn-of-the-century, entirely disappeared. The English officer is 'shot in the breast'. Cloete was of the old school. Yet strangely, for all the detail of Hetta standing over her husband's body, 'her legs apart' smashing skulls and dying with a bayonet in her side, there is a lack of conviction in Cloete's writing.

Cloete was exploiting the popular myth that the Boer women formed a corps and fought alongside their men. The closest and only documented instance of Boer women fighting was when Helena Wagner of Zeerust spent five months fighting as a man without her identity being revealed. For the rest, although some Boer women pleaded to be armed and to be allowed to fight, none of them fought. Cloete, realising the 'romantic' and sensationalistic potential of such a myth, simply spices his battle scene with Hetta, thereby completing the perverse and well-tried formula of combining sex with violence.

In this episode and many others like it, the action becomes an end in itself. This is a general tendency in the fiction and it would be difficult to find examples to contradict it. Even in a novel like Kit Denton's *The Breaker* (1973), in which the action culminates in one of the officers being emasculated by the Boers, the protagonist, Harry Morant's violent reaction to it, is a separate episode. In no way does the narrative rely on the details of the battle to add credibility to his reactions.

In the 'new romanticism', gratuitous violence is glorified for its own sake. This is certainly true of popular fiction and films since the 1960s, and has culminated most profitably in the *Rambo* films. In this context, it is probably not inappropriate to speculate about the relationship between the 'new romanticism' and the tolerance of, and glorification of violence especially in films and on television.

The same attitudes towards violence obtain in South Africa's most recent contribution to war fiction: the *Grens Roman* (Border Novel), which has emerged in response to the South African involvement in Angola. The formula for the *Grens Roman* as for Boer War fiction, is to use the battle scene as a focal, though separate, event. Character and thematic development do not depend on the detail of the violent action. The various battle scenes merely provide heroics and punctuate the narrative.

Endnotes

1 The sub-title of this poem provides the only biographical information I have been able to find: 'The Tale of a Returned Australian Continganter done into verse'.
2 Vaughan 1906: 23.
3 Fussell 1975: 23.
4 *Henry IV Part 1* Act V Sc. 1.
5 Vaughan 1906: 22.
6 Parker 1913: 258.
7 Ibid: 412
8 Cathcart 1927: 35–6.
9 Gibbs 1957: 103.
10 Emmanuel 1901: 248.
11 Munnik 1913: 140.
12 Bancroft 1912: 279–80.
13 Ibid: 281.
14 Fiedler 1964: 29.
15 Blackburn 1900: 203–4.
16 Kipling 1904: 159–60.
17 Kipling, R., 'Piet' in *Rudyard Kipling's Verse* 1912.
18 Quoted in Julian Ralphis *War's Brighter Side* 1901: 242.
19 Viljoen 1904: 296–8.
20 Reitz *Commando: A Boer Journal of the Boer War* 1929: 12–13.
21 Leipoldt 1980: 204–5.
22 Van Wyk Smith 1978: 2–3.
23 Cloete 1963: 233–4.

'But blackened rafters, gaunt against the sky,
Like grim uplifted fingers, ever seem
To call down some swift vengence from on high.'

(F.C. Kolbe)

CHAPTER FOUR

CONCENTRATION CAMPS, MARTIAL LAW AND MILITARY JUSTICE: 'Shoot straight you bastards'

> ' … this is war-time, when we have no law, only justice.'
>
> Douglas Blackburn, *A Burgher Quixote*[1]

Popular fiction does not try to change the world; it simply tries to reflect it. That is, it tends to reflect the majority view, which is why it is so useful to literary and social historians. 'Serious literature' is inclined to regard the world ironically; it is indirect, ambiguous, and given to allusion. The attitudes and values in serious literature are often ahead of their time and are often, in fact, unpopular. Popular fiction on the other hand, tends to comfort our prejudices, not challenge them.

This is what distinguishes the work of say George Griffith, Henry Gibbs and Wilbur Smith from that of Rudyard Kipling, C. Louis Leipoldt and Herman Charles Bosman. Kipling, Leipoldt and Bosman tell their stories in language densely packed with allusion and ironic comment. The scale and complexity of their insight accumulate as their tales unfold into a comprehensive, fate-driven vision of human affairs, challenging and engaging the readers' intellects and touching their compassion.

Lesser writers, on the other hand, are at best content to take sensational issues and events and relate them in ways that merely reflect the preoccupations of their times. They make little or no attempt to examine any of the undercurrents that give rise to the kinds of action they describe. Thus, their writing is notably devoid of irony or scepticism about human motives. Consequently, their writing is readily accessible to literary historians on the lookout for evidence of how the mass of ordinary people understand and react to their times. Popular perceptions of the controversial issues surrounding the Boer War are a case in point: the concentration camps, martial law, and military justice.

'Methods of barbarism'

Perhaps the most controversial of these issues was the concentration camps – one of many grim precedents (along with barbed-wire and trench warfare), destined to be overshadowed by the Stalags and Gulags of the 20th century.

All in all, nearly twenty-eight thousand white people and fourteen thousand black people died in the camps. There were many reasons for these deaths: the food was appalling; lack of basic hygiene, together with the intense summer heat and winter cold, and overcrowding, resulting in dysentery and cholera. Emily Hobhouse alerted the British public early on.[2] For her pains, the British authorities refused her permission to land when she returned to South Africa a second time. At least her agitation had the virtue of having the camps investigated and improved to some extent. Nonetheless, the camps were, and have remained, a source of much bitterness among the Afrikaner people.

A spate of novels in Afrikaans devoted to the suffering of women and children in the camps accompanied the rise of Afrikaner nationalism from 1935 onwards. With the approach of the centenary of the Great Trek and the build-up of tension before World War II, many Afrikaners saw the British suppression of Afrikaner nationalism as an 'English war'. So seriously did the Smuts government take this rise of Afrikaner nationalism, that it banned E. Steenkamp's *Helkampe* (1941). Meanwhile, J.R.L. van Bruggen's *Bittereinders* (1935) and Sannie Visser's *Via Dolorosa* (1942) both attained cult status in their time.

Understandably, few of the early English-speaking writers mentioned the British concentration camps in their novels. For imperialists, the camps constituted an embarrassment best ignored. Those who braved the issue felt forced to elaborate unconvincing explanations to justify their existence. It is all the more interesting therefore to turn first to a novel by the vechtgeneraal and 'Bittereinder', Ben Viljoen, who might be expected to have exploited this emotive topic for its full propaganda value.

In *Under the Vierkleur* (1904), Viljoen was intent on bringing the facts and conditions in the camps to the public notice. However, he had another purpose: he used the camps to represent the nadir of Boer aspirations. The old ways are dead. Any attempt to rebuild them is doomed. Yet, for all the undeniable suffering of the women and the many deaths, the tone is one of reconciliation. When the hero, Danie, reaches the camp in Middelburg in search of his family, a British sentry directs him to the correct tent:[3]

> "It's the third down the second street, on the right, sir," answered the man politely; "but old Linde died some months ago … ."

Viljoen does not try to score any easy points. The sentry could easily have been caricatured as a bully or sadist with too much power over the weak and helpless. Instead, he is polite and helpful. And similarly, when Danie finds his mother and sisters, the scene is marked by restraint:[4]

> The flaps of the tent were not drawn back, but hung loosely, closing its entrance. With his blood pounding at his pulses, he cautiously drew one of them aside, and peered in. His mother and two sisters, dressed in such poor mourning as they had been able to collect, sat despondently on their rough, unmattressed cots. Their faces were browned by the long camp life, but otherwise how changed! Their cheeks and temples were thin and shrunken, their faded eyes, tired by much weeping, lacked lustre, even interest. Nevertheless, as the tent flap was lifted and the unexpected light broke in on their dismal surroundings, they looked up startled at the face within the entrance. None of them recognised him. Well, if that white-haired old woman was his mother, these two thin, sickly women his pretty sisters, why,

> perhaps he, too, had changed more than he thought. He stifled his disappointment.

If one considers the intensity of feeling the camps gave rise to, this description is remarkable for its restraint. Viljoen avoids the temptation to catalogueing the physical suffering, preferring to focus on the sense of loss and futility of it all, summed up by Danie's disappointment at not being recognised by his family. The war has the power not only to change physical appearances but to dull perceptions. The consequence is an apathy as dreadful as death itself. But, Viljoen is not concerned with the dead but with the living. Danie rouses his mother and sisters with his visions of the future:[5]

> "… we are going back, – going home! And six months at Baakenhoogte will bring the shine and the flesh and the roses back. We will build the old place up as it was before, – all the kraals and the shed and your flower gardens in the same old places. There is some of the house yet standing. I saw the place a year ago. It shall be all the same!"
>
> But with the assurance, the thought of his father came to him, and he bit his lip and was silent. No, it could never be quite the same again.

The realities are there: the desolation, the imperatives of hard work, the death of his father. Given Viljoen's bitter opposition to the Treaty of Vereeniging and his self-imposed exile first in Madagascar and later in the United States, where he was part of Buffalo Bill Cody's travelling circus, *Under the Vierkleur* is a remarkably restrained account of the war. It is worth reading today to remind ourselves that little is to be gained from dwelling bitterly on the past.

Whereas Ben Viljoen focused on the living, Olive Schreiner concentrated on the dead. But, then her's is a different kind of writing with a different kind of purpose, though her description of the camps is no more extensive than Viljoen's:[6]

> Near one of the camps in the Northern Transvaal are

> the graves of two women. The older one died first, on the twenty-third of the month, from hunger and want; the younger woman tended her with ceaseless care and devotion to the end. A week later when the British Superintendent came round to inspect the tents, she was found lying on her blanket on the mud floor dead, with the rations of bread and meat she had got four days before untouched on a box beside her. Whether she died of disease, or from inability to eat the food, no one could say. Some who had seen her said she hardly seemed to care to live after the old woman died; they buried them side by side.
>
> There is no stone and no name upon either grave to say who lies there … our unknown … our unnamed … our forgotten dead.

The lament at the end of this extract echoes Schreiner's 'The Cry of South Africa', a cry no less meaningful a hundred years later:[7]

> Give me back my dead
> Whom thou hast riven from me
> By arms of men loud called from earth's farthest
> bound
> To wet my bosom with my children's blood!
> Give me back my dead,
> The dead who grew up on me!

Both story and poem give evidence of the same passionate conviction and commitment to life and abhorrence of war.

So much then for restraint and compassion. By way of contrast, the following extract gives a fairly accurate picture of what sort of arguments were advanced to convince the reading public that Emily Hobhouse was simply an interfering busybody intent on stirring up trouble. J. Qallan Dixon's *Genevieve de Brabant* (1904), must rate as one of the worst novels ever written about the Boer War. No publisher is given on the title page, so presumably the author had to resort to publishing it himself. Nonetheless, the views he advances are disturbingly representative of a considerable body of opinion at the time. As to the literary and propaganda techniques the author employs, they have a familiar ring to them:[8]

> It was said that word had been received from the Boers by General Kitchener, asking him to do away with the Concentration Camps, as they (the Boers) had been informed of the high mortality rate in them, but which had been highly exaggerated. This and other dreadful untruths, such as the ill treatment of women and children, had been and were continually given to the enemy; in fact, everything and anything to keep up and stir up hatred against the British, and which was at this time the only way in which the real enemies of peace could now keep the remnants of the Boer army in the field. The latest rumour, being the killing by the British of wounded Boer prisoners, was proved to the Boer generals to be entirely without foundation.
>
> General Kitchener explained to them that such reports emanated from enemies of Britain, and kept the war party strung up, and this they were not doing for any love of the Boers personally.
>
> Kitchener himself visited the camps, and found from the lips of the prisoners themselves that they had no complaints, but were well treated. This news he communicated also to the Boers in the field, adding: "We will either have to arm your men with arms to again fight us, or keep them safe in the camps."

The unsuspecting reader might be tempted to imagine that the war was a matey affair, played according to rules adhered to on both sides, and the combatants were the mutual victims of some unspecified 'real enemies of peace'. As for rumours about the mortality rate and the treatment of women and children, Emily Hobhouse and Millicent Fawcett published enough factual information during 1901–2 to force the British government to acknowledge that the situation was desperate.

On the other hand, Lord Kitchener made every effort to avoid the camps and thus escape responsibility for having to do something about them.

Perhaps Dixon's special pleading is understandable given the times in which he wrote. Perhaps he was genuinely taken in by British propaganda. However, Edna Drummond (*The Burning Land*, 1979), who wrote some seventy-five years later also found it necessary to excuse what Campbell-Bannerman described in 1901 as 'methods of barbarism':[9]

> Orders were issued to the British soldiers to burn down any farm whose owner was known to shelter members of a commando. The livestock was to be slaughtered or commandeered; the women and children to be put into special camps for safety and protection from hostile natives. It was an order that met with no enthusiasm. The British had always been surprisingly controlled where other armies rushed in to rape and plunder, and putting a torch to simple farms built by the hands of their owners was not to their liking. When the women and children began dying in the camps through disease and lack of supplies – most of which had been blown up by the Boers en route – they relished the task even less.

Those novelists who dealt with the camps most successfully did not try to explain the reasons for their existence, but describe their characters trying to come to grips with the realities of sickness, hunger and death. Perhaps the most dramatic depictions of life in the camps are to be found in Manfred Nathan's *Sarie Marais: A Romance of the Boer War* (1938); Nora Stevenson's *So Much has Happened* (1939), Giles Foden's *Ladysmith* (1999) and Stuart Cloete's controversial *Rags of Glory* (1963):[10]

> Catalina and Martha worked with the sick. The death of her children had changed Martha, made her a fury, defying death, the new enemy, determined to save the

> other little ones. But what odds they fought. Most of the women believed water in any form to be fatal. They would not wash their children's fevered bodies, sponge their faces, or even give them any water to drink. Dogs were bought from Kaffirs and killed for their blood, which was poured fresh and hot down sick children's throats to give them strength, before anyone could stop these desperate mothers.
>
> Mr Tucker sent for help, for another doctor, for more nurses, for medicine. He got nothing. The epidemic was so widespread. Death lay like a winding sheet open over the veld.

Cloete, like Nathan and Stevenson, avoids trying to account for the camps and exonerating those responsible for them. He concentrates on the suffering that he sees as the result of ignorance on both sides. The situation was intolerable and could only get worse. Cloete was one of the few writers to acknowledge that the women's ignorance of basic hygiene in close quarters was a major factor in the spreading of disease. But then he had the advantage of being able to draw on several decades of academic research.

A striking feature of those stories that touch on the concentration camps is that Afrikaans-speaking authors writing in English were all at pains to illustrate the need for understanding, tolerance and reconciliation between the survivors of the war and their descendants. While it might have been expected that these Afrikaner writers would have viewed the camps with bitterness, I have not found one who wrote in English who blamed the British for pursuing a policy of attrition. The suffering is acknowledged and was in no way minimised, but the focus in the end is on reconciliation and reconstruction.

The same cannot be said for those who wrote in Afrikaans, especially in the 1930s or '40s who were committed to another political agenda. Ironically, the 'Bittereinder', Ben Viljoen, set the pattern. Certainly, in Sampie de Wet's short story, 'Concentration Camp', one of the most uncompromising accounts of the plight of women and children in the camps, one of the main themes is still reconciliation. The narrator tells her daughter many years after the war of how, as a child, when she was in the Middelbult camp, she saved a little boy from the usually fatal 'stomach sickness'. Later, when they both grew up they married each other. Throughout the forty years of their marriage it is the husband, Sarel, who tries to temper his wife's bitter memories. In retelling the story to her daughter, she is forced to admit:[11]

> It wasn't the khakies who treated us so badly. Your father always said many of them did not know what was happening in the camps. It was the handsuppers and the joiners, our own people working for the English. It was they who were so hard on the women. I heard them talking to Mrs Van Niekerk as I would never talk to a servant. Sometimes they threw her meat ration in the dirt and made her pick it up there. For a while there was a joiner in charge of the camp.
>
> It was he who made a small barbed-wire enclosure, with no shade and no protection from the wind, and there he put the women who had broken the rules. Their children used to stand and cry outside the wire. After Miss Hobhouse came they stopped all that. I saw Miss Hobhouse myself. She was a tall thin Englishwoman with long feet. We used to laugh about her feet, but she was very good to us women and children.

De Wet, along with Herman Charles Bosman, is one of the few writers who acknowledges the existence of the 'handsuppers' and the 'joiners' – the Boers who had thrown in their lot with the British before the war was over. They were regarded as traitors by the Boers who continued the struggle against the British. Perhaps the most famous 'joiner' of all was General Christiaan de Wet's brother, Piet, who changed sides after he was captured in 1901. Those who occupied positions of trust and responsibility in the camps were especially despised. A number who tried to treat with the Boers in the field on behalf of the British were shot as traitors. This is the subject of Bosman's story 'The Traitor's Wife'.

Sampie de Wet did not idealise women in the camps. There were those women who faced the challenge of survival with stoic fortitude, but there were also women like Mrs Van Niekerk:[12]

> Mama said Mrs Van Niekerk was a feckless woman. When she got her ration of coarse meal she sifted out all the bran and threw it away. Then she made vetkoekies and all her children ate as much as they wanted. Sarel Van Niekerk used to bring me a few cakes too. The next day the little ones cried with hunger because all the meal was finished and they had no bread. Mrs Van Niekerk cried aloud, cursing the khakies between her sobs, and saying, "They are killing all the women and children by starvation. They won't give us food to eat."

The final irony of the story is that Sarel, Mrs Van Niekerk's son, who nearly died but who survived to marry the narrator, grew up, wore khaki and 'died in Italy fighting for the English'.

The last word on the subject of the concentration camps deserves to be given to Lord Milner, chief architect of the war. For, although there is no substantiation for the view that the concentration-camp policy was an exercise in genocide, Milner admitted: 'The abuse so freely heaped upon us for everything we have done and not done [in the camps] is not without some foundation.'[13]

Martial law

Martial law was another feature of the Anglo-Boer War, like the concentration camps, that writers were reluctant to explore until after World War I. Mention has already been made in Chapter One of W.C. Scully's novel *The Harrow* (1921), which treats the subject at length and it might be argued from a more prejudiced point of view than any other.

However, we turn again to Ben Viljoen's *Under the Vierkleur*, for one of the earliest and certainly one of the most interesting accounts in the fiction of a trial under martial law. Danie the hero is captured while on commando. Such is the military mind that everything he has done during the previous year is turned into a capital crime. His predicament is similar to Gideon Scheepers', with whom he is obviously meant to be compared.

Scheepers, a Cape Boer, was captured a few months before the end of the war. He was severely wounded, but once he had recovered was put on trial for treason, convicted and shot. There was such an outcry, both in South Africa and overseas, that such executions of Boers were stopped. Understandably, Scheepers' fate found a ready response in Afrikaans fiction. Probably the best-known novel that treats the issue at length is A. Roodt's *Kaapse Rebel* (1945).

In *Under the Vierkleur*, Danie is indicted on thirteen counts, conviction on any one of which could result in his execution. Fortunately, a British officer, whom Danie had captured and then released some months earlier, intercedes for him and his sentence is commuted. Danie is kept in prison for the last six months of the war, ignorant of his fate.[14]

> "Daniel Linde," he said, "stand up." Danie was helped to his feet. The colonel continued, "This court finds you guilty on all counts charged in the indictment against you, and sentences you to be shot to death, the sentence not to be carried out until after its confirmation by the commander-in-chief of His Majesty's forces in South Africa."

This episode is ample illustration of a remark made in Leipoldt's *Stormwrack*:[15]

> Martial law gives plenary and absolute power to the military authorities … . It is a negation of all law.

Just how much martial law is a 'negation of all law' and incidentally, justice, is the central theme in Leipoldt's fine novel *Stormwrack*.

When a commando calls at the farm of one of the leading members of the community, the full implications of martial law are felt throughout the district. Although the Rekkers are an old established Afrikaner family and have a certain sympathy for the Boer cause, it does not extend to becoming involved in the war. They refuse to help the commando, whereupon their house is burned to the ground. One of their servants is shot while trying to run for help, and young Martin Rekker is forced to join the Boers at gun point. When the British soldiers arrive on the scene, they arrest old man Rekker on suspicion of having assisted the enemy. The only grounds for their suspicion is that the family is Afrikaans-speaking and is known to have supported the Afrikaner Bond. The British proclaim Rekker's son a rebel who, if captured, could be shot for treason.

Later, two local Boers are tried for treason. One of them, a halfwit from the village, is accused of shooting a wounded British soldier. The village is forced to gather in the square outside the gaol and witness the proclamation of his sentence. Some days later, sixteen leading citizens are compelled to watch his execution. Leipoldt had, of course, already explored this theme in his great narrative poem 'Oom Gert Vertel'.

Leipoldt does not depict the actual execution in *Stormwrack*, preferring instead to explore the effect it has on a wide variety of characters, all of whom represent different points of view. The approach is not dissimilar to that used in Greek tragedy where scenes of violence take place off stage. By depriving the violent act of any sensationalism, the halfwit's execution becomes no more than a sordid and shameful event and a fitting comment on the 'heroics' usually associated with war.

Leipoldt makes the point that if people allow themselves to be dictated to by events, passively giving up their resistance to what they know is wrong, the first casualties are compassion and common sense. Martial law, Leipoldt says, is not only the negation of all law, it is also the negation of civilisation based on tolerance and compassion.

Military law

In contrast, military law is based on the needs of the institution it serves by regulating the behaviour of its members. However, military law is as subject to corruption and manipulation as any other system of law; and because of the nature of the institution it serves, its solutions tend to be absolute. War does not encourage the notion of the sanctity of life. Whatever the issue, military justice is ruthless in protecting its own, as the Dreyfus case illustrated so completely.

Harry Morant's execution in Kit Denton's *The Breaker* (1973) is described in theatrical terms, complete with heroic dialogue, flashes of gunfire and all the panoply and pageantry that is usually associated with such scenes in gung-ho fiction. Morant is depicted as the victim of an unjust and corrupt system, sharing his last cigarette with a brother officer who is to be executed with him, and manfully refusing a blindfold. The knowledge that this scene is the fictional account of events that actually took place in the Northern Transvaal in 1902, is intended to give the story added poignancy.

In Denton's novel, as in real life, Morant is accused by a British court martial of shooting defenceless Boer prisoners, and a Lutheran minister, whom he suspected of passing on intelligence to the Boers. There is little doubt where Denton's sympathies lie. Throughout the trial, Morant is portrayed as the victim of vested interests. The prosecution's case rests on proving that Morant was acting on his own initiative by taking no prisoners, but if the defence can prove he was acting under orders, British prestige (and particularly Lord Kitchener's reputation), will suffer.

The exigencies of British honour – and more to the point, the claims of British propaganda – demand that Morant be found guilty and executed, to demonstrate the impartiality of British justice to the Boers and to the world at large.

As Denton presents it, Morant is found guilty and sentenced to be shot by a firing squad to cover up evidence that might harm the reputation of his military superiors. Morant is portrayed as a victim of ambition and hypocrisy. He remains cool even though he soon realises he is doomed. As he faces the firing squad, his last moments are described with characteristic verve:[16]

> There was a silence and Harry was looking up into the sky, deep and warmly blue. The voice sounded a thousand miles away when it called the firing party to aim, and he looked down again, surprised to see them so close, the muzzles staring at him. He pitched his voice down to them.
>
> "Shoot straight, you bastards. Don't make a mess of us!"

> They saw the flame, but not the smoke that followed it.

In one of Herman Charles Bosman's most famous short stories, 'Mafeking Road', Bosman touched directly on the question of military law and its possible tragic consequences. After the relief of Mafeking, when the Boers were in retreat, young Stephanus van Barnevelt says:[17]

> "I wouldn't go back to Mafeking for anybody … unless, maybe, it's to hand myself over to the English."
>
> "We can shoot you for doing that," the veld-kornet said. "It's contrary to military law."
>
> "I wish I knew something about military law," Stephanus answered. "Then I would draw up a peace treaty between Stephanus van Barnevelt and England."
>
> Some of the men laughed again. But Floris shook his head sadly.

Stephanus does go back, intending to put his 'hands-up to the English'. His father, Floris, follows him into the night:[18]

> … Floris did not speak about what happened that night, … we saw him riding out under the star-light, following after his son and shouting at him to be a man and fight for his country … . Floris did not mention Stephanus again, his son who was not worthy to be a Van Barnevelt.

It is not military law that is responsible for Stephanus's death, but his father's ideals of family and national honour. But it is military law that makes it a capital offence for Stephanus to 'draw up a peace treaty between [himself] and England'.

Bosman leaves us with a puzzle. How does a man reconcile the conflicting demands of family, military caste and national pride with the immediate and concrete claims of human relationships? Whatever the answer, the reader cannot avoid the realisation that war can drive men to extreme and terrible acts, the consequences of which can haunt them for the rest of their lives. Within the context of the military apparatus, individual conscience and motive are rendered irrelevant. As Captain Vere says in Melville's *Billy Budd*: 'War looks but to the frontage, the appearance'.[19]

ENDNOTES

1 Blackburn 1903: 112.
2 Emily Hobhouse. 'I began to compare a parish I had known at home of 2 000 people where a funeral was an event – and usually of an old person. Here some twenty to twenty-five were carried away *daily* … . The full realisation of the position downed upon me – it was a death rate such as had never been known except in the times of the Great Plagues … the whole talk of death – who died yesterday, who lay dying today, who would be dead tomorrow' quoted in Pakenham 1979: 507.
3 Viljoen 1904: 377–8.
4 Ibid: 378.
5 Ibid: 380.
6 Schreiner, O., 'Eighteen-Ninety-Nine' in *A Century of South African Short Stories* (ed. Jean Marquard, 1978).
7 Schreiner, O., 'The Cry of South Africa' in *A Century of South African Poetry* (ed. Michael Chapman, 1981).
8 Dixon 1904: 174–5.
9 Drummond 1979: 411–2.
10 Cloete 1963: 476.
11 De Wet 1956: 92.
12 Ibid: 92.
13 Lord Milner quoted in Spies 1977: 171.
14 Viljoen 1904: 349–50.
15 Leipoldt 1980: 160.
16 Denton 1973: 266.
17 Bosman 1969: 51.
18 Ibid: 52.
19 Melville 1891: 389.

A

BOER OF TO-DAY

A STORY OF THE TRANSVAAL

BY

GEORGE COSSINS

AUTHOR OF

"ISBAN ISRAEL," "THE WINGS OF SILENCE"

&c.

LONDON

GEORGE ALLEN

1900

CHAPTER FIVE

BRITISH VIEWS OF THE BOERS: 'I do not love my empire's foes'

Ho, sing me a song both deep and strong,
Like the thunder of hoofs as they roll along:
Let the music ride with a swinging stride,
Like the gallop of steeds in their strength and pride.
When they reach at their bridles and foam and fret,
For I sing of a rider: De Wet, De Wet.

Through the black, still night comes a stamp and beat,
And the dark is a-clatter with horses' feet,
With the rattle of arms, as they wheel and pass,
And the dull deep thunder across the grass,
Who rides by night, when the moon is set?
And the night owl answers, 'De Wet, De Wet'.

B. Shadwell[1]

While it is commonly recognised today that racism is the greatest cause of conflict in southern Africa, the history of relations between the white inhabitants is no less conflicted. Territorial and commercial ambitions fuelled by greed, arrogance and different world views have played predictable parts.

The British imperial view

As might be expected the British imperial views have been well documented. Innumerable accounts exist of the impression the Boers made upon the British settlers and visitors who came to administer, hunt, botanise or merely to look at the country. While not all descriptions of the Boers by the British are unfavourable or unfair, it is generally true to say it was the derogatory opinions that took root in the popular mind.

The British humiliation at Majuba; the disastrous Jameson Raid; and the well-publicised grievances of the Uitlanders during the late 1890s served only to inflame prejudices kept alive by generations of British writers and politicians.

Although some writers of popular fiction attempted to escape from the snare of contemporary prejudice, most early novels are populated with grotesque caricatures of the Boers. In the main, the Boers are described as nasty, smelly, dirty, uncouth and ignorant – 'the Boers are notoriously of the great unwashed order'.[2] They were purported to be obsessively cruel to 'kaffirs', and implacably opposed to any form of progress: 'There is nothing that the Boers hate and fear more than novelty either in peace or war.'[3] This last remark, written in 1897, reflects a deeply held prejudice that was destined to cost the British dearly at Spioen Kop, Stormberg and Magersfontein, and still later after the capture of Pretoria in June 1900, when the war moved into its guerilla phase. The Boers were also held to be religious hypocrites and cowards:[4]

> … as to honour … there's no meaning to them in the word – not to a wily old Boer who would stick at nothing in his country's name and feel persuaded he was doing the Lord a very valuable service.

It was frequently lamented that the Boers did not fight 'fair and square':[5]

> The boer is a great fighter – so long as he has secured a hiding-place amongst rocks, and can shoot at his enemy without fear of retaliation. He also loves to keep his horse tethered close at hand, in order that he may be enabled to make a bolt of it, should the foe show any sign of an advance. But he does not relish

> tackling any man, be he black or white, in the open, and only does so when there is literally no alternative offered him.

To Hume Nisbet it was self-evident that an Englishman:[6]

> … was unable, by reason of his nationality and training, to comprehend such depths of atrocity and moral depravity as are practised and boasted about as slimness by this wily and degraded nation of savages.
>
> Their skins are similar in shade to our own. They read from the same Bible. But their hearts are blacker, and their minds deeper smirched with ignorance, than the most benighted of savage races who at present people the globe.

Or, as Sir Garnet Wolseley wrote to the Colonial Secretary a little over a year before Majuba:[7]

> [the Boers] … have all the cunning and cruelty of the Kaffir without his courage or honesty … they could not stand up against our troops for an hour.

These widely held preconceptions were rudely shattered when the British confronted actual Boers on the battlefield.

It is an ancient maxim of war not to underestimate the enemy. It was just this trap that many British generals fell into with disastrous results. One irony of the war was that it was the so-called anti-progressive Boers who most rapidly and successfully adapted to the new conditions, while the supposedly innovative British seemed incapable of developing strategies in advance of those used in the Crimea in 1855.

Because the imperialists were largely the victims of their own propaganda, they were generally unable to perceive the Boers as anything other than backward and inferior. Many writers wedded to the imperial cause depicted the Boers as overly cunning and treacherous rather than admit to British short-comings. Thus, an exercise in what amounted to national self-deception, aided and abetted by government propaganda and the jingoistic press, sought to explain away one British defeat after another.

The pattern is set

John Barrow, an early visitor to the Cape, at the beginning of the 19th century set the pattern and tone for much subsequent writing about the Boers. Although he was writing strictly about the Trek-boers, what he had to say was generalised by subsequent writers to apply to all the Boers:[8]

> Placed in a country where not only the necessities, but almost every luxury of life might by industry be procured, he has the enjoyment of none of them. Though he has cattle in abundance he makes very little use of milk or of butter. In the midst of soil and climate most favourable to the cultivation of the vine, he drinks no wine. He makes use of few or no vegetables nor roots. Three times a-day his table is loaded with masses of mutton, swimming in the grease of the sheep's tail. His house is either open to the roof, or covered only with rough poles and turf, affording a favourable shelter for scorpions and spiders; and the earthy floors are covered with dust and dirt, and swarm with insects … . His apartments, if he happens to have more than one, which is not always the case among the grazing farmers, are nearly destitute of furniture. A great chest that contains all his movables, and two smaller ones that are fitted to his wagon, are the most striking articles. The bottoms of his chairs consist of thongs cut from a bullock's hide. The windows are without glass; or if there should happen to be any remains of this article it is so patched and daubed as nearly to exclude the light it was intended to admit.
>
> The boor notwithstanding has his enjoyments: he

> is absolute master of a domain of several miles in extent, and he lords it over a few miserable slaves or Hottentots without control. His pipe scarcely ever quits his mouth, from the moment he rises till he retires to rest, except to give him time to swallow his sopies, or a glass of strong ardent spirit, to eat his meals, and to take a nap after dinner. Unwilling to work, and unable to think; with a mind disengaged from every sort of care and reflection, indulging to excess in the gratification of every sensual appetite, the African peasant grows to an unwieldy size, and is carried off the stage by the first inflammatory disease that attacks him.

Nor did the women fare any better:[9]

> The women of the African peasantry pass a life with the most listless inactivity. The mistress of the family, with her coffee-pot constantly boiling before her on a small table, seems fixed to the chair like a piece of furniture. The good lady, born in the wilds of Africa, and educated among slaves and Hottentots, has little idea of what, in a state of society, constitutes female delicacy. She makes no scruples of having her legs and feet washed in warm water by a slave before strangers; an operation that is regularly performed every evening. If the motive of such a custom were cleanliness, the practice of it would deserve praise, but to see the tub with the same water passed round through all the branches of the family, according to seniority, is apt to create ideas of a different nature. Most of them go constantly without stockings and shoes, even when the thermometer is down to the freezing point. They generally, however, make use of small stoves to place their feet on. The young girls sit with their hands before them as listless as their mothers. Most of them, in the distant districts, can

> neither read nor write, so that they have no mental resources whatsoever.

Barrow's patronising distaste for a people he clearly despised for what he perceived as a lack of 'refinement', limited resources and the manner in which they '[lord] it over a few miserable slaves of Hottentots without control' is echoed again and again in the fiction associated with the Anglo-Boer conflicts.

Slaves and slavery

The Cape was virtually untouched by the Age of Enlightenment, which transformed European perceptions of the possibilities of life. The contrast between the people living an isolated, conservative and rural existence inland from the southern tip of Africa, and the visitors from industrialised Europe, could hardly have been more marked. Misconceptions were bound to occur. For example, the development of the indenture system by the Boers after the emancipation of the slaves in 1807, led to accusations, which found an echo in the fiction that the Boers were perpetuating a system of slavery under another name. The Boers' treatment of black people is commented on by most authors. In theory at least, British writers were outraged that the Boers should treat black Africans as being beyond the pale of accepted morality simply because they were 'heathen'.

In Rev. Henry Adams' *Perils in the Transvaal and Zululand* (1887), one of the characters, Mr Baylen, describes the way in which the Boers go about acquiring labour for their farms, to two young boys, Redgy and George, who are fresh from England. Having described a Boer massacre of a Bechuana village, Mr Baylen says:[10]

> "It was the most shocking sight I have ever witnessed."
>
> "Horrible indeed sir!" exclaimed Redgy.
>
> "What provocation do you suppose they had given the Dutchmen?"
>
> "Most likely none at all," was the answer. "The Bechuanas in general are peaceable enough, but the

> Dutch – the Boers that is – are bent on having slaves to work for them; and if they can't get them by what they consider fair means, will get them by foul."
>
> "What do they consider fair means?" asked Redgy.
>
> "Buying them off their parents," answered Baylen. "They will go to a village and demand the help of a number of women to work in their fields or gardens. These women, who dare not refuse, take their children with them, and then they will try to bargain for these, in order to make slaves of them. But the Bechuanas are a very affectionate people, and can very seldom be induced to sell their children. Therefore, as the Boers would tell you, they are obliged to take them by force."
>
> "You are joking with us, sir, are you not?" said George.
>
> "Indeed I am not. They think that not only is it fair and right that the natives should be obliged to work without pay for them, but that it is their duty to oblige them so to work."
>
> "On what possible grounds, Mr Baylen?"
>
> "Because they are an inferior race, over whom the Boers have a natural right. This is no pretence. They really think so. The Boers are, after their fashion, a very religious people. They believe Almighty God has given the black races to be their servants, and that they are carrying out His will when they reduce them to slavery. Some of them even believe that it is their mission to kill all except those who are thus kept in bondage. They liken themselves to the Israelites when they entered the Promised Land, and the natives to the Canaanites, whom they were to exterminate."

If one goes by the literature, Mr Baylen is merely expressing generally held convictions about the way Boers treated black people. Most importantly, their cruelty and racism is shown as an extension of their religious fanaticism. Whether this is an accurate perception or not, it was one that was widely held and deeply entrenched. An interesting aside for the modern reader is the parallel between these early perceptions and the way successive Nationalist governments won the Dutch Reformed churches' approval for their Apartheid policies.

Adams, writing in 1887, was no less politically motivated. He was intent on reinforcing the moral imperative of British imperial interests in southern Africa. Where did the Rev. Adams get these ideas from? He had never been to Africa, and, like so many of his contemporaries, he had to rely on second-hand accounts. David Livingstone's highly popular public lectures and published accounts of his travels were just such sources. It is interesting to compare Adams' episode with an account taken from Livingstone's diary:[11]

> They came with the prestige of white men and deliverers; but the Bechuanas soon found, as they expressed it, 'that Mosilikatze was cruel to his enemies and kind to those he conquered; but that the Boers destroyed their enemies, and made slaves of their friends.' The tribes who still retain the semblance of independence are forced to perform all the labour of the fields, such as manuring the land, weeding, reaping, building, making dams and canals, and at the same time to support themselves. I have myself been an eye-witness of Boers coming to a village, and, according to their usual custom, demanding twenty or thirty women to weed their gardens, and have seen these women proceed to the scene of unrequited toil, carrying their own food on their heads, their children on their backs, and instruments of labour on their shoulders. Nor have the Boers any wish to conceal the meanness of thus employing unpaid labour; on the contrary, every one of them, from Mr. Potgieter and Mr. Gert Krieger, the commandants, down-wards, lauded his own humanity and justice in making such an equitable regulation. "We make the people work for us, in consideration of allowing them to live in our country."

This new species of slavery which they have adopted serves to supply the lack of field-labour only. The demand for domestic servants must be met by forays on tribes which have good supplies of cattle. The Portuguese can quote instances in which blacks become so degraded by the love of strong drink as actually to sell themselves; but never in any one case, within the memory of man, has a Bechuana Chief sold any of his people, or a Bechuana man his child. Hence the necessity for a foray to seize children. And those individual Boers who would not engage in it for the sake of slaves can seldom resist the twofold plea of a well-told story of an intended uprising of the devoted tribe, and the prospect of handsome pay in the division of the captured cattle besides.

Whips and whipping

The Boers' reputation for cruelty to 'kaffirs' remained a constant theme in Boer War fiction. Most often, the topic is not detailed much beyond emotional reportage and moral indignation. Occasionally, though, some writers are not content to rely on stock responses. Victor Rousseau Emmanuel was one of the earliest authors to use satire to expose and exploit different levels of significance that mere reportage might miss. In the following extract from his novel, *Derwent's Horse* (1901), much of the effectiveness of his comments is derived from the way he moves without pause from a bland journalistic statement about an event, to satirical comment on its justice:[12]

> One day old van der Walt tied up a Kaffir to a tree and flogged him for theft. This is the natural and proper destiny for a Kaffir, and far more suitable than fastening him to a trekking waggon-wheel and using him for a brake, which savours of cruelty, or burning him to death in his hut, which is a sin.

Who chooses the 'chosen' race?

Few writers committed to the Empire could contain their resentment at what they perceived as the Boers' view of themselves as a 'chosen people'. Bertram Mitford says of one of his Boer characters in *Aletta* (1900):[13]

> He implicitly believed that the whole Dutch race in South Africa were under special Divine protection, and the Anglo-Saxon under the Divine curse … .

What was especially annoying to Mitford, and to others who harboured similar feelings, is not only that the Boers should conceive of themselves as a 'chosen people', but that they should have the effrontery to believe that the British were godforsaken. Significantly, the character to whom the view above is credited, is the villain of the novel, implacably dedicated to opposing British interests in southern Africa.

Rhodes believed that one of the moral foundations of the Empire was that British civilisation was mankind's greatest achievement, and that the British had a divine mission to bring it to as much of the world as possible. The British too, saw themselves as a 'chosen people'. It is no small wonder then, that the Empire's writers used every opportunity to discredit any rival claims that might challenge their position as 'God's chosen'. The Boers were certainly numbered, if not specifically by Kipling, then by most of the imperialist writers of the time as being among the 'lesser breeds without the law'.[14] That the Boers should go their own way, refusing to fit in with what Rhodes and his fellow imperialists saw as the unfolding of God's grand plan, was a continual affront.

George Cossins, in his novel *A Boer of To-day* (1900), reveals how, even if the Boer could be 'civilised' and 'tamed' he would never be able to throw off the claims of blood. Jan, the young Afrikaner hero of this novel, leaves his home in the Transvaal to visit his uncle De Villiers, in the Cape. It is there that his education begins:[15]

> Little by little, he learned to reverence women, to honour true manliness, to understand the English idea

> of fair play, and to blush for the 'tricks' which, as a child he had been taught to consider not only fair but desirable.

What 'true manliness' is, is suggested a little earlier. His uncle remonstrates with Jan for kicking a youth in a fight:[16] 'You must never kick a man; it is not Eng – I mean, manly, Jan.' Much later, having had the benefit of an Oxford education, Jan says in despair:[17] 'I hardly know what I am, I seem pulled both ways.' The bonds of blood and breeding prove too strong. Oxford notwithstanding, he reverts to kind:[18]

> Jan was true to his race. Give a Boer a thousand erven and he immediately dreams how happy he would be with two thousand; but when the two thousand are his, he casts covetous eyes on the Kaffirs near him, and is still not happy till their land also comes into his hand. The paradise of the Boers consists in unlimited territory, numberless slaves, abundant game, and no taxes … .

… a paradise indeed.

In a not too disguised manner, and with somewhat greater ambitions than a couple of thousand erven, the British had, since 1805, set about annexing considerable portions of southern Africa on the pretext that the indigenous inhabitants could not govern themselves. These portions proved to have exploitable assets such as diamonds and gold. In many respects, the Boer ambitions, as depicted here, were in fact the principles on which the British Empire was founded and flourished.

Cossins was the only British author writing at the time of the war who attempted to explore the complex relationship between the Boers and the blacks. That he failed is not surprising. However, he did succeed in conveying the need for each side to recognise each other's humanity.

His novel opens at the time of Sekukuni's revolt, during President Burgers' term of office in the old South African Republic. Jan, barely a teenager, discovers a young 'kaffir' who had just seen his family slaughtered by the Amaswazi, led by a Boer commando. The young black boy's suffering has little effect on Jan:[19] 'Jan touched the boy with his foot – for he was only a Kaffir'. Their confrontation is a microcosm of the racial situation in South Africa. Yet, later when both of them are presented with separate opportunities to betray each other, they refrain from doing so. Some inner compulsion forces them to acknowledge that they share in a common tragedy:[20]

> In spite of racial differences two pairs of hands touched lightly and ashamedly, and the boys turned away in different directions, Mahaan full of gratitude, Jan half glad, half disgusted that he had given way so far as to clasp hands with a kaffir.

Cossins was clearly ahead of his time. Many later authors, such as Stuart Cloete in *The Hill of Doves* (1942) and *Rags of Glory* (1963), depicted black people in the role of the faithful family retainer. But none of these writers made any attempt to explore the emotional significance that the master/servant relationship might have had for the Boers and their black servants. Cossins, though, is aware of the subtle interplay of emotions that might have existed between the two boys as they tried to come to terms with their differences and acknowledge that the qualities that bind them together are greater than the differences that forced them apart.

Cossins had his limitations. His novel never questions the notion of 'racial superiority'. Nor is it ever made clear why Mahaan should be 'full of gratitude'. *A Boer of To-day* may fail because of the author's limitations in developing plot, theme and character. However, in the opening chapters Cossins goes a long way to showing a side of the Boer character and the complexity of interracial relationships that had been almost universally ignored till then.

It is seldom that black characters are given the opportunity to voice their opinions about the Boers. When they do, what they have to say is predictable. The following extract from Henry Gibbs' *The Tumult and the Shouting* (1958) is atypical, but then Gibbs was writing in an era that had become acutely aware of the race issue:[21]

> "Hate them?… . "No," she said at length. "The Boers have magnificent qualities. They are courageous. No adversity can weaken their determination. Their loyalty to each other is beyond criticism. They have won great achievements out of spirit and fortitude. No … I pity them. They are frightened to let anyone admire them for their good qualities. They insist upon others seeing them only as masters. It is a tragedy when a people of such greatness permit themselves to be so weak."

Next to racism, the other great 'ism' anticipated in South Africa well before it became a burning issue in the rest of the world, was sexism. Boer women and the way they were treated by Boer men has long been cause for comment among English-speaking writers. The picture painted by Barrow at the turn-of-the-18th century is pervasive. Tant' Sannie in Schreiner's *The Story of an African Farm*, was an example many writers were inclined to follow.

Writing in 1900, Fox Russell, in *The Boer's Blunder*, expressed the following sentiments:[22]

> A Boer would never dream of concealing anything … from his vrau; she was to be treated just as if she were one of the sterner sex; indeed it was very possible that she might be called upon to handle a rifle and fight with men. No idea, therefore, of sparing her feelings, would ever enter into the Afrikander's calculations.

In a world that now strives for equality between the sexes, the sentiments expressed above would probably be received differently from the way they were intended in 1900. Nevertheless, the conviction held by many writers of popular fiction that the Boers had scant respect for the feelings of their womenfolk, persisted until well after the war was over. With few exceptions in the early novels, Boer women were depicted as dirty, ignorant, uncouth and, above all, 'unfeminine'; so much for the stereotype. When it came to describing an individual, Russell's Tant Cloete conforms to type:[23]

> … an enormous fat woman, with the face of a virago, showed herself over the tail-board of the great, lumbering vehicle, and glared at the two men, her arms stuck akimbo … .

When she walks she '[rolls] her great carcase'. Each exclamatory caveat, which makes up her entire conversation, is 'accompanied by an imperious wave of a very red and dirty arm'.[24]

It is worth comparing Tant Cloete with C.R. Prance's Tante Rabella, created a generation later. For Prance, Tante Rabella is one of those 'backveld women of 'Voortrekker' stock who, like the Saga women, could at need do a man's work both in battle and at time of peace'.[25] Prance says that it is these women, made in an heroic mould, who belong to a 'natural aristocracy'.[26] Tante Rabella is indeed a far cry from Tant Cloete.

Many English-speaking South African writers in the 1920s and 30s, such as Pauline Smith and Prance, emphasised the Boers' dignity, simplicity and humanity. In his autobiography, *Towards the Mountain*, Alan Paton recorded the enthusiasm with which he initially greeted the 1937 Trek and dedication of the Voortrekker Monument. At that time, many writers of English fiction were committed to the union of the two white groups. They actively sought to soothe the old wounds in their writing. Consequently, at that time, individual portraits of the Boers and their women were much more sympathetic than they had been in stories written before World War I.

Women, the victims of war

Olive Schreiner's portrait of women as victims of war in her short story 'Eighteen-Ninety-Nine' is very different from her picture of Tant' Sannie in *The Story of an African Farm*. In the following extract, a mother and her daughter-in-law receive news from the front that Jan, the son and husband, has been killed:[27]

> The old woman leaned forward and grasped the boy's arm. "Read it over again," she said, "from where they

found him." He turned back and read slowly. She gazed at the page as if she were reading also. Then, suddenly, she slipped out at the front door.

At the back of the house she found her daughter-in-law still walking up and down, and the Kaffir woman with a red handkerchief bound round her head and the child sitting across her hip, sucking from her long, pendulous breast, looking on.

The old woman walked up to her daughter-in-law and grasped her firmly by the arm.

"He's dead! You know, my boy's dead!" she cried, drawing the apron down with her right hand and disclosing her swollen and bleared face. "Oh, his beautiful hair – Oh, his beautiful hair!"

The old woman held her arm tighter with both hands; the younger opened her half-closed eyes, and looked into the keen, clear eyes fixed on hers, and stood arrested.

The old woman drew her face closer to hers. "You … do … not … know … what … has … happened!" She spoke slowly, her tongue striking her front gum, the jaw moving stiffly, as though partly paralysed. She loosed her left hand and held up the curved work-worn fingers before her daughter-in-law's face. "Was it not told me … the night he was born … here … at this spot … that he would do great things … great things … for his land and his people?" She bent forward till her lips almost touched the other's. "Three … bullet … wounds … and four … bayonet … stabs!" She raised her left hand high in the air. "Three … bullet … wounds … and four bayonet … stabs!… Is it given to many to die so for their land and their people!"

The younger woman gazed into her eyes, her own growing larger and larger. She let the old woman lead her by the arm in silence into the house.

In their grief these two women stand for all women in time of war. Their only solace is a bitter one. Jan died a hero. The wife mutely confronts the brevity and barrenness of her marriage. She has not even been left a child through whom she could contemplate the future. And yet, for all this, Schreiner knows that life goes on. The image of the 'Kaffir woman' with the child at her breast affirms the primacy and continuity of life.

Herman Charles Bosman does not see the war-torn Boer woman as a symbol, but he does see her with an Afrikaner's eyes. In 'The Affair at Ysterspruit', the narrator is a young inexperienced school teacher, whose enthusiasm for 'huisbesoek'[28] is charged by his passion for gathering story material about the war from the Marico locals. It is on just such a 'huisbesoek' that the young school master encounters Ouma Engelbrecht.[29] The picture she paints of her dead son, Johannes, flatters his image of the Boers and he encourages her to show him a photograph. For: 'It was always with a thrill of pride in my land and my people that I looked on a hero of the Boer War [when shown] a photograph of a burgher of the South African Republic.'

However, in this case, as the school master picks up the portrait he realises that Johannes, who died of bullet wounds in the affair at Ysterspruit, was a National Scout. That is, he had betrayed the Boer cause and fought for the English. The tragedy does not lie so much in Johannes' fate but in Ouma Engelbrecht's, whose own people find her an embarrassment, and who is ignored and forgotten. She is left with only her grief for solace. Bosman's Ouma Engelbrecht is no universal symbol but the portrait of an alienated woman as she lives in obscurity with her grief. She is rooted in a time and place where nothing is as it seems.

Betrayal was of course one of the skeletons in the Afrikaner cupboard left over from the war. The fact that Bosman returned to this theme in four of his short stories: 'The Affair at Ysterspruit', 'The Traitor's Wife', 'Mafeking Road', and 'Peaches Ripening in the Sun', probably accounts to some extent for his lack of popular appeal for many years in the Afrikaner community. Bosman's interest was not in political over-simplifications but in the complexity of human motives. The myths of national solidarity held no attractions for him. Hence it is 'with a queer jumble of inarticulate feelings'[30] that the school master leaves Ouma Engelbrecht.

In the following extract from 'The Traitor's Wife', the narrator, Bosman's other persona – Oom Schalk Lourens – remembers Serfina Roux. Her husband had been an admired leader of the commando to which Oom Schalk belonged, but for reasons never disclosed, had surrendered to the English. Leendert Roux and his wife know that as far as the commando is concerned, his life is forfeit. The scene is set just after Serfina has betrayed Leendert to the commando and he has been captured and shot:[31]

> Serfina looked even more shadowy than she had done in my dream when she set off back to the homestead along the footpath through the thorns. The sun was just beginning to rise. And I understood how right Jurie Bekker had been when he said that she was just like the Transvaal, with the dawn wind fluttering her skirts about her ankles as it rippled the grass. And I remembered it was the Boer women that kept on when their menfolk recoiled before the steepness of the Drakensberge and spoke of turning back.
>
> I also thought of how strange it was that Serfina should have come walking over to our camp, in the middle of the night, just as she had done in my dream. But where my dream was different was that she had reported not to me but to our veld-kornet where Leendert Roux was.

To Oom Schalk, there is something about Serfina that defies definition. However, it is with the image of the Boer women inexorably encouraging their menfolk to cross the Drakensberge that much of her quality comes into focus. It was the women who had the vision to see the possibilities of the world beyond the mountains, and it was they who drove their men to seek freedom in a new land. The end justified the means. So it is with Serfina, although the story hints that Serfina's motives may not be entirely based on patriotism. What is left unclear is the exact nature of her relationship with the man who takes over as commandant when Leendert surrenders to the English. Once again, things are not as they seem. To the end of the story, Serfina remains dreamlike, illusive and uncanny.

Of love and marriage

A marriage proposal has long been a useful literary device to explore social convention and to reveal characters' limitations. It is at such pivotal moments that the suitor's needs must reveal his sensitivity, generosity and depth of emotion to prove himself worthy of the object of his passion.

Perhaps the most celebrated proposals in English literature are Darcy's and Mr Collins's to Elizabeth Bennet in Jane Austen's *Pride and Prejudice*, and Mr Causubon's to Dorethea in George Eliot's *Middlemarch*. In each case, the suitors reveal themselves for what they are.

The prototype of the proposal scene in South African literature is that of Piet Van der Walt to Tant' Sannie in *The Story of an African Farm*. It is with the same gentle humour touched with compassion that Pauline Smith describes Jan Beyers' attempts to woo and win Andrina in *The Beadle*. In Boer War fiction the marriage proposal has often been used to illustrate just how lacking in finer feelings the Boers are. For Francis Bancroft in *Thane Brandon* (1913), an old Boer's proposal to a young attractive widow, is an opportunity to further the author's ideological aims:[32]

> "Is it time to make love and my man not yet in his grave six months?"
>
> "That! That's nothing," interpolated the old Boer mildly; he had produced a square black bottle from which he drank occasionally with gurglings expressive of his enjoyment of the contents. "Six months, say you? Why, woman, it was as we were riding home from my first wife's burying that I bespoke Katerina Plessis – she was my second wife. That's the way to do it; for when the Lord takes a man's wife or a woman's husband, He does so as to give a change for another

> man or woman."
>
> He chuckled fatuously behind the waggling beard as he dug claw-like, iron-hard finger-tips into Johanna's shapely arm. She slithered agilely beyond his reach with a little affected scream. "God save us, old man! Your nails! They're long as aasvogel's talons; sharp as wild cat's claws!"
>
> Her words added to his hilarious content and he drank a long deep draught, cleared his throat afresh, spat profusely into the heart of the burning logs and drawled nasally his further reminiscences.
>
> "Ja! Ja! – but I was a good man to them both and many sons and daughters they bore me – seven-and-twenty in all those two women bore me. You'll have plenty of children and grand-children – yes, and great grand-children, too – ready to hand the day we wed, my girl," he added, addressing Johanna with a leer.
>
> "Shut up your nonsense!" she cried, tossing her dark head and affecting conventional displeasure, and the old man laughed again deep in his chest.
>
> "Nay! nay! Why this foolish bashfulness, girl? This comes of your going among the foolish folk living in Pretoria – no true Transvaalers but just piebalds, neither Britons nor Boers. But as I say, mense, seven-and-twenty children have I bred and reared here in the backveldt, and maybe the Lord will yet send me more sons; that is what I hope for. Our country needs many, many sons to replace those lost in the war. And who knows, mense – who knows but that our children will one day retake the land we must lose to-day?"

The old man has the last word. He may not be much of a marriage prospect, but he appears to have more political insight than perhaps Bancroft intended.

In the interests of British even-handedness, the *Boys' Own Paper* had occasion to publish the following portrait of the 'typical' Boer going a-courting:[33]

> When a Boer youth goes away on a courting expedition he is a sight for the gods. He will be dressed up regardless of expense, his hair will be well oiled, and parted over his forehead, and his face will have been scrubbed until it shines again; his horse will be groomed to perfection, his saddled cleaned, and his stirrup-irons, bits, and spurs burnished to the consistency of silver, and he will mount, and, digging the spurs into his horse, will start off at a hand gallop to visit his inamorata.
>
> After a three months' courtship the marriage will take place, and the neighbours, for fifty miles around, will drive over, and the quiet farm will be given over to riotous merriment for three days and nights, after which the guests will depart, and the young man will settle down to dream away the balance of his life in a placid calm, unless some unforseen circumstance, such as the present war, occurs to call him away to more stirring scenes.

Redressing the balance

Bertram Mitford was one of the few early writers to attempt a balanced picture of the Boers. He set out in *Aletta* to convince his readers that not all Boers are nasty, ugly and ignorant.[34]

> If Ratels Hoek was a creditable example of the better class of Dutch farm, no less was its owner an excellent specimen of the better type of Dutch farmer. Stephanus De la Rey was a tall, handsome man of about fifty. He had a fine forehead, blue eyes, and straight, regular features, and the masses of his full brown beard had hardly yet begun to show threads of grey. His character was in keeping with his general appearance, for though quiet-mannered, he was the most straight-forward and genial of men, and was

> immensely looked up to and respected far and wide by such few English as the neighbourhood contained, no less than by his own compatriots.
>
> His wife was a bright, cheerful, brisk-mannered little woman, who, as we have already heard it stated, was half English in that she owned an English mother.

For many writers the only way to make the Boers acceptable was to anglicise them. In George Cossins' novel *A Boer of To-day*, Jan De Villiers ...[35]

> ... had the lightest, most whimsical manner of dealing with worries and annoyances of any man I ever saw. They called him 'Mark Tapley' on the fields, for nothing seemed to distress him except dishonesty and vice. He was tremendously down on the I.D.Bs. as a fraternity, but I know that he helped one of them when he was at the point of being arrested. The man had a sickly wife, and that was enough for De Villiers. "Look here," he said, "you can't go to gaol and leave her to fret her heart out; you stay here and I'll make a bolt for it."

De Villiers could be an English country squire. He has all the right Whig attitudes. Ironically, the true test of his assimilation of English values is in the gallant way he is prepared to break the law. What makes this doubly ironic is that the Illicit Diamond Buying (IDB) Laws were enacted in order to protect those who were busy plundering the Kimberley diamond fields, namely Rhodes and his cronies.

All too often the moral universe of imperialism was little more than a charade for preserving and presenting British self-interest in the best light. The magnates who controlled the diamond fields had made the trade in diamonds a criminal offence (except through their own agents), although British commercial policy at the time was committed to unrestricted trade and competition. However, when it came to IDB, the official rationale was couched in moralistic terms. If the diamond price was undermined by unrestricted buying and selling, the market would be flooded and the price would fall, leading to the impoverishment of many people who had invested in or had depended on the industry for their livelihood.

What was not mentioned was that by criminalising illicit diamond sales, the De Beers mining magnates were able to manipulate prices and keep their profits at levels acceptable to themselves and their shareholders. As might be expected, those who did the actual physical work were paid as little as possible. Moreover, the British had managed to bully the Orange Free State into parting with the diamond fields for the bargain-basement price of £90 000. De Beers had a virtual monopoly of world diamond sales.

Presumably it is this monopoly that John Buchan referred to with such tact as the 'delicate equipoise of diamond values' in *Prester John*.[36] It is worth noting that IDB continues to be prosecuted today for much the same reasons and with much the same justification as it was over one hundred years ago.

Mitford's De la Rey and Cossins' De Villiers are atypical of the way Boers were depicted in early popular English fiction. The writers may have protested that it was their intention to show that not all Boers were unwashed, ignorant and bigoted, but what made these Boers so admirable and acceptable was their 'Englishness'. Both Mitford and Cossins were convinced imperialists and they used their novels to vindicate the spread of British civilisation, as Rhodes conceived it, to as much of the globe as possible.

Language chauvinism

At the turn of the 19th century, the fledgling language Afrikaans, otherwise known as the Taal, was cause for much comment by writers of popular fiction, nearly all of it negative. As might be expected, 'Die Taalstryd' (the language struggle) is and has been intimately associated with the Afrikaner struggle for national identity. As that struggle was waged against the English, it is not surprising that the Afrikaans language should come in for as much criticism by the British as everything else identified with the Boers. Nor has the controversy surrounding Afrikaans disappeared with time. During the 1976 riots against the imposition of Afrikaans as a language of instruction in black schools, and the revolution of the 1980s, Afrikaans was known as 'the language of the oppressor'. Opposition to it was one of the rallying points of the struggle against Apartheid. Ironically, these are perceptions with which many of the Uitlanders, living in Kruger's republic, could have had sympathy.

Part of the early resentment against the Taal can be traced to Kruger's decree that only Dutch could be taught in state schools. It was further decreed that only Dutch would be allowed in the courts. The outcry from the predominantly English-speaking Uitlander population was predictable.

In times of intense patriotism, as Michael Streak has remarked:[37] 'Language was the tool of the ideological imperialists and formed part of the British desire to civilize the world.' Every opportunity was taken by writers of British imperial persuasion to denigrate the Taal. One of the favourite and presumably most effective ways of doing so was to let the criticism come from characters who should be favourably disposed to it. For example, in Hume Nisbet's *For Right and England*, when a 'burgher of the more advanced class of Transvaalers'[38] learns that President Kruger 'planned to make it a punishable offence for the English language to be taught in schools, or in private,'[39] he says: 'Does the maniac think it possible to substitute our vile and illiterate dialect for the language of Shakespeare?'[40] In George Griffith's *Briton or Boer?* the villain of the piece, Kruger's Secretary of State, Dr Leyds, describes the language he is helping to entrench as 'combinations of unpleasant sounds and imperfect grammar which our burghers are pleased to call a language.'[41]

While it is difficult to see how a language can be 'illiterate', Nisbet and Griffith point to two aspects of the Taal that came in for special abuse: its unpleasant sound (to English ears) and its so-called primitive state of grammatical development. Many people who did not speak the Taal held the perception that it did not deserve the status of a language. At best the Taal was described as a 'dialect', though of which language it was, was not specified. As late as 1917 in Horace Rose's *Haidee*, the Taal is referred to merely as a collection of 'guttural sentences'.[42]

The minority view is best expressed in Louis Leipoldt's novel *Stormwrack*:[43]

> "Language," said the pastor reflectively, "is a great factor in building up national consciousness. But one can make too much of it, and I think some of us are doing that. There is first the feeling of inferiority in not being able fluently to speak that which is one's own, and secondly the impression that because others do not speak one's language they are at heart unfriendly towards it and despise it. Here both come in to play. English, with its fine literature, its tremendous commercial importance and its official prestige, has an unassailable position. Dutch, which is difficult – far more difficult than English, because it is partly an inflected language, Mr Bisley – is losing ground. Now there is a feeling that our dialect Dutch, which is not inflected, which is easy to speak and generally understood even by those who are illiterate, should be looked upon as our language. Well, I have no feeling against it. It may in time become a great language, like English, but at present it is a baby in swaddling clothes. Unfortunately there are many of us who cannot, or will not, see that. They want us to force the pace … there are some of us who would seek in this matter of language an apple of discord. They go so far as to make language a test of patriotism."

Leipoldt's novel was written in the early 1930s and reflects his and many of his contemporaries' desire for tolerance and unity. The fact that English is the 'language of Shakespeare' appeared to prove irrefutably to many writers, the superiority of English over the Taal. It was a short step from that assumption to the conviction that people who speak the 'language of Shakespeare' must therefore be superior to those who don't. All that is proved, of course, is that language chauvinism is no different from any other chauvinism, and that the war itself was, among other things, for language supremacy.

After the war, it was possible for an increasing number of English-speaking authors to take a more dispassionate view of the Boers. For the first time, the Boer point of view expressed by such writers as

General Ben Viljoen in *Under the Vierkleur* (1904), Johanna Brandt in *The Petticoat Commando* (1913), G.G. Munnik in *Major Greville V.C.* (1913), and as we have seen in *Stormwrack* by Louis Leipoldt, began to emerge. What these writers had to say must have been uncomfortable to many English readers who had had an almost undiluted diet of jingoistic propaganda until then. A character in Munnik's novel puts it thus:[44]

> Our enemies – and we have many … represent us as an ignorant, dirty, mean-spirited people, scarcely removed from Kaffirs. If they take to the field, however, they will find out their mistake. We are a small nation, but a proud one, and our patience is not inexhaustible.

Much mismanagement in southern Africa by the British stemmed from their arrogant assumptions about themselves, and their mission to spread British civilisation. The Boers were almost always judged by the lowest common denominator, as Munnik suggests. As a consequence, it was almost impossible to see the Boers as a people to be respected or to be reckoned with. This lack of sensitivity probably found its most repellent expression in what purports to be a love letter addressed to the city of Bloemfontein. It was published in *The Friend* shortly after Lord Roberts occupied the city in March 1900. As an indication of how persuasive the spirit of British imperialism was, it is worth noting that the author of the letter, Julian Ralph, was not even British. He was an American journalist who espoused the imperial cause with passion:[45]

> Come, little Miss Bloemfontein, sit down beside me and let me hold your dimpled hand and look into those eyes which have caught the wonderful blue of these heavens, and the tints of your gardens and your bowery streets. I think our whole army like you, you belle of the Boer aristocracy. You certainly change your lovers lightly and easily, but soldiers are reported not to mind a little coquetry when they are far from home. You have tripped out to meet us so enticingly,

you have led us into your bower with your warm little hand, and you have spoken so kindly to us, that we dislike to think you were quite the same to your earlier beaux in their homespun suits, their flapping hats, and their lavish indulgence in whiskers and beards, which, as you must know, are the cheapest of luxuries – prodigalities in which misers indulge to make a show and save a barber's bill.

You might have been hateful to us and we could not have blamed you, for we came too nearly, as certain other soldiers came to the Sabine sisterhood, with blood in our eyes and weapons in hand, fancying that you would cling to your old love, and never dreaming he would run away and leave you unprotected in this placid and pretty little boudoir that you have set up here. You won't forget that little episode, will you, Miss Bloemfontein? And you did take note, didn't you, my dear, that when we found you deserted, all forlorn, we changed from lion to lamb, from blustering warrior to soft-spoken wooer.

The spirit of resistance was not dead though. An anonymous citizen of Bloemfontein replied. It is to *The Friend*'s credit that the following letter was published, though it is probably a further indication of the relative naïvety of the times that it was.[46]

To Mr. Englishman – a loveless letter

Come, tall Mr. Englishman, and sit down beside me, but for the love of heaven, do not look into my eyes, lest they scorch you with a fiery 'hate of hate'. The blue of mine eyes may be perilously near that blue which men have named electric, and such an electric shock of scorn would they shoot that you would wish yourself amidst the turmoil of war again, some of whose bolts and bombs have taken the lives of our fathers, brothers, friends!

You will not wonder then that I do not like your

whole army or any part thereof, although it may have done me the great and unwished-for honour of liking me – or you, the conqueror of the land, which is mine by the same right as your little island is yours – the right of old tradition which is so great a factor in the history of nations, and in which our land abounds; the right of residence which has been ours since our peacefully ruled and hitherto prosperous little Free State was created – the right of love for the land of our birth – the right of pride in our despised beaux, with their home-spun suits and lavish beards and whiskers, who have gone out to fight with such bravery for their cause and country.

Surely, Mr. Englishman, you of all men should be able to appreciate this factor in them, you who pride yourself of being the bravest man of the bravest of living nations. Were this factor missing in them, would you not have been here five long months ago? Surely you, I say, should be able to overlook such small matters as the bad cut of their coats and the length of their beards. You should know that greatness does not lie in outward seeming.

Please do not say "Miss Bloemfontein tripped out to meet us so enticingly." Say, rather, "little Miss Uitlander," who has, as you rightly think, by no means hitherto scorned our homespun youths, and to whom we extended a loving hand when she came, and who now, in return for this, unnecessarily flaunts your colours in our faces, and welcomes you too kindly. Much bitter sorrow was there, oh sir, when you entered this loved home of ours. I and my sisters, who felt as would your English dames, were another William the Conqueror to take their island home from them, lay in dumb anguish and writhed when the word went forth, "we have fallen into bondage," "our enemy hath us in his grasp" – and our cup of bitterness was more than full.

Although *The Friend* denied Miss Bloemfontein the last word, in subsequent weeks a number of anonymous pamphlets appeared on the streets of Bloemfontein condemning the British occupation. One of these was entitled:[47]

'Sulk or Duty'
In reply to *The Friend* of March 16th, 1900
Duty of every true Africander

The following extract gives an accurate flavour of the tone:

> We shall not hear the voice of the people of the land for many weary weeks; it can in no way make itself heard. A lying press has been established which represents the Jingo portion of the Community – and gives voice to the strangers in our land.
>
> We are advised by *The Friend* not to 'sulk' but to do our duty. That is why every true Africander should strive untiringly to do – his duty – but not in the way *The Friend* would point out to us.
>
> We have another goal in view.
>
> *The Friend* would have to forget the grossly unjust and overbearing policy England has followed in South African affairs.
>
> We must recognise a 'friend' in the country that has stolen our Diamond Fields from us – has tried to break Africanderdom – who would steal our land from us – and possess our Sister Republic's rich Gold mines – England – who would rob us of our National Life – and in compensation for all these bitter wrongs we are told to 'so manage the affairs of this land that England herself will be proud to recognise us among the best of her children'.

This article is further evidence that relations between Bloemfontein and the British occupying forces (especially those responsible for official propaganda) were not as cordial as Julian Ralph would liked to have maintained. An interesting point is that the author, Maude Bidwell, regarded herself as an Afrikaner, notwithstanding the fact that she was English-speaking as was the rest of her family, the Fichardts. The Fichardt children were brought up by English nannies and steeped in English culture. This was true too of the future Prime Minister of the Orange Free State Colony, Abraham Fischer's family.

Maude Bidwell became an author in her own right and produced a book for children: *Breath of the Veld* and a volume of reminiscences, *Pen Pictures of the Past*, published only in 1986. Her sister, Ella, who married into the Fischer family, wrote a novel in English, which she had translated into Afrikaans: *Die Loutering van Petrus*. Ella's son, Bram Fischer, later played a leading role in the revolution that brought about the overthrow of Apartheid.

The British stereotypes of the Boers in and out of popular English fiction contributed to the clumsy prosecution of the war. Certainly, British perceptions had no way of accommodating the refinement and sophistication of such Boer families as the Fischers, Fichardts and the Reitzs. The best they could do was to patronise them.

Since then, especially in the 1930s (as Leipoldt's *Stormwrack* indicates), there has been an increasing acknowledgement in the fiction of the Boer as a people caught in the web of history, rather than as 'types' to be classified, labelled and described according to a formula. Ironically, outside of fiction, their descendants have not fared so well. The old stereotypes persist.

Endnotes

1 Bernard Shadwell quoted in Van Wyk Smith 1978: 253.
2 Russell 1900: 38.
3 Griffith 1897: 153.
4 Bancroft 191: 104.
5 Nisbet 1900: 215–6.
6 Ibid: 253.
7 Wolseley, Sir G. (British High Commissioner) Letter to Sir Michael Hicks Beach, October 1879, quoted in Pakenham 1991: 86.
8 Barrow, J. quoted in Streak 1974: 12–13.
9 Ibid: 13.
10 Adams 1887: 129–30.
11 Livingstone 1857: 30.
12 Emmanuel 1901: 38–9.
13 Mitford 1900: 9.
14 Kipling, R,. 'Recessional' 1912: 328.
15 Cossins 1900: 31–2.
16 Ibid: 21.
17 Ibid: 44.
18 Ibid: 200.
19 Ibid: 5.
20 Ibid: 15.
21 Gibbs 1957: 157.
22 Russell 1900: 3–4.
23 Ibid: 181–2.
24 Ibid: 182.
25 Prance 1937: 19.
26 Ibid: 17.
27 Schreiner 1978: 99.
28 In the early 20th century teachers in rural schools in the Transvaal were required to visit the homes of their pupils and get to know the parents of the children they taught. This practice 'huisbesoek' ensured that schools and teachers assumed a role and place in such communities almost as influential as the church and the predikant. Bosman was sent

as an uncertificated teacher by the Transvaal Education Department to the Groot Marico in the Western Transvaal. Like the character in his story he used the opportunity to gather a wealth of story material which later appeared in print.

29 Bosman 1963: 122.

30 Ibid: 126.

31 Ibid: 91.

32 Bancroft 1913: 268–9.

33 Quoted in *Ormond Lodge*, 'The Boer Boy' in 'The Best of British Pluck' *Boys' Own Paper* (Philip Warner ed.) 1976.

34 Mitford 1900: 24.

35 Cossins 1900: 56.

36 Buchan 1961: 204.

37 Streak 1974: 53.

38 Nisbet 1900: 35.

39 Ibid: 24.

40 Ibid: 35.

41 Griffith 1897: 28.

42 Rose 1917: 128.

43 Leipoldt 1980: 63.

44 Munnik 1913: 74.

45 Ralph, J. *The Friend*, Bloemfontein, 17 March 1900 in *War's Brighter Side* 1901: 32–33.

46 Ibid: 70–71.

47 Bidwell, M., Pamphlet 'Sulk or Duty', Bloemfontein, March 1900.

"'What price Majuba!' cried Harkaway,
cutting down a brawny Boer, over six feet in height."
Bracebridge Hemyng: *Jack Harkaway in the Transvaal*

CHAPTER SIX

HEROES, HEROINES AND OTHERS: 'A fool's way from first to last'

We, nursed in high traditions,
And trained to nobler thought,
Deem death to be less bitter
Than life too dearly bought:
Sharp spurs have we to honour,
But ye without their aid
Rush on the deadly breaches,
And storm the barricades.

James Rhoades, 'Dulce et Decorum Est'[1]

As a general rule the heroes and heroines who populate the pages of Boer War fiction are little more than their creators' mouthpieces, reflecting their attitudes, values and prejudices. Broadly speaking, heroes in the early novels reflect and stand for the necessary virtues and values of the Empire. But, with the passage of time, values have changed. Since World War II, the relaxation of sexual taboos and the popularisation of the study of psychology have increasingly shifted the emphasis and revised notions of 'maleness', 'manliness' and 'existential-angst'. Heroes of post-World War II fiction are very often depicted as being disenchanted with life – the unhappy victims of their passions.

Following World War I the number of novels in which the main character is a woman greatly increased. An obvious explanation for this trend can be attributed to the changes brought about by war, which widened the roles women played in society, for example in the armaments industry. The agitation of the suffragettes for the vote escalated the fuller participation of women in society.

Part of the reason for the emergence of the female protagonist in popular literature may have been the fact that more women were writing than previously. On the other hand, an explanation may be sought in the growing preoccupation writers had with a perceived need to contribute to the reconciliation of the two white antagonists and to the building of a Union of South Africa.

Traditionally, women have tended to be the chief mediators in domestic squabbles. As the Anglo-Boer conflict came to be seen more and more as a domestic or civil war, the choice of a heroine instead of hero as the leading character, may have enabled authors to portray reconciliation in the fiction more effectively.

The two most striking examples of this development are Daphne Muir's *A Virtuous Woman* (1929) and Manfred Nathan's eponymous novel based on the popular legendary figure of the Afrikaans ballad, *Sarie Marais* (1938).

One of the earliest and least typical, and therefore most interesting of these early heroines is Hansie, in Johanna Brandt's part-autobiography, part-novel, *Petticoat Commando* (1913). Johanna Brandt was a remarkable woman. She organised Boer espionage in Pretoria after Kruger fled the Republic. These events provided much of the plot for *Petticoat Commando*. Stuart Cloete based one of the sub-plots of his *Rags and Glory* on her character and exploits. In *Petticoat Commando* she fictionalises herself as the high-minded heroine, Hansie. Perhaps the most memorable moment in the book describes how, when the exhausted British troops marched into Church Square in Pretoria, one soldier gasped exhaustedly: 'Thank God, the war is over', to which Hansie replied: 'Tommy Atkins, the war has just begun.'[2]

He is an English gentleman

The Boer War hero is almost without exception, a 'gentleman'. I have found only one who is a member of the working classes: Steve, 'a member of the factory operative class'[3] in Arthur Laycock's *Steve the Outlander* (1900). However, Laycock did not see fit to give Steve a lower-class accent as he had done for the other working-class characters in the novel. This was probably insurance against alienating the class-conscious reader who was presumed to be more willing to accept a working-class hero as long as there was little to remind him of the hero's working-class origins. For the rest, all the major characters in the early fiction have the assurance and sense of their own responsibility within the class system, expected of them by an equally class-conscious readership.

Perhaps the best example of the young men who kept the Union Jack flying for England in South Africa, is David Crawfurd in John Buchan's *Prester John* (1916). Although *Prester John* is not a Boer War novel, (there are only two mentions of the war in the book), David provides a bench-mark against which the ideals of the typical Boer War hero can be measured:[4] 'He has to take all the risks, recking nothing of his life or his fortunes, and be well content to find his reward in the fulfilment of his task.' Imperialism was not taken lightly. It implied responsibility with humility.

One of the earliest examples of what it meant to be 'British', a 'gentleman' and to be living in 'foreign parts', is found in Rider Haggard's *Jess* (1887). Silas Croft, on whose farm the hero, Captain Niel, is working, explains to his niece just what it is that distinguishes John Niel from the neighbouring Boers:[5]

> "You see my dear … he's quiet and he doesn't know much about farming, but he's willing to learn, and he's such a gentleman. Now, where one has Kafirs to deal with, as on a place like this, you must have a gentleman. Your mean white will never get anything out of a Kafir; that's why the Boers kill them and flog them because they can't get anything out of them without. But you see Captain Niel gets on well enough with them."

In addition to being a 'gentleman', Niel is described as having other indispensable qualifications: courage and determination.[6]

> Indeed, he had a sort of bulldog-sentiment about him that led him to believe that, if he made up his mind to do a thing, he would do it somehow, unless he should

> be physically incapacitated by circumstances beyond his control … . We owe more to sturdy, determined, unconvincible Englishmen like John Niel than we realise, or, perhaps should be willing to acknowledge in these enlightened days.

There was a general belief, if one is to judge by the fiction, that the uniquely 'British virtues' of 'gentlemanly conduct', of being an amateur, of a sense of 'fair play' and possessing a dogged determination were enough to equip any Englishman to deal with all the vicissitudes of administering and farming in Africa: the drought, the locusts, 'lazy Kaffirs' and treacherous Boers.

Heroes were expected to be decisive, but considered. Colvin Kernshaw, in Bertram Mitford's *Aletta* (1900), for example:[7]

> … is a tall, well-set-up man of about five-and-thirty, with clean cut features and a dark moustache. His brown eyes are clear and searching and there is a certain quickness about his speech and movements which is totally dissociated with any suggestion of flurry.

Colvin is obviously a man of decision, in the prime of life, who, for all his 'quickness' is not inclined to take hasty decisions. The uprightness of his character and his fair-mindedness are reflected by his views of the growing polarisation between the British settlers and the Boers:[8]

> [Colvin] took a judicial view of the situation, and, while recognizing that it had two sides, and that there was a great deal to be said for both, he distinctly declined to allow any political considerations to make any difference to the relationship in which he stood towards his Boer neighbours and their families, with several of whom he was on very good terms indeed.

Colvin's tolerance was not uncommon among heroes of the early fiction, especially that written by authors who had direct experience of the country. Colvin may be a imperialist but he is no jingo.

Yorke Harbeton, in *With Robert to Pretoria* (1902), is typical of G.A. Henty's young heroes:[9]

> Yorke Harbeton was, as he said, nearly sixteen, and was a typical public-school boy – straight and clean-limbed, free from all awkwardness, bright in expression, or, as he himself would have called it, 'cheek'; was a little particular about the set of his Eton jacket and trousers and the appearance of his boots; as hard as nails and almost as tireless; a good specimen of the class by which Britain has been built up, her colonies formed, and her battle-fields won – a class in point of energy, fearlessness, the spirit of adventure, and a readiness to face and overcome all difficulties, unmatched in the world.

There is little doubt that Henty's novels will not be remembered for their contribution to English literature. However, there is wealth of evidence to suggest they played an important part in showing how the age and especially young imperialists perceived themselves. In some ninety-odd novels, by Henty, young readers were able to participate vicariously in the great events of the day, while at the same time identifying themselves with heroes who lived by the unequivocal code of honour founded on British notions of 'decency' and 'fair play'.

The following quotations, taken almost at random from the Boer War novels of G.A. Henty and Bracebridge Hemyng, provide a composite picture of the typical turn-of-the-century youthful hero. They are inevitably the products of British public schools:[10] 'So you were at Rugby!' his hearer [Rhodes] broke in. 'I am a public-school boy myself, and there is always a fellow feeling among public-school boys, even if they were not at the same school.' Heroes are typically good at games, especially cricket. They are resourceful: 'Young Jack Harkaway was one of those smart fellows who can put a hand to anything.'[10] Heroes are 'gentlemanly' and gracious, if distant with women:[11] 'Like most boys of that age, Yorke, though very fond of his sisters, regarded them as mere girls.'[12] Yorke's cheerful good humour guarantees his 'readiness to face and overcome all difficulties, unmatched in the world.' Yorke's public-school background (those 'seminaries for the English governing class', as Hilaire Belloc[13] called them), his 'self-possession' and physical fitness were all that was considered necessary to administer the British colonies and win Britain's wars. In these novels, 'brains' are never seen as necessary for success. The 'swot' is universally despised. 'Yorke is no fool, but he has no great application, and his school reports show that, although not at the bottom of his form, he is never more than half way up.'[14] In other words, he is an intellectual mediocrity, though this is not how his readers would have perceived him. Like his counterpart in Henty's *With Buller in Natal* (1901), Yorke is 'a splendid rider and an excellent shot'.[15] Henty's young heroes provided a pattern for many authors who were writing for a similar audience. Their social background is sufficiently middle class to be comfortably familiar to the middle-class reader while they are neither too clever nor too stupid and are therefore easy to identify with.

Nonetheless, whatever his other capabilities, the young hero is always an outstanding sportsman. Games of all kinds, especially team sports, had become increasingly organised and popular during the 19th century and were seen within the context of the Public School system as a necessary adjunct to producing morally superior young men. The hero of the Rev. H.C. Adams' *Perils in the Transvaal and Zululand* (1887) 'swims like a fish, and dives like a cormorant; and can manage a boat.'[16] The ability to shoot straight was mandatory.

One of the more endearing characteristics shared by all of these young heroes is a firm belief in honour. Jack Harkaway answers a call for help with:[17]

> "Help is at hand," Jack cried. "I am an Englishman, and it is my mission to take vengeance on those cowards [the Boers]."

This was written when the fact of having been born an Englishman seemed to carry with it a moral imperative to defend the weak and helpless, and to wreak vengeance on all cowards and villains. In F.S. Brereton's *One of the Fighting Scouts: A Tale of Guerilla Warfare in South*

Africa (1903), the eighteen-year-old George Ransom extracts the following oath from a trio of Boers:[18]

> "Let this be warning to you, and go your way, promising never again to lift rifle against the invaders. Leave your weapons where they are, and pile your bandoliers on top. Now repeat the words after me: I swear by the Lord above to cling to the promise I have made to the British Government. I declare that I will never fire on the enemy's scouts, and that I will give no information to my countrymen."
>
> Each of the Boers held his hand in the air, and solemnly took up the oath, looking very shamefacedly at George the while.

It probably passed the undiscriminating reader by that George is demanding the Boers take an oath to become traitors. Ironically, the ambivalence of the British position is highlighted by the way George refers to the British as 'invaders', thus turning the Boers and their 'countrymen' into victims of imperial aggression. This was, of course, neither George's nor his creator's intention. Self-righteousness is one of the marks of a 'gentleman' in these novels, and self-righteousness is sufficient unto itself.

Brereton continued writing long after the Boer War was over. In his novels about the 1914–18 war the youthful heroes of *Under Haig in Flanders* and *With the Allies to the Rhine* are cast in the same mould as George. The titles he chose for his novels indicate that Henty's influence persisted well into the 20th century.

The dashing 'heroes' of Boer War fiction provide a vivid indication of readers' expectations and of the authors' ability to exploit the conventions within which they wrote. One of the most successful authors of fiction for the young was Bracebridge Hemyng, the creator of the Jack Harkaway series. Hemyng began writing the Jack Harkaway serials for *Brett's Boys for England* in 1871. They were an instant success. Thirty years and three generations later found young Jack, son of Jack Harkaway, grandson of Jack Harkaway, in South Africa fighting for the honour of the Empire in *Jack Harkaway in the Transvaal*; or *Fighting for the Flag* (1902) and *Jack Harkaway's War Scouts among Boer Guerillas* (1902). Jack Harkaway's influence as a source for youthful fantasy lasted long after the turn of the century. Siegfried Sassoon mentions in his *Memoirs of a Fox-Hunting Man* (1924) that he had a horse called Harkaway III.

In *Jack Harkaway in the Transvaal* the young hero's credentials are established as follows:[19]

> BOOM! It was the sound of gunfire at Mafeking, on a beautiful night, with stars brightly shining, and a cool breeze blowing from the west.
>
> "Halt! Who goes there?" cried a sentry.
>
> "Friend," was the rejoinder.
>
> "Pass, friend, and all is well."
>
> The person who had been challenged by the sentry was young Jack Harkaway, who, at the age of sixteen, had been gazetted subaltern in the 7th Hussars, a few weeks after being sent with his famous regiment to South Africa to fight the Boers.
>
> The regiment remained at Ladysmith under the command of Sir George White; and young Jack Harkaway – who in a short time, had gained the reputation of being a smart officer was sent to Mafeking with dispatches for Colonal Baden-Powell, and remained with him on the staff … .

It was not unusual for boys of Jack's age and younger, to serve in the army. Hardy's 'Drummer Hodge' was probably no more than twelve or fourteen. Any doubts about Jack's suitability as a hero are dispelled a page later, when he confronts the villain of the piece, who in his view is a renegade Boer:[20] 'If I were in command, I would hang you before breakfast to-morrow.' Whatever faults Jack may have, self-doubt is not one of them.

The danger is that one can take this sort of writing too seriously. It was, after all, intended largely for a heartily undiscriminating and intensely patriotic juvenile audience who liked lots of action and clear-cut lines between good and evil.

For sheer 'dash', though, there can be few heroes in popular literature who could thrill their readers as Jack did:[21]

> Getting up, the dog snarled and barked, baring his gums and showing his teeth.
>
> With a spring he flew at Harkaway, who, standing with his back to the animal, did not notice the aggressive movement.
>
> "Look out, Jack," cried Fred Dawson, "the Dutchman has set the dog on you."
>
> Alarmed at this intimation, Jack had just time to turn round and draw his sword, in the use of which he was proficient.
>
> As the dachshund, which was a magnificent creature, was about to jump at his throat, his eyes red as fire, and his mouth flecked with foam, Jack made a circle in the air with his sword, and, bringing it down with tremendous force, severed the dog's head from its body, just as if, at a military tournament, he had been cutting a dead sheep in half.
>
> It was a splendid feat, which Fred Dawson and Brick highly applauded, clapping their hands.
>
> Half-a-dozen evil-looking loafers, who seem to have been recruited from the scum of the earth, incited by the cries of the Kafir, swooped from the bar outside into the room, brandishing various weapons.
>
> They looked very fierce and grotesque in their border attire.
>
> Some having knives stuck in their belts, Harkaway stood in front of his companions, sword in hand, and defied the uncouth mob to come on.
>
> He did not desire to be engaged in a brawl which was not his own seeking, but he had to defend himself.

Phew! Some dachshund. Some blow. No wonder Fred and Brick applauded. And to top it off, the 'scum of the earth' brandishing weapons various! Hemyng knew his audience. He had had success using similar situations and costume effects for over thirty years.

But that was not all. Not only did Hemyng write rousing patriotic tales for boys. There was another side to his fictional output that was probably unknown to his youthful audience: a series of popular novels about prostitutes and social depravity: *The Prostitute Class Generally* (1861), *Revelations by a Private Policeman* (1884) and *The Women of Paris: A Romance* (n.d.). One wonders what Freud would have made of his literary interests.

A-HUNTING WE WILL GO

A mandatory part of a hero's credentials was the ability to shoot straight. South Africa's teeming game provided the hero with ample opportunity to test his marksmanship, before the serious business of war started.

Just as the diamond and gold fields far outstripped myth and fable, so did the actual slaughter of game far exceed anything the literary imagination could conjure up. John Bisset recorded in his memoirs, *Sport and War* (1875), that when the sixteen-year-old Prince Alfred toured South Africa in the 1860s, a hunt was arranged for him in which some 600 head of game were slaughtered in a single day. The hunts described in fiction seem mild in comparison:[22]

> "Buck! A herd of fifteen, I think!" said George suddenly, pointing to some brown and white dots across the veldt … .
>
> "Then off we go, and my best shirt that I kill the most!"

Once the hunt is over, fifteen pages later, it is dismissed with: 'We've had our sport and enjoyed it.'[23] The author records, without any sense of irony or horror, that a black servant has to follow after the hunters to administer the *coup de grace* to the maimed animals. It may be tempting to pass moral judgement on attitudes to hunting found in this and many other novels of this period. But, the 19th century was an age in which Africa's 'plenty' seemed inexhaustible. The need to preserve its game was not the issue. Indeed it is worth asking why, today, in an age of conservation, *Jock of the Bushveld* continues to sell as well as it does. Human nature is much more complex than fashions in 'political correctness' admit.

Attitudes to hunting in fiction have certainly changed since the turn of the 19th century. For example, when the reader first meets Wilbur Smith's hero Sean in *The Sound of Thunder* (1968), he is returning from a four-year-long hunting trip in the lowveld with a wagon piled high with more ivory than even Selous could have dreamed of. There is no suggestion, though, that Sean has been spending his time enjoying himself. He views his efforts as hard and dangerous work:[24]

> ... this exhausted little caravan carried the teeth of five hundred elephant; ten tons of ivory; the harvest of Sean Courtney's rifle; ivory that he would convert into nearly fifteen thousand gold sovereigns once he reached Pretoria.

Sean's rifle, although the outward sign of his masculinity and the emblem of his authority, is not a toy like George's, but a tool. The elephant he hunts do not provide him with sport but with the means to redeem his lost fortune. Their value is purely utilitarian. For Mitford and Brereton's heroes, hunting justifies itself. It is fun. For Smith's hero, hunting is a means to an end; it has no 'romance' or 'glamour'.

'The last of the gentleman's wars'

The Second Anglo-Boer War was known as 'the last of the gentleman's wars'. If the fiction is anything to go by, it was and still is perceived as the last war in which both sides subscribed to a common 'code of honour'. That reality and popular perception were not always in accord, is not at issue. But events such as the telegram of condolence that Lord Roberts sent to President Kruger when he heard of General Joubert's death did much to reinforce the view that this was a war in which it was still possible to believe in 'gallantry towards the foe'. Early authors wrote about such chivalric behaviour with conviction;

those of succeeding generations with nostalgia.

The chivalric code has been a feature of English literature since the Middle Ages. It had passed through many mutations via Spencer to Sir Walter Scott and into the 20th century where it was upheld by the heroes of such writers as Captain W.E. Johns, the creator of Biggles. Johns claimed that when he was shot down during the Battle of Britain by the ace Ernst Udet, Udet landed in a nearby field, 'saluted my dead gunner, got me to a doctor in the village and said 'Bad luck. My turn tomorrow'.' But, like so many writers of popular war fiction, Johns could not often distinguish between fantasy and reality.

An alternative and much metamorphosed chivalric hero appeared in Jane Austen's and Thackeray's gentlemen officers, whose good manners and gallantry are often merely facades behind which they can pursue their nefarious ambitions. Clearly, part of the reading public was becoming more sophisticated or cynical. But a sizeable portion still demanded heroes who lived by the conventional chivalric code.

In the hands of Ouida, the hero remained pure and true. So much so, that her most complete chivalric hero, reflecting the English passion for animals, is a horse. In her novel *Under Two Flags* (1867) Forest King saves the honour of the Guards of England. He set the standard by which all other 19th century heroes must be judged for bravery, beauty, strength of purpose and gentleness of temperament.

An example of this kind of gallant hero is Captain John Niel of Haggard's *Jess*, who rescues the heroine's sister from an outraged ostrich – a variation on the traditional dragon – or in the African context, lions, elephant or stampeding buffalo. Niel's heroic deeds lead to much misunderstanding, confusion and heart-ache as he tries to preserve his and everyone else's honour. This is the stuff of popular 'romance': heroic action, misunderstandings, mistaken identities and a dedicated belief in the power of love and self-sacrifice. Nowhere in Boer War fiction is there a suggestion as E.M. Forster says that 'there is a grain of resentment in all chivalry'.[25]

The heroes in Boer War romance all act from a deep conviction of the sanctity of love and friendship. The same principle endures with some variations in Wilbur Smith's *The Sound of Thunder* (1966). The sexual mores may be different and the description of violence more savage, but the hero tries to act in a manner befitting a code of honour that is ultimately chivalric.

Courtly love, which demands that the hero serves an unattainable beauty, is another ingredient. In *The Sound of Thunder*, the heroine Ruth disguised as a boy and pledged to the hero's best friend, seeks the hero's protection, perhaps shades of Lancelot and Guinvere. As is usually the case in romantic fiction, mutual attraction proves irresistible. Having once fallen, they deny themselves each other in the name of marriage and friendship. Smith's story has more in common with Ouida and Marie Corelli than is first apparent, and the device of disguising the heroine as a boy is well within a romantic comic tradition that goes back to at least *Twelfth Night*.

The Pre-Raphealites' re-discovery of the Middle Ages, and the work of such poets as Tennyson also contributed to the aura of high idealism. For example in Francis Bancroft's *The Veldt Dwellers* (1912), the hero, George Brandon, is symptomatic of the age that gave him birth:[26]

> Surely, nowhere had he seen, in form, appearance and expression a closer living resemblance to Tennyson's conception of the noblest of men. His lips moved as he breathed the vision thus conjured from the recesses of the brain:
>
> *His hair a sun that raged from off a brow.*
> *Like hill-snow high in heaven; the steel-blue eyes,*
> *The golden beard that clothed his lips with light.*
>
> He thought of George Brandon's mighty arms, and chest and limbs. He thought of his handsome face, of his simple sincerity, genuine kindness and good faith.

George Brandon lives up to this impression. He is an admirable man whose abilities set him apart from the common. He is, in fact, an inspiration to all who know him, almost a latter-day Arthur living in the Northern Transvaal, struggling honourably, but vainly, to reconcile his conflicting loyalties to his people, the English, and the land that gives him sustenance, the Transvaal. In every way he measures up to what the age demanded of its (literary) heroes.

The plaudits that Francis Bancroft (Mrs Francis Carey Slater) earned when *The Veldt Dwellers* was published confirm that *The Times* reviewer at least approved of the hero:[27]

> Mr Bancroft has written a powerful and impressive story. Taking a difficult theme he deals without prejudice or extenuation. The book … is an inevitable march to doom, the strong man falling through his very strength and love, the woman inter-meddling with things too violent for her and bringing on her own fate … has something of the air and structure of an Icelandic Saga.

This and the following review from *The Throne* is a fitting reminder that reviewers are as fallible as the rest of humanity.[28]

> South Africa has proved a rich mine for novelists. In *The Veldt Dwellers* by Francis Bancroft, it has inspired another novel that will surely live; a book that may not have the selling powers of *The Dop Doctor* but it is in a way equally remarkable as a literary achievement.

A house divided against itself

Bancroft's hero was one of the first to give an indication of the manner in which succeeding generations of heroes would be patterned. For, with the gradual perception of the Anglo-Boer conflict as a civil war, the hero, racked by his conscience as he confronts his divided loyalties, appears more frequently in the literature. Variations on George Brandon's question in *The Veldt Dwellers*:[29] "How can I fight my own race and blood?" are voiced by major characters, for example, in Norman Mckoewn's *The Ridge of White Waters* (1934), Manfred Nathan's *Sarie Marais* (1938), Francis Brett Young's *The City of Gold* (1939) and C. Louis Leipoldt's *Stormwrack*, also written during the 1930s. Bancroft's protagonist also anticipates the hero of an even later generation, typically found in such novels as Henry Gibbs' *The Tumult and the Shouting* (1958), Stuart Cloete's *Rags of Glory* (1963), Wilbur Smith's *The Sound of Thunder* (1966) and Kit Denton's *The Breaker*

(1973). This hero was, more often than not, the victim of his own passions rather than the victim of conniving, treacherous Boers. In other words, Bancroft shows the shift that was beginning to take place in Boer War fiction from the external to the internal landscape. Of course, the authors of this fiction were still heavily committed to the world of action and excitement, but the influence of popular psychology was beginning to make itself felt.

One of the most fascinating, and certainly most unusual of these divided heroes, was Andrew Quakerley in C. Louis Leipoldt's *Stormwrack*. In the synopsis of the novel, Leipoldt describes him as follows:[30]

> Andrew Quakerley, the descendant of an English county family, whose ancestors settled in South Africa in the early part of the last century, finds himself laird and chief citizen of a small village in the Cape Colony when the Anglo-Boer War breaks out. He is passionately devoted to English ideals, but at the same time has, by intermarriage and the influence of the environment, come to realise the aspirations of his fellow citizens of Dutch descent. The conflicting loyalties at war within him are described.

Quakerley's dilemma is South Africa's dilemma. Like so many South Africans he has relatives fighting on both sides. The implications are slow to dawn on him. He should take a leading part in the political life of the Colony, but he prefers to remain aloof from the world of ambition and intrigue, devoting himself to his garden on which he lavishes all his creativity:[31]

> As he stood idly looking at his garden, Andrew Quakerley presented the appearance of a man who had grown old with singularly little disturbance of his serene virility. His neatly trimmed beard, with some reddish strands still apparent among the grey, his sparkling eyes, his clear, wholesome skin, and his loose, well-made tweed suit which set off his tall,

> spare, but finely proportioned figure, combined to give the impression of an alert, healthy, vigorous old man, whose oldness had in it no attribute of decline. A handsome, well-shaped man, would have been the verdict of whoever saw him standing there, and no stranger would have guessed that he had recently celebrated the seventy-fifth anniversary of his birth.

The garden, symbol of order and harmony, represents his life's work. It is also the buffer he has built between himself and the world. But the war gradually forces him into a position he cannot avoid. His Free State relatives are fighting for the Boers. Later, he is one of sixteen leading members of the community forced to witness the execution of two local Boers accused of treason. Quakerley is caught between the British and the Boers and is alienated by both. His tragedy comes to a head as a battle is fought over his garden. The following morning the old man surveys the destruction:[32]

> … too grief-stricken to cry, for the consolation of tears is denied to age … . He had never felt the sharp, searing pain that he experienced now. The sheer cruelty, the hideous savagery of it all. He was quite unprepared for the devastation he now saw before him.

His death and the garden's destruction are metaphors for the indiscriminate destruction wreaked on the country. The divided, uncommitted protagonist, Quakerley, illustrates the point that life cannot be lived in idealised isolation, but must be suffered in reality.

Between 'romanticism' and realism

After the Great War, a radical shift took place in the traditional concept of the hero in popular fiction whose strength of character was meant to excite admiration. Self-doubt now becames the guiding principle. The single most important event that changed Western man's perception of himself and the universe, causing him, as Paul Fussell[33] says, to lose his innocence, was the World War of 1914–18. But the war itself is insufficient to explain such a paradigm shift completely.

Since at least the mid-nineteenth century, if not before, Western Man's concept of himself had been under severe assault. Marx, Darwin, Nietsche, Freud and Einstein had prepared the ground for the final disillusionment that came with World War I. The long established verities and ideals that had sustained the orderly governance of society and had given individuals a sense of their own identity and purpose could no longer be maintained. After the Great War it was no longer possible to believe unconditionally in 'honour' and 'glory'. The failure of the traditional ruling classes to provide competent, innovative and inspired leadership, rang the death knell of the class system. Cracks in the system had appeared during the Anglo-Boer War, but the scale of events was much smaller so that traditional values, structures and perceptions had not been seriously challenged. But for the perceptive observer the cracks were there nonetheless, as the popular literature attests. However, after the 1914–18 war, the Depression, the rise of the totalitarian state and World War II, heralded the arrival of existential man. Man now inhabited a haphazard universe in which the individual had little control over his life.

One of the first things that distinguishes the early protagonists in Boer War fiction from those who have appeared since World War II is that the earlier protagonists are not appreciably introspective or self-aware. They did not suffer doubts about themselves or the causes they served. Sean Courtney, Wilbur Smith's hero in *The Sound of Thunder* (1966), provides a useful benchmark for how heroes have become embittered, alienated, cynical, and often consumed with 'existential angst', reflecting the psycho/socio-crisis of man in the latter half of the 20th century compared to the heroes at the end of the 19th century.

Smith's hero lives in a hostile world, surprisingly similar to that inhabited by Tom Wolfe's corporate raiders. Sean is driven by ambitions, emotions and guilts that he only dimly understands. Above all, he is haunted by a sense that he has been betrayed by life. For all that, Sean tries to live by a set of principles clearly derived from the chivalric tradition. At the same time he is the victim of his own passions and the world's cynicism. He has little insight, and blunders about his world in a state of baffled existential rage.

In Wilbur Smith's *The Sound of Thunder*, the formula according to which Sean is created is as much a comment on Smith's readers and what they expected of their heroes as it is, by way of contrast, a reflection of the world view of those who preceded Smith between the wars and earlier. The unrealistic or idealised 'romanticism' is still there, but it is now tinged with sado-masochism. An episode in the opening chapter illustrates this point vividly:[34]

> Sean beat him again, with the rope, but this time coldly – not for the sake of retribution. Dirk did not break. For ten hissing strokes, each of which ended with a wicked snap across his buttocks, Dirk lay silent under the whip. His body convulsed slightly at each lash but he would not speak, and Sean beat him with a sickness in his own stomach, and the sweat and shame and guilt running into his eyes, swinging the sjambok mechanically with his fingers clawed around the butt of it, and his mouth full of the slimy saliva of self-hatred. When at last Dirk screamed, Sean dropped the sjambok. Sean reeled back against the side of the wagon and leaned there gasping – fighting down the nausea, which flooded acid-tasting up his throat.
>
> Dirk screamed again and again, and Sean caught him up and held him to his chest.
>
> "I'm sorry Pa! I'm sorry. I'll never do it again, I promise you. I love you, I love you best of all – and I'll never do it again," screamed Dirk, and they clung to each other.

This episode is nauseating indeed. Wilbur Smith is one of the most popular and successful writers of the last thirty years. It is worth speculating, why? Does Smith's hero articulate contemporary man's nostalgia for a simpler world; a world in which violence might be clothed in and justified by the trappings of chivalry? Does Sean represent post-Freudian man's anxieties and frustrations with a world that no longer takes authority, manhood, and sex for granted?

In *The Sound of Thunder* the war provides its hero with the most complete masculine activity through which he can set the seal on his manhood. But the chivalric code of honour, the warrior's code, sits uneasily with what are essentially his 20th century identified crises and sado-masochistic tendencies. Whatever the case, Smith's sales attest to the fact that at some profound level he is writing about issues in a way that appeals to a vast number of contemporary readers.

Much of Sean's violence and feeling of nausea result from frustration, from feeling powerless. His physical courage is not in doubt, but physical courage is not enough. Whenever he acts, he acts blindly, lashing out in the only way he knows how, and, while Smith may be able to provide his hero and readers with some sort of catharsis, in the end Sean does not have the certitude of his 19th century predecessors, nor the insight of the 20th century anti-hero.[35]

> Again Sean opened his mouth but this time the sound he uttered was without form. The way an old bull buffalo bellows at the heart shot, that way Sean gave expression to his grief. A low shuddering cry that carried to the men in the rocks around and to the Boers in the saucer above.
>
> He made an attempt to touch Saul. He stared at him.
>
> "Nkosi." Mbejane was appalled at what he saw on Sean's face. His tunic was stiff with his own dried blood. The graze across his cheek was swollen and inflamed and it wept pale lymph. But it was the eyes that alarmed Mbejane.
>
> "Nkosi." Mbjane tried to restrain him, but Sean did not hear. His eyes were glazing over with the madness that had taken the place of his grief. His head hunched down on his shoulders and he growled like an animal.
>
> "Take them! Take the bastards!" And he went up and over the rock in a twisting leap with the bayoneted rifle held against his chest.
>
> "Come on!" he roared and went up the slope so fast that only one bullet hit him. But it did not stop

> him and he was over the lip, roaring and clubbing and hacking with the bayonet.

Sean articulates the dilemma of modern man who feels powerless in the face of an inimical universe. Inarticulate bitterness drives him. What can he do, given his limitations, but rage and flail blindly? Like Walter Mitty he is caught in a double bind. The fantasies that he acts out through violence of one kind or another, ultimately reveal his own powerlessness and emptiness of his existence. As the ultimate individualist, he owes no allegiance to society. In fact, society is identified as the enemy. Nor was he the first Boer War hero in fiction to rage against the world.

Howard Rumbold is the protagonist of no less than four Boer War novels by Henry Gibbs published slightly earlier: *The Splendour and the Dust* (1955), *The Winds of Time* (1956), *Thunder at Dawn* (1957) and *The Tumult and the Shouting* (1958). Howard too, is his own worst enemy.[36]

> Hatred filled Howard. Over the years he too had acquired a long memory. Hatred bred hatred. Others could interpret what God did or did not intend. He was only a man and his hands twitched with a longing to fasten on sweaty bearded necks and ensure their owners never sang hosannas again. They did not expect that. Ah no! They believed Almighty God bestowed on them alone a right to enshrine hatred like a heavenly symbol, they even called it holy wrath, before which they might genuflect in pious devotion.

Howard is unlike George Brandon of an earlier generation, in that he is not without blemish. Although he is big and strong (a condition common to almost all Boer War heroes) he has been deafened by a Boer carbine that exploded near his head, and he is consumed with bitterness. Howard is bitter because he married a Boer woman whose loyalty to her people is greater than her love for her husband. At the base of his embitterment is a strong resentment for the values, particularly the

Boers' religious hypocrisy, which are responsible for estranging his wife from him. But there is another dimension to his bitterness. He is acutely aware of the contribution, as he sees it, the Boers have made to the racial disaster in South Africa. At the end of the novel he confronts the dilemma of being reconciled with his wife while at the same time abandoning the beliefs he thinks are necessary to achieve racial harmony.[37]

> He watched [Gervase, his wife] walk away towards the house. At the back of his mind lurked a conviction that the piccaninns present a basic problem. So did the Coloured. He thought of Shalini, the unfortunate girl who helped Gervase, the devices and misery they and others endured in attempts to try for white. It was a mess. Sooner or later every mess caused trouble. History was littered with preventable calamities, caused solely because men kept their heads in the sand rather than face up to problems, until finally disaster engulfed them. The recent war proved it. What other solution than education and participation equal to ability existed here?
>
> Yet another basic problem existed within the one he saw. Now Briton and Boer might work together, overcome the ravings of crazed racial fanatics like Oost. But on this point every Boer would oppose him as stubbornly as their ancestors opposed the abolition of slavery. Between her and himself, well, he knew no woman with a greater right to piece of mind, with or without him. Yet every man was a link joining the past to the future. Which imposed the greater claim on him: her new confidence or the future of their children? Was it right to keep peace in his home and by doing so go against his beliefs even if it imperilled a future generation?

Howard Rumbold has the distinction of being one of the very few heroes in Boer War fiction who addresses the racial question directly.

A FOOL'S WAR ... A SAHIB'S WAR

The war was officially a 'whiteman's war' and it is portrayed as such in the fiction. Kipling was the only writer to attempt to give another point of view. The narrator in his short story 'A Sahib's War', Umr Singh, is the only black protagonist in the fiction. Umr Singh looks dispassionately on the British and Boers alike. He owes allegiance to neither side. His loyalty is to the British officer, Kurban Sahib, to whom he is 'knit as it were by a blood tie'.[38] Although it might appear that Kipling's purpose is to illustrate how such individuals could, through the mighty ties of Empire, be drawn into the conflict, it is soon clear that his intention is to comment indirectly on the Boers' dishonourable and cowardly conduct and tactics, without appearing biased. The fact that Umr Singh is not white, not a Christian, and does not share the same values that may be presumed to be common to the British and the Boers, makes his condemnation of Boer treachery all the more damning. Umr Singh is a man of principle and honour, and apparently an objective observer. His criticism of the way in which the British fought the war is only Kipling thinly disguised:[39]

> A fool's war from beginning to last; for it is manifest that he who fights should be hung if he fights with a gun in one hand and a purwana in the other, as did all these people. Yet we, when they had had their bellyful for the time, received them with honour, and gave them permits, and refreshed them and fed their wives and their babes, and severely punished our soldiers who took their fowls. So the work was to be done not once with a few dead, but thrice and four times over. I talked much with Kurban Sahib on this, and he said, "It is a Sahib's war. That is an order."

Kipling's many poems, articles and satirical pieces that appeared in *The Friend* reiterated similar criticisms again and again. But Kipling was no 'Little Englander'.[40]

> They shot us? Assuredly they shot at us from houses adorned with a white flag; but when they came to

> know our custom, their widows sent word by Kaffir runners, and presently there was not quite so much firing. No fee-ah! All the Boer-log with whom we dealt had purwanas signed by mad Generals attesting that they were well disposed to the State. They had also rifles not a few, and cartridges which they hid in the roof. The women wept very greatly when we burned such houses, but they did not approach too near after the flames had taken good hold of the thatch, for fear of the bursting cartridges. The women of the Boer-log are very clever. They are more clever than the men. The Boer-log are clever? Never, never, no! It is the Sahibs who are fools. For their own honour's sake the Sahibs must say that the Boers are clever; but it is the Sahibs' wonderful folly that has made the Boer-log. The Sahibs should have sent us into the game.

British indignation over an enemy who refused to 'play by the rules' is thinly disguised as Umr Singh's outrage at Boer treachery. Two of the main complaints levelled at the Boers were that they exploited the white flag to lure the British into ambushes, and that they frequently signed declarations once they surrendered stating that they would no longer take part in hostilities, using the opportunity to rejoin their commandos as soon as they had managed to re-equip themselves. The not too suble suggestion is that the Sikhs and Gurkhas who did not harbour any such foolish, 'romantic' notions as the British, would make short work of the Boers. They would not be hamstrung by any fanciful notions of 'fair play' and 'fighting by the rules'.

British values triumph in the end. Umr Singh's master, Kurban Sahib, is shot in a Boer ambush. He and Sikandar Kahn contemplate vengence:[41]

> Then we entered with bared swords … . Indeed, these Boer-log do not understand the steel, for the old man ran towards a rifle in the corner; but Sikandar Khan prevented him with the blow of the flat across the hands, and he sat down and held up his hands, and I put my fingers on my

lips to signify they should be silent. But the woman cried and one stirred in a inner room, and a door opened, and a man, bound about the head with rags, stood stupidly fumbling with a gun. His whole head fell inside the door, and none followed him. It was a very pretty stroke – for a Pathan.

Then they were silent, staring at the head upon the floor, and I said to Sikandar Kahn "Fetch the ropes! Not even for Kurban's sake will I defile my sword." So he went to seek and returned with three long leather ones, and said, "Four wounded lie within, and doubtless each has a permit from a General," and he stretched the ropes and laughed. Then I bound the old man's hands behind his back, and unwillingly – for he laughed in my face and would have fingered my beard – the idiot. At this the woman with the swine's eyes and the jowl of a swine ran forward, and Sikandar Kahn said, "Shall I strike or bind? She was thy property in the division." And I said, "Refrain! I have made a chain to hold her. Open the door." I pushed out the two across the verandah into the darker side of the thorn trees, and she followed upon her knees and lay along the ground, and pawed at my boots and howled. Then Sikandar Kahn bore out the lamp, saying that he was a butler and would light the table, and I looked for a branch that would bare fruit. But the woman hindered me not a little with her screechings and plungings, and spoke fast in her tongue, and I replied in my tongue, "I am childless to-night because of thy perfidy and my child was praised among men and loved among women. He would have begotten men – not animals. Thou has more years to live than I but my grief is the greater.

I stooped to make sure the noose upon the idiot's neck, and flung the end over the branch, and Sikandar Kahn held up the lamp that she might well see. Then appeared suddenly, a little beyond the light of the

> lamp, the spirit of Kurban Sahib. One hand he held to his side, even where the bullet had struck him, and the other he put forward thus, and said, "No. It is a Sahib's war." And I said, "Wait a while, Child, and thou shalt sleep." But he came nearer, riding, as it were, upon my eyes, and said, "No. It is a Sahib's war." And Sikandar Kahn said, "Is it too heavy?" and set down the lamp and came to me; and as he turned to tally on the rope, the spirit of Kurban Sahib stood up within arm's reach of us, and his face was very angry, and a third time he said, "No. It is a Sahib's war". And a little wind blew out the lamp, and I heard Sikandar Kahn's teeth chatter in his head.

Kurban Sahib's ghost is an example to both these 'lesser breeds', Boer and Indian, without the law, and is able to inspire Umr Singh with a higher ideal than his honour or even his grief; that of keeping the war a 'white man's war'.

Nor was India the only part of the Empire to respond to the call to arms. Volunteers came from Canada and New Zealand, with Australia providing the largest contingent. Kit Denton's novel *The Breaker* (1973) is based on the life and execution of Australian folk hero Henry Morant. It is the most recent fictionalised account of the Australian involvement in the Anglo-Boer conflict; J.H.M. Abbot's *Tommy Cornstalk* (1903) being the earliest. The intervening 70 years have seen many changes of fashion and perception. One of the more colourful changes has been the emergence of myths and folk tales about such characters as Ned Kelley who roamed the outback in a homemade suit of armour. Henry Morant was just such another character. Not much is known about him. However, his trial and execution in Pietersburg, Northern Transvaal, in February 1902, have inspired several books, a play and a film, *Breaker Morant.*

Denton's novel exploits the controversy surrounding the trial of Henry Morant and his execution. Was he guilty of the cold-blooded murder of defenceless Boer civilians, or was he the scapegoat for a military establishment cover-up? Morant was a gentleman born and bred (his courage like all Anglo-Boer War heroes is unquestioned). Morant represents both natural and civilised man. Herein lies his status as a 'romantic' hero. Yet, much of his behaviour contradicts the chivalric code. He can be both gallant and brutal with little capacity to reflect on the motives for his actions. Like so many 'romantic' heroes in this type of fiction, Morant is also a man with a mysterious past. It gradually emerges that he has been disinherited by his aristocratic family for disgracing them with loose living and mountainous gambling debts. Sent to Australia to protect the family honour and assuage his father's anger, he lives a life of violence, sex and drink, acquiring a passing reputation as a breaker of horses and balladeer:[42]

> "Love me little, love me long"_
> Laggard lover penned such song;
> Rather, Nell, in other style,
> Love me much, a little while.
>
> If that minstrel ever knew
> Maid so kissable as you
> (Like you there was never such) –
> He'd have written, "Love me much!"
>
> Other loves have passed away:
> Springtimes never last alway!
> 'Twill be better, will it not,
> To think that once we loved a lot?

War provided the ideal setting for Morant to indulge his thirst for excitement and his desire to avoid responsibility. As the leader of a group of irregular cavalry engaged in playing the Boer guerillas at their own game, he is free of the restraints of military discipline. He is passionate and loyal, and inclined to act spontaneously without regard to consequences. But his fatal instability is revealed when one of his fellow officers is caught in an ambush and castrated. Morant then issues the fatal order:[43] 'Don't bring me any more prisoners,' that ultimately leads to his own death in front of a firing squad.

Morant is depicted as much of a casualty as the woman whose house he burns to the ground and as the defenceless prisoners he guns down in revenge for a brother officer's castration. He is the victim of his emotions, events beyond his control and finally of a corrupt miltary hierarchy determined to save face and preserve its own reputation. The courtroom scene is the real battlefield in which two worlds confront each other: the imperial and the colonial. There is no doubt where the author's sympathies lie. The military establishment are arrogant, hide-bound and legalistic. The Colonials are disingenuous and generous. Morant's humour seldom deserts him, and he lends strength to his fellow accused. In the face of everything, he remains a paradoxical figure of honour; paradoxically a chivalric hero.

Perhaps it is fitting that the last word on the chivalric code should be expressed by Johanna Brandt already mentioned at the beginning of this chapter who felt that all the devices of literature should be employed to further the 'romantic' cause of freedom.

In *Petticoat Commando* she fictionalises herself as her heroine Hansie and is therefore free to use all the fictional techniques of 'romance'. For example, describing how the Boers stole a herd of horses right from under the noses of the British occupying forces in Pretoria, she rhapsodises:[44]

> A moment more and every man was provided with a steed, another moment and they tore across the veld in a mad, exultant flight, while behind them shots rang out and the bullets fell beside them in the grass.
>
> Eleven horses in all! Noble thoroughbreds, well trained and sensitive to voice and touch.
>
> No fear of cruel treatment from your captors, beautiful steeds! The life you are entering upon may be full of hardship for you, but it will be free and wild, and you will be tended with all care and gentleness. These men are brave and strong, and it is only the cowardly and weak who would inflict on you one single and unnecessary pain.
>
> Serve your new masters well. Be swift and sure when Death is on your track. God only knows what the future holds for them of suffering and woe.

Noble men, noble horses, exulted language, all in the service of a noble ideal. These are the hallmarks of the chivalric code.

Hansie was destined to survive into the late 20th century when she made a brief appearance in my own short story on the Boer War, *The Black Cat* (1988).

Endnotes

1 Rhoades, J., 'Dulce et Decorum Est' in Smith, Van Wyk, 1978: 54.
2 Brandt 1913: 33.
3 Laycock 1900: 1.
4 Buchan 1916: 202.
5 Haggard 1887: 23.
6 Ibid: 96–97.
7 Mitford 1900: 15.
8 Ibid: 20.
9 Henty 1902: 7.
10 Ibid: 116
11 Hemyng 1902: 15.
12 Henty op sit: 6.
13 Belloc quoted in Hammond and Jablow 1970: 184.
14 Henty op sit: 7.
15 Ibid: 23.
16 Adams 1887: 17.
17 Hemyng 1902: 3.
18 Brereton 1903: 38.
19 Hemyng 1902: 3.
20 Ibid: 4.
21 Ibid: 5.
22 Bisset 1903: 14.
23 Ibid: 30.
24 Smith 1966 (1968): 5.
25 Forster 1967: 209.
26 Bancroft 1912: 36.
27, 28 Two press opinions on the frontispiece of Bancroft, 1913.

29 Bancroft 1912: 44 .
30 Leipoldt 1980: 248.
31 Ibid: 5.
32 Ibid: 215.
33 Fussell 1975: 18–27. This is a superb study of the Great War.
34 Smith 1966: 8.
35 Ibid: 256–8.
36 Gibbs 1958: 6.
37 Ibid: 286–7.
38 Kipling 1904: 79.
39 Ibid: 89.
40 Ibid: 89–90.
41 Ibid: 96–98.
42 Denton 1973: 276.
43 Ibid: 179.
44 Brandt 1913: 140.

"Webb seized her by the throat, and clutched a dagger which gleamed in the sunshine."

CHAPTER SEVEN

ROMANCE:
'Never cease to love me'

> What grief of love had he to stifle,
> Basking so idly by his stone,
> That grimy soldier with his rifle,
> Out in the Veldt alone?
>
> Herbert Trench 'I Heard a Soldier'[1]

The history of 'romance' is rooted in the stories of chivalry and courtly love celebrated throughout Europe by troubadours during the Middle Ages. Since then romance has gone through many changes, for, like everything, it has had its fashions. The Gothic novels of Horace Walpole and Mrs Radcliffe in the 18th century, the sentimental novel in early Victorian fiction, and more recently the works of Denise Robins, Georgette Heyer, Ursula Bloom and Barbara Cartland show how these fashions have changed in response to their readers' tastes.

What is important in 'popular romance' – as Miss Prism in Oscar Wilde's play *The Importance of Being Earnest* reminds us – is that: 'The good end happily and the bad, unhappily.'[2]

If lovers and readers need to be rewarded with a happy ending, they also need to be kept in suspense, or, as Algernon says in Wilde's play: 'The very essence [of romance] is uncertainty'.[3] The 'romantic mix' must include impediments hurled in the lovers' path to force them apart. Their story is the story of their struggles to be reunited. Marital bliss may be held out as the ultimate reward but it can only be achieved after much suspense, suffering and conflict. Once the lovers have survived their ordeal and the wedding bells begin to chime Algernon complains:[4]

> I really don't see anything romantic in proposing. It is very romantic to be in love. But there is nothing romantic about a definite proposal. Why, one may be accepted. One usually is, I believe. Then the excitement's all over.

War as the backdrop to romance provides the essential elements of uncertainty and excitement. Will those so obviously meant for each other survive to be rewarded with wedded (but boring) bliss? Peace is usually associated with the humdrum dullness and predictability of marriage. War is the proper pursuit of heroes.

Courtly love and chivalry

One of the most popular ways in which 'romance' was depicted in the early Boer War fiction was as a chivalric quest: the hero conceives of a great passion and goes off to war to prove himself worthy of the woman he loves. In the tradition of courtly love, his love is spiritual and unconsummated. This notion obviously has much in common with the conviction that war is a necessary cleansing fire. In any event, the hero's bravery and constancy are, as a rule, rewarded in the end. It is rare indeed for the lovers to be denied each other at the end of a Boer War novel.

Whatever the case, love is always portrayed as the antithesis of war. Love stands for life, growth and belief in the future.

In keeping with the chivalric ideal, the early fiction tends to depict love as ennobling and morally uplifting, even to the extent of reforming the villainous, as in L.T. Meade's *A Sister of the Red Cross* (1901):[5]

> Until he met Mollie he had never honestly and truly, as he thought, cared for any one … . But love will work wonders even in a nature like Major Strause's.

Unconsummated passion is the essence of courtly love. Desire is as essentially spiritual. More often than not, as for example in Arthur Laycock's *Steve, The Outlander* (1900), where sex cannot be avoided, it is depicted as one of the 'lower appetites' which, like all forms of self-indulgence, indicates a base and weak character:[6]

> "Oh, yes," he said sarcastically, "many of the men were kind and friendly to you. I noticed. The beasts! I had difficulty holding myself in check when I saw those leering, sensuous rascals ogling you as they talked their filth."

Often, as in *Steve, The Outlander*, the trade-mark of the villain is that he has dishonourable designs on the heroine and threatens to submit her to a fate worse than death:[7]

> "Come Ella; come with me! You'll be mine. You *are* mine! Curse it! no man shall have you but I!"
>
> She looked with alarm into his bloodshot eyes. His face was flushed with excitement, yet a look of gloating triumph was plainly written upon it. Intuitively, she apprehended her imminent danger. His desperate words rang in her ears.

In this type of fiction bloodshot eyes and a flushed face are mandatory markers of the villain's unspeakable intentions. Similarly, in F.A.M. Webster's *African Cavalcade* (1936), a generation later, the villain's moral degeneracy is indicated by the unreasonable demands he makes on his wife:[8]

> In the privacy of their bedroom he continually pestered her with his attentions, for an excessive amorousness was another of his less pleasing qualities.

COLD SHOWERS AND ROUGH TOWELS

Victorian attitudes to sex persisted well into the 20th century. It was widely held in the medical profession in the latter part of the 19th century that sexual over-indulgence could lead to blindness, cancer or madness. A well-known palliative for masturbation was cold showers and rough towels.

A number of writers including Rachel Anderson, Margaret Dalziel, Margaret Mare and Alicia Percival, have all remarked on the distorted conservative sexual values of those authors in the mainstream of the 'romantic tradition'. Paradoxically, as society has become more sexually permissive, writers of popular romance such as Denise Robins, Ursula Bloom and Barbara Cartland have maintained the tradition in which virginity and chastity are the ultimate standards by which to judge the heroine. Against all odds the courtly love motif survived into the 20th century. For it is one of the aims of such writers, like their earlier counterparts Ouida and Marie Corelli, to proclaim the virtues of the 'moral life'.

However, in recent years there has been a marked shift in what is permissible in mainstream 'popular romance'. Publishing houses such as Mills & Boon and Silhouette are catering more and more for their readers' perceived taste for more explicit sex scenes. So too, with the passage of time, moral idealism in Boer War fiction has gradually disappeared and the sexual element has become more explicit, at the same time losing its associations with moral degeneracy. Nor is sex any longer the prerogative of the villain of the piece. In fact, sex ultimately becomes an ideal, a form of fulfilment in its own right, with women occasionally taking the lead, as for example in Robin Collins' *The Four Coloured Flag* (1958):[9]

> "Love me, Danie," she whispered.
> "I know nothing," he said humbly.
> "It matters not."

It is one of the canons of the early fiction that love, as opposed to sex, has power to uplift those who are in need of inspiration and moral resuscitation. It was left almost entirely to Rider Haggard in his first African novel, *Jess* (1887), to point out the limitations of love as a panacea, and the dangers inherent in pursuing it as an ideal. Describing the growing attachment between his hero, John, and the eponymous heroine, Jess, Haggard allows himself to digress briefly by way of allegory to comment on love's promises:[10]

In short, they were walking along that easy, winding road which lead to the mountain paths of love. It is very broad, like another road that runs elsewhere, and, also like this last, it has a wide gate. Sometimes, too, it leads to destruction. But for all that it is a most agreeable one to follow hand-in-hand, winding as it does through the pleasant meadows of companionship. The view is rather limited, it is true, and homelike – full of familiar things. There stand the kine, knee-deep in grass; there runs the water; and there grows the corn. Also you can stop if you like. By-and-by it is different. By-and-by, when the travellers tread the heights of passion, precipices will yawn and torrents rush, lightnings will fall and storms will blind; and who can know they will attain at last that far-off peak, crowned with the glory of a perfect peace which men call Happiness? There are those who say it can never be reached, and that the halo that rests upon its slopes is no earthly light, but rather, as it were, a promise and a beacon – a glow reflected whence we know not, and lying on this alien earth as the sun's light lies on the dead bosom of the moon. Some declare, again, that they have climbed its topmost pinnacle and tasted of the fresh breath of heaven which sweeps around its heights – ay, and heard the quiring of immortal harps and the swanlike sigh of angel's wings; and then behold! a mist has fallen upon them, and they have wandered in it, and when it cleared they were on the mountain paths once more, and the peak was far away. And a few there are who tell us they live there always, listening to the voice of God; but these are old and worn with journeying – men and women who have outlived passions and ambitions and the fire heats of love, and who now, girt about with memories, stand face to face with the sphinx Eternity.

It is not often that one comes across such a pessimistic view. *Jess* is one of the very few Boer War novels in which the hero and heroine are not rewarded with each other in the end. Jess dies tragically and John has to make do with her sister, Betty.

The New Woman

One of the most significant events in literature which signalled a reappraisal of the role of women in society, and the depiction of the heroine on literature, was Nora's declaration in Ibsen's *A Doll's House* (1879) that she had duties to herself more sacred than those imposed upon her by society as a mother and wife. Nora's statement of faith is as convenient a moment as any from which to trace the emergence of the New Woman who become such a feature of the fiction of the last two decades of the Victorian era.

As with so much else concerning the development of South African literature, Olive Schreiner's *The Story of an African Farm* (1883) provides a bench mark coming as it did so soon after *A Doll's House.* Schreiner's work stands in much the same relation to the romantic literature of the colonial world as Ibsen's social dramas did to the theatre of his day. Schreiner's heroine, Lyndall, declared her independence of thought on religion and love in a way that shocked her readers just as Nora had shocked theatre audiences throughout Europe a few years earlier:[11]

> "It must be nice to believe in the Devil," she said; "I wish I did. If it would be of any use I would pray three hours night and morning on my bare knees, 'God, let me believe in Satan.' He is so useful to those people who do. They may be as selfish and sensual as they please, and, between God's will and the Devil's action, always have someone to throw their sin on. But we wretched unbelievers, we bear our own burdens; we must say, 'I myself did it, I. Not God, not Satan; I myself!' That is the sting that strikes deep."

> "Waldo," she said gently, with a sudden and complete change of manner, "I like you so much, I love you." She rested her cheek softly against his shoulder. "When I am with you I never know that I am a woman and that you are a man; I only know that we are both things that think. Other men when I am with them, whether I love them or not, they are merely bodies to me; but you are a spirit; I like you."

Notwithstanding Lyndall's bold declaration, it is interesting to see how physical attraction and passion are still regarded as separate from, and inferior to, a spiritual union. If anything, Lyndall's sentiments reflect Schreiner's own spiritual conflicts and physical timidity. The era was, after all, one of intense sexual repression. As Ronald Pearsall says in *The Worm in the Bud*[12], it was a generation 'preoccupied by sex, rather than occupied by it.' Schreiner's problem, which made her so different from her contemporaries, was her refusal to lapse into conventional religious piety. For all that, as her relationship with Havelock Ellis and her later writings attests, she never compromised her intellectual integrity. She continued to confront her own inner conflicts, no matter how painful, with the same sort of courage she displayed in fighting for more public social issues. The same cannot be said of the vast majority of popular romance writers.

Prior to Ibsen and Schreiner, the works of Richardson and Mrs Radcliffe provided the model for the heroines of Victorian sentimental fiction. They were all young and beautiful. It was a formula Jane Austen ridiculed in *Northanger Abbey*. Ann Eliot's beauty, it will be recalled, was faded and haggard at twenty-seven. Heroines were most often passive in all matters concerning love, believing marriage to be their unquestionable destiny. Coupled with this passive acceptance was a vague religiosity usually expressed in good, if unspecified, works and prayer.

The sentimental fiction of the 19th century is full of young, beautiful, morally impeccable heroines, incapable of the slightest physical effort, and given to fainting at the least provocation. Increasingly, though, after the appearance of Nora, heroines became less frail and more capable. For example, the heroine in L.T. Meade's *A Sister of the Red Cross* (1901),[13] exhibits the kind of capability one would expect of a nurse in the frontline. Mollie, the heroine, is efficient and proud of her calling. Other stereotypes, mainly associated with chastity and virginity, were longer in disappearing.

Meade's novel is an early example of a kind of fiction that has become increasingly popular: the 'hospital romance'. Generally, in this type of romance the titles are self-explanatory: *The Rebellion of Nurse Smith* (1967), and *Light in the Ward* (1966) and so on. Part of the attraction of Meade's novel is that it combined the horrors of the battlefield with the horrors of the hospital ward, enabling the reader to participate in two vicarious experiences with the additional thrill of a love story.

Rider Haggard's *Jess* signalled an interesting shift in emphasis. The heroine, Jess, represents the emergent New Woman, while her sister is cast in the mould of the sweet but mindless stereotype. The formula anticipated by Haggard, of presenting the hero with a choice between two women, one relatively emancipated, the other clinging and submissive, recurs with increasing frequency between 1890 and 1910. The same formula is found in Meade's novel. Mollie's position is similar to Jess's. She is in love with a man her sister mistakenly believes reciprocates her own affection. Like Jess, Mollie is determined to do the honourable thing and disguise her own feelings. Although Meade's heroine, like Haggard's, is racked by her conscience and sense of duty, there is no indication on the part of the author that the course of love must end in disappointment and disillusionment. In keeping with Haggard's pessimistic view, Jess is killed tragically at the end of the story without revealing her secret, and her sister gets the man. In Meade's novel, Mollie triumphs over temptation, keeps her honour and is rewarded in the end when the hero claims her in preference to her sister.

Although the course of true love never runs smoothly, it seldom ends in disappointment. Mollie's credentials as a heroine are established by her impeccable integrity:

> For she knew also that he might have been the one man in all the world for her. She might have given him

> a woman's first great, tender love. For Mollie, whose deepest affections were hard to touch, when once won, would have been won forever; and Gavon Keith might have won her. Yes, she knew it; she was too honest to disguise her own feelings. He was in trouble too, and this very night he had taken her into his confidence. Such confidence was dangerous. She knew she was on the edge of a precipice; and although there was that within her which was strong enough to resist temptation, yet temptation was keen, bitter, dreadful. She was in danger of loving the man whom Kitty [her sister] loved. The predicament was a terrible one.

In these novels this sort of scene stands in relation to the heroine much in the same way that the battle scene stands in relation to the hero. It is essentially a test of mettle. Just as the hero must prove his physical courage, the heroine must prove her moral courage. As Mollie stands on the 'edge of a precipice' she is tempted to give Gavon 'a woman's first great, tender love'. Fortunately, she has 'that within her which [is] strong enough to resist temptation.' Here, essentially idealistic and sexless love fulfils the conventional role of ennobling the heroine. The 'romantic' worldview is one in which men are depicted as creatures of action and women as the guardians of morality.

In the canon of courtly love, from Tristram and Iseult onwards, one of the most important articles of faith is that unconsummated love has the power to exalt the lovers. Consummated or profane love, on the other hand, is associated with the gross appetites that mankind shares with animals. Haggard represents a minority view. Nowhere in the fiction is there a similar pessimistic attitude towards romance. Many writers do not shirk from using love to explore exploitation, betrayal and vice, but the general tone throughout is that romance ultimately leads to an attainable peak where, even if the peace does not pass all understanding, it can still be called happiness. For the most part, though, fulfilment remains the ultimate reward for the lovers once the war has ended.

This happiness is not always seen as the prerogative of heterosexual relationships. In Charlotte Moor's *Marina de la Rey* (1903) the heroine sees her mission in South Africa as civilising and educating Dutch girls. She conceives a great affection for her prize pupil, Marina. Christine's aunt speculates about her niece and her pupil:[14]

> "Ah," thought the Aunt, "these young things want each other! not all my tenderest love could make up to Tacine for youth and companionship! But, oh! The poor loving little starved heart, will it ever find a lasting all-satisfying love to rest on, in these wilds!"
>
> Which all-satisfying love, as my readers may guess, was in her opinion only obtainable from a man.

It could be argued that Moor is describing feminine friendship in terms of a convention that was perfectly acceptable to her contemporaries. On the other hand, the effusive and sensuous way in which Christine responds to Marina must leave the modern reader, at any rate, with a nagging doubt about the author's intentions. When Christine first sees Marina:[15]

> The touch of this girl sent a thrill through her; she had that exquisite soft, womanly caress in her fingers which is rare and irresistible; it made Christine long to kiss her.

The writing of the time is curiously naïve. What would cause at least a raised eyebrow in the modern reader, was often stated without any sense of irony or ambiguity.

For all that, Moor was firmly entrenched in a tradition that saw love as uplifting and all-conquering. Just how all-conquering becomes evident when the nominal hero, Ronald, is inspired by Christine to reform and give up his black mistress with whom he had been 'wallow[ing] in Circe's pig-sty'.[16] As Christine becomes more interested in Ronald, her inspired feelings for Marina diminish. Africa and the war test Christine and Ronald, and ultimately they are rewarded with each other.

Boer War fiction is populated with men who have been saved from themselves by women of sublime beauty and chastity.

Sex vs love

If love can resurrect the morally polluted, in Moor's book, sex has its triumphs too. During the pursuit of Kitchener's scorched earth policy, a detachment of British troops arrives at a farmhouse where it is suspected Boer commandos have been harboured. Orders are given to set the farmhouse alight:[17]

> The women resisted, they would not go out, nor remove their belongings, as the soldiers gave them leave to do. At last most of them had to be removed by force, to the accompaniment of howls from the children, who tore at the men like tiger cubs, when suddenly Helene rushed to her bedroom and locked herself in.
>
> Fearful of some hidden danger, perhaps of explosives, the Captain ordered the door broken in, but the first man who entered fell back with an oath and a scarlet face of astonishment.
>
> Marina flew in, full of terror as to what might have happened. There stood Helene, with her defiant face, streaming black hair, and a look of almost frenzied determination, perfectly naked, and perfectly unashamed, her magnificent figure drawn up to its full height. In her desperation, not knowing what other weapon to use, and feeling the instinct of the wild creature to tear itself when caught in a trap, she had rent off every shred of clothing, and stood defying the whole band of men, a beautiful Fury.

The thought of a hardened detachment of troops, who cannot have had any contact with women for at least six months, if not longer, being cowed by the sight of a 'perfectly naked … [female] figure drawn up to its full height' may stretch the credulity of the modern reader.

Of all the early Boer War novels, *The Dop Doctor* (1910) by Clothilde Graves illustrated, perhaps more vividly than any other, traditional and conventional attitudes to 'romance', while at the same time exposing the author's unconscious feelings about sex. Graves' novel is well within the romance tradition of ideological conservatism, committed to upholding old verities and values and traditional class structures. However, Graves tries to elevate her novel above the level of more conventional 'romance' that was disposed to avoid overt discussion of socio-political questions. In contrast, Graves confronts all the contemporary controversies: religious, social, sexual and the Feminist Question.

The story, set largely in Mafeking during the siege, concerns the morally uplifting effect of a beautiful and pure young girl, Lynette, on a drunken English doctor, Owen Saxham. In keeping with the quest tradition, Lynette inspires Owen to give up the demon drink, change his ways and prove himself worthy of her by his selfless conduct during the siege.

Graves' language is at least as revealing as her subject matter must have been shocking to her early readers. There is one rape, several references to abortion and prostitution, and one relationship that is arguably lesbian. The only constant in this novel is that love and sex are two separate things. The heroine's ever-present fear is that 'the smiling face of Love [might] turn out to be nothing but a mask hiding the gross and brutal leer of Lust.'[18] (Graves is heavily committed to the capitalisation of abstract nouns.) One of her most consistent attitudes is that man is a lustful creature. His feelings for the opposite sex can only be condoned if they are exalted by the purity of the relationship. Throughout the novel, the ideal of courtly, unconsummated love as a spiritual force is constantly juxtaposed with profane love, which is the expression of man's lustful, animal nature. Lynette's experiences are such that 'The close approach of any man, even the thought of such contact, turned her deadly faint, checked her impulses, stopped her breath.'[19] If ever there was a case of sexual hysteria masquerading as noble virtue, it is to be found in Lynette. Like many Victorian heroines of a generation earlier, she is of a sensitive nature. The slightest stress makes her hover, Ophelia-like, on the brink of madness. The explanation given for her fragility is that as a child she was raped.

As early as 1885, W.T. Stead had exposed the traffic in young girls who were required to satisfy the penchant of a substantial section of Victorian male society had for deflowering virgins. Nor was child abuse anything new to Victorian literature. Children from Oliver Twist and Nicholas Nickleby onwards have been portrayed as victims of the adult world, but Lynette must rate as one of the earliest victims of child molestation in English literature. However important her rape is to the reader's appreciation and understanding of her subsequent behaviour, it is not half as revealing as the way in which the rape is communicated to the reader. Reflecting on what is without doubt a terrible experience, the omniscient author comments:[20]

> That night in the tavern in the veld had branded a child with premature knowledge of the ferocious, ravening Beast that lies in Man concealed.

Not content to let the episode speak for itself – child rape is appalling enough as it is – Graves is determined to squeeze everything she can out of it in her efforts to shock her readers. Her premise is that all men are sex-maniacs. Secondly, Graves asserts that it is a woman's plight, sooner or later (in this case sooner) to fall victim to man's uncontrollable lust. Lynette's childhood experiences fill her with missionary zeal to release all women 'who are the slaves and martyrs of the unrelenting, merciless, dreadful pleasures of Man'.[21]

While sex may be a 'ferocious, ravening Beast that lies in Man concealed' waiting to pounce on and devour Innocence, the power of Beauty to overcome moral degradation is truly inspirational. Graves' hero, Saxham, has come down in the world. He has lost his position in Society, his wealth, his professional standing and the girl he was going to marry, and has taken to drink and lost his self-respect. He is ready to be saved from himself. When he sees Lynette for the first time:[22]

> Something stirred in the secret depths of him, and came to life with an awakening thrill exquisitely poignant and sweet. For this slight, unsophisticated, convent-bred creature, slender as a lily, reared in innocence among the blameless was rich as her frail, lovely mother had been before her in the mysterious allure of sex … . Thoughts of the stored-up golden honey seen gleaming through the translucent waxen

> cells of the virgin comb made the senses reel as you looked at her, if you were man born of woman, with your passions alive and keen-edged in you, and your blood had not lost the lilt of the song that it has sung in healthy veins of the sons of Adam since Woman was made for and given to the Man. For Artemis may invite, if unconsciously, the hot pursuit of the hunter; the shy close-folded nymph among the sedges may awaken the primal desire of Pan among the reeds … . Saxham, even in the years of his degradation, had scarcely sunk to the level of the crook-shinned, hairy thighed, hoofed satyr.

Graves was pursuing a moral crusade. Like so many writers of popular romantic fiction, from Marie Corelli to Denise Robins, Graves was motivated by a desire to improve the world; especially a world as she saw it that was slipping into the swamps of egalitarianism and socialism.

Growing realism

Francis Bancroft's two novels *The Veldt Dwellers* (1912) and *Thane Brandon* (1913), published shortly after *The Dop Doctor*, show an interesting shift of attitude to 'romance' while yet clinging to some of the idealistic conventions that characterised most of the popular fiction, immediately preceding their publication. In Bancroft's novels there is a greater acknowledgement of the role of sex in determining the quality of romantic relationships. The moral idealism is still there. Love still has the power to uplift and is used as a marker of sensitivity and integrity. But sex is given greater recognition, and is faced more readily as a means of giving powerful expression to love.

With the pursuit of realism in fiction there is a diminishing of high idealism. It is now possible for Johanna in *The Veldt Dwellers* to say to her suitor:[23] 'If you want me, speak as a man speaks to the woman he wants – and take me once and for all.' He replies equally plainly: 'I love you as a man loves the woman he means to mate.'[24] Nonetheless, coexistent with this recognition of the role of sex is the notion of the exalted nature of love. The sentiment behind the following remarks is symptomatic of the vision of sacrifice in the cause of a noble ideal, characteristic of so many Victorian heroines in light romantic fiction:[25]

> "… it's like this that a woman feels when she loves a man, she would welcome even death from his hands … yes if he took her up and threw her into that still, dark pool lying down there" – she pointed towards the river-bed – "she would be content to let her flesh and her bones, her softness and her beauty – all that made her dear to the man – rot, and moulder away down in the cold bed of darkness and slime and filth because it was his hand that threw her there!"

This statement of faith by the heroine Margery is in essence no different from those expressed by Mollie in *A Sister of the Red Cross*, or from the basis on which Jess decides to suppress her emotions in Haggard's novel. The heroine is an individual of immense moral courage and commitment to her ideals. Her integrity is her most important distinguishing mark.

Not surprisingly, attitudes to 'undying love' fluctuate and are not at all consistent. In G.G. Munnik's *Major Greville, V.C.* (1913) the heroine pleads:[26] 'Never cease to love me, Maurice … I couldn't live if you did.' On the other hand, a much more cynical view is expressed in Bertram Mitford's *Aletta* (1900):[27]

> Propinquity! He had seen repeated instances of this, had even experienced some. The girl or woman who "could not live without you" today might be voting you a bore of the first water by this time next year, or even earlier.

Which merely goes to show that the men in Boer War fiction can be as idealistic or as cynical about women as the men in any other fiction, or out of it.

The 1930s saw a significant development in the use of 'romance' in fiction about the Boer War. The intention of much of the writing of this period appears to be an attempt to contribute to the building of a united nation in which the white antagonists are reconciled. With this purpose in mind, many writers used the notion of love between individuals on opposite sides of the conflict to stand symbolically for the divided nation, which could be healed by a marriage between Afrikaans and English-speaking South Africans dedicated to seeking a common destiny. Marriage, whether it predates or postdates the action, is depicted as not merely the union of two individuals but as the union of two peoples. For example, the strains placed on Gideon Reineke and his English-born wife, Deborah, in Norman McKoewn's *The Ridge of White Waters* (1934) obviously have symbolic overtones. After the Jameson Raid, Deborah finds herself in the dilemma of all those with divided loyalties in times of war. Her choice is between the land of her birth and her family:[28]

> A cleavage in Johannesburg on racial lines would bring her nationality again to the foreground, and she was consumed with fear lest it turn her family against her. For all her sins of omission she loved England still, but Jurie and Jan and Dora had a closer claim. If necessary, she would bury the other love deep in her heart rather than risk losing theirs. She would even borrow some of Gideon's deceit and pretend she was really a Boer at last.

Deborah remains resolute, despite the fact that her husband is away on commando. Her family is broken up and she is sent to a concentration camp until the end of the war. Gideon is led to believe she has been collaborating with the British. Nonetheless, she remains steadfast in her love for him and helps him overcome the bitterness of defeat. Such is the rehabilitative influence of her love that when Gideon returns to the ruins of his farm at the end of the war he has a flash of insight into what the future might hold for him and his people.[29]

> Very often he had heard it said, especially since the war had brought an increase of mutual respect, that the English and the Dutch should work together, that they were, in effect, man and wife. But the idea had not got hold on his mind. Despite the fact that he was married to an English woman, the union appeared unnatural in the nation; contrary to the will of God. But now a new inspiration filtered in. With the recollection still vivid in his mind of his joy at finding how well his wife had kept faith with him, he asked himself why such a marriage should be impossible.

The message is clear: with mutual trust and forgiveness a union could be achieved that would weld the nation together. The Reinekes' marriage is portrayed as a metaphor for the way in which love can overcome prejudice and provide a basis for hope in the future. Their marriage survives, strengthened by the ordeal it has come through. War which we saw in an earlier chapter has the power to test and strengthen individuals, can do the same for nations.

Love and marriage

As the 20th century advanced, 19th century views on female sexuality lingered as did 'romantic' notions of war. Manfred Nathan's *Sarie Marais* (1938), had very definite views on female sexuality.[30]

> Though Sarie was a young woman, and, like all her sex, would come to realise in time that love was a woman's whole existence, she never looked into her feelings on the subject, although, in common with most girls, she had vaguely contemplated the future possibility of marriage. All the more, as love was an important part of a woman's life, it must be a matter for consideration. Women, as a rule, do not fall in love as suddenly and passionately as men. Though love does not take note of personal attributes, it is, for a

> woman, not to be entered into heedlessly. Sarie was not of the superficial kind who are entrapped by a few flattering words – though Philip was too serious and sincere to think of making love lightly. Women, on the whole, view love more objectively than men, and Sarie was no exception to her sex. Once the problem was directly presented to her she must regard it in all its bearings, and weigh the pros and cons.

An impetuous but essentially inexperienced young man in love with an innocent girl is conventional enough. This is the sort of situation Hemingway, for example, used in *The Sun Also Rises* (1926), and *A Farewell to Arms* (1929), in which youth and innocence are the chief victims of war. In a novel that takes an otherwise interesting view of the war from the standpoint of a young Boer girl, and is not afraid to face many of the issues English-speaking authors had hitherto avoided, Nathan's strangely archaic depiction of romance relies on the conventions of 19th century popular literature. It was as if the 20th century had not dawned, and James Joyce, D.H. Lawrence and Hemingway had not published a book.

With the advent of the 1940s, sexual relationships in Boer War fiction are faced in a much more direct manner than before. Sex is generally acknowledged as an integral part of 'romance'. In Kathleen Sinclair's *The Sun Climbs Slowly* (1942), the heroine Charlotte and her husband Jan confront the fact that their marriage is disintegrating. Jan says: [31]

> "One cannot command one's affections, Charlotte. And a good share of a happy marriage is made in bed, my darling; and that is where ours has been wrong from the beginning."

There are not many 'bad' marriages in Boer War fiction prior to the 1940s. But where they do occur there is no attempt to analyse the marriage in terms of what such relationship demands of the husband and wife. Increasingly after 1940, perhaps with the effect of the social stigma attached to divorce decreasing, there is a greater willingness to acknowledge that marriages succeed or fail for a multiplicity of reasons, not the least of which is sex. The demands made on marriage within the context of war became worthy fictional material and the breakdown of marriage is yet another metaphor for the destructive forces of war.

MISCEGENATION

From the 1950s onwards a further element was added in the fiction, perhaps in response to the growing awareness of the colour issue in national politics; an element already anticipated in South African fiction from opposite points of view in Millin's *God's Stepchildren* (1924) and Plomer's *Turbott Wolfe* (1926): miscegenation. For example, in Henry Gibbs' *The Tumult and the Shouting* (1957), the protagonist, Howard Rumbold, is moved to awareness of the plight of the Coloureds by a young coloured girl, Ruth. It is doubtful what attracts him first:[32]

> ... the swell of her hip silhouetted upon the rough stone wall ... her big firm breasts scarcely moving under the loose old plain-coloured dress ... Howard felt pity for her. At a pinch she might pass for white, her skin almost fair, a heady temptation, and she was intelligent.

Ruth's intelligence is tacked on to the list of her other attributes, almost as an afterthought. What is revealing is the suggestion that much of her sexual attraction lies in the fact that she can almost pass for white. In keeping with white political prejudices, the darker the skin, the less acceptable is sex between white and black. In one of the few early Boer War novels in which a white man takes a black mistress, Moor's *Marina de la Rey* (1903), the relationship is portrayed as being clearly indicative of the man's degradation.

In *The Tumult and the Shouting*, Ruth's desirability has wider implications. She has two love affairs with white men. This in itself is noteworthy. Sex is not seen as the apotheosis of fulfilment and commitment as it was in the earlier fiction, but as an appetite. This does not mean to say that it is divorced from emotional commitment. Simply, it has been de-mythologised and placed in the context of other drives and needs. The first affair Ruth has is with a young boer, Danie Duplessis, who treats her badly (and eventually murders her). The second is with a wounded British officer, Major Gervase Fortune, who acknowledges her humanity. It is fairly obvious, given the other sexual relations across the colour line in the novel, that Ruth's experiences at the hands of Duplessis and Fortune are meant to point to essential differences between the Boers and the British. On the other hand, Ruth sees sex as a weapon to use against the white man to better her lot in life. Initially, she intends taking a lover 'to fascinate, thwart, tantalize, deny him until he is burnt with lust to possess her and she could (then) shape his will on the soft anvil of her body.'[33] But Danie, while enjoying her sexually, is armoured by his racial prejudice against ever becoming vulnerable to her.

Because her attitudes to life are essentially practical, she does not resent Danie marrying a white woman while continuing their affair:[34]

> She harboured no grudge against the nonnie for having captured Danie and understood that if it had not been her it would have been another, perhaps one who concealed in her veins a dark flow of Baster blood and who only passed for white, women more venomous and cruel than any to Baster women who could not pass, first to scold, first to strike, first to accuse of thieving and abnormal vices, first to use a sjambok, first to invent ways to drive them into the brothels of Johannesburg, ja and first to fall on their knees to pray in devout supplication for mercy, terrified lest their blood darken the skin of their children, staring into their cots with dilated anguished eyes a thousand times a day, peering at tiny blemishes through a magnifying glass while their lips moved in fearful prayer, women whose dread of being debased by pure white women drove their men to seek wealth and influence, envious of uitlander women like this

nonnie Danie would make his wife who was kind and even said when she was wrong or made a mistake because she would not pretend, except of course to keep Danie in order or to find out if her wiles could make him give in to her.

This was written in a country where official reports and statistics about who had got what percentage of 'coloured' blood had severe political implications. The length of the sentence notwithstanding, this extract represents on the face of it an attempt to confront the tragic complexity of the racial situation in South Africa. There is little doubt where Gibbs' sympathies lie. He touches on a tender nerve. Those who 'try for white' live in a state of perpetual terror lest they be found out. All this points to a society in which there is little regard for human dignity or worth.

However, it is part of Gibbs' intention to show that love can overcome even racial prejudice. Much later, when Ruth helps to conceal Gervase from the Boers, the proximity into which they are thrown and the dangers they share leads to a growing intimacy between them:[35]

> No, she told herself while he kissed her, deep in her heart she realised now that she dared not deceive him in the way she planned so cunningly for though he kissed and touched her he did not do so like a white man making use of a Baster woman but in ways any man must with any woman, part of their seeking each other out in this terrible thing called life.

Gervase helps Ruth overcome her racial prejudices and makes her feel she is a woman. But it is not theirs to be united. Her murder is conveniently arranged to allow Gervase to marry one of his own kind. In fact, none of the relationships which span the colour line result in marriage, except for that of Adam Rumbold who turns against the British, fights for the Boers and is eventually tricked into marrying a coloured girl he has been led to believe is a Boer woman. The intended irony is obvious. Adam becomes the victim of his own racial prejudices. Poetic justice is done. What is only marginally less obvious is the extent of Gibbs' own racial prejudices, which have been disguised by the apparently sympathetic manner in which he treats Ruth's tragedy.

Mittee (1951) by Daphne Rooke was published a few years before *The Tumult and the Shouting*, and treats the question of miscegenation in even greater detail. *Mittee* is narrated by Selina, a coloured girl, friend and servant to Mittee, the eponymous heroine. Selina is seduced by the man Mittee is to marry. Characteristically, once he has 'had' her he is filled with remorse and dread that anyone should find out. At the same time he is still at pains to maintain the fiction of his superiority:[36]

> Afterwards, he stirred me with his foot and said, "You mustn't tell anybody about this, Selina."
>
> "No, Paul."
>
> "You must call me Baas Paul," he said uneasily.
>
> "Baas Paul."
>
> "I'll give you a little present."

Selina soon discovers she has more than a little present. She is pregnant. Like Gervase's relationship with Ruth, this one is essentially an illegitimate union that cannot be resolved. Paul continues to exploit Selina. The only way she can break free of his will is to murder him.

Few writers of Boer War fiction have exploited the theme of sex or love across racial barriers subsequently. Most of them have preferred to use romance for little more than decorative purposes and to keep the pages turning. Robin Collins, in *The Four Coloured Flag* (1958), is typical in this regard. The war is seen as just one of those rituals whereby a young man wins his spurs; sex is another such ritual. Today, the seamy sex scene is an obligatory ingredient for financially successful writing. Stuart Cloete and Wilbur Smith, perhaps more successfully than others, have managed to exploit sensational sex in their novels. Smith has, to date, written only one novel with an Anglo-Boer War theme, *The Sound of Thunder* (1966), which is a sequel to his *When the Lion Feeds* (1964), set in the period before the war. Cloete, on the other hand, had written about the war in *The Hill of Doves* (1942), *Rags of Glory* (1963) and *Watch for the Dawn* (1974). The sub-plot of *Rags of Glory* is concerned with the white slave trade in late 19th century England. Although probably a good ploy for attracting and holding readers, much of what Cloete describes about the white slave trade belongs to an earlier era.

During the course of the last hundred years, Boer War fiction has gradually lost its air of genteel respectability. The early writing was dominated by middle-class writers who shared and enshrined the values of their class. Although the middle classes dominated Victorian society, they modelled their values and thought processes on what they thought were the values and thought processes of the upper classes. An enormous amount of 'double think' must have dominated middle-class perceptions as they strove to evolve a self-image, 'mistaking the genteel for the pure, and distressed by the all too evident intrusion of the animal in man'.[37]

Much early Boer War fiction reads as though writers were trying to reassure the reading public that their view of morality did prevail and the idealised picture they portrayed, was a reality. In matters of 'romance', as in war, the late Victorian and Edwardian writers of popular fiction showed a remarkable naïveté, almost a reluctance to acknowledge man's true nature. The rapid and popular dissemination of Freud's writings and World War I were destined to disillusion humanity in both regards. Notwithstanding increasing cynicism on such matters in the 20th century, the prevailing notion throughout much of Boer War fiction was that, once the hero had won his spurs in battle, he could return home to claim his reward in the arms of the woman he loved. Thus, the chivalric code had not entirely disappeared.

Endnotes

1 Trench 1907: 176.
2 Wilde 1963: 275.
3 Ibid: 255.
4 Ibid: 258.
5 Meade 1901: 214.
6 Laycock 1900: 100.
7 Ibid: 194.
8 Webster 1936: 100.
9 Collins 1958: 36.
10 Haggard 1887: 32–33.
11 Schreiner 1883: 193.
12 Pearsall 1978: 6.
13 Meade 1901: 105.
14 Moor 1903: 76.
15 Ibid: 59.
16 Ibid: 112.
17 Ibid: 285.
18 Graves 1910: 44.
19 Ibid: 192.
20 Ibid: 183.
21 Ibid: 294.
22 Ibid: 249.
23 Bancroft 1912: 64.
24 Ibid: 65.
25 Ibid: 147–148.
26 Munnik 1913: 29.
27 Mitford 1900: 55.
28 McKoewn 1935: 135.
29 Ibid: 382.
30 Nathan 1938: 74.
31 Sinclair 1942: 59.
32 Gibb 1957: 57.
33 Ibid: 62.
34 Ibid: 64.

35 Ibid: 130.
36 Rooke 1951: 26.
37 Pearsall 1971: 1.

FRANCHISE
JUSTICE FOR
UITLANDERS
TRANS
VAAL

CHAPTER EIGHT

SATIRE'S STING:
'A true disciple of swift'

Go to the front, forsooth! Not they;
The streets of Cape Town they invaded,
Held the hotels in mighty force,
And all the drinking-bars blockaded …
Above the popping of their corks
They cannot hear the sounds they dread –
The shrieks of sorely wounded men,
The sound of shrapnel overhead;
Above their conversation's hum
The roar of lyddite does not come.

Lionel James, 'Truth[1]

While it may be true that love and war bring out the best in humankind, they also provide ample opportunity for the parading of hypocrisy, self-interest and self-delusion. The Second Anglo-Boer War, as much as any other war, afforded cartoonists and satirists the opportunity to lampoon and ridicule politicians, soldiers, the greedy, the gullible, financiers, and fanatics, Boer and British alike.

Unfortunately, the passage of time has blunted the wit and obscured the relevance of these pieces, rendering many of them almost unintelligible today. Like the turn of the century cartoons the satire has lost its bite, while the humour is often laboured and obvious. What raised the passions and ire then, seldom has more than passing interest for those of us who have to face the hypocrisies and stupidities of our own times. Satire that transcends time and place is the product of a rare sort of genius, such as that possessed by Aristophones or Swift that is, at once, both typical and universal.

Some of the better known contemporary writers who seized the moment include H. H. Munro *Alice in Pall Mall* (1900), Frank Harris *How to Beat the Boer: A Conversation in Hades* (1900), G.K. Chesterton *The Napoleon of Nottinghill* (1904), Hillaire Belloc *Mr Clutterbuck's Election* (1908) and of course, Rudyard Kipling, 'Fables for the Staff', published in *The Friend* in 1900. Their work, rooted as it is in those times, is almost unreadable today.

Working within the absurdist tradition created by Lewis Carroll in *Alice Through the Looking Glass* (1872), Munro created his own Alice. She questions a War Office Spokesman, the White Knight (The Marquess of Lansdowne), about the tactics and weapons used in the Boer War ridiculing bureaucratic red-tape.[2]

> "… have you ever conducted a war in South Africa?" [asked the White Knight]
>
> Alice shook her head.
>
> "I have," said the White Knight with a gentle complacency in his voice.
>
> "And did you bring it to a successful conclusion?" asked Alice.
>
> "Not exactly to a *conclusion* – not a *definite* conclusion, you know – nor entirely successful either. In fact I believe it's going on still … . But you can't think how much forethought it took to get it properly started. I dare say, now, you are wondering at my equipment?"
>
> Alice certainly was; the Knight was riding rather uncomfortably on a sober paced horse that was prevented from moving any faster by an elaborate housing of red-tape trappings.
>
> "Of course, I see the reason for that," thought Alice; "if it were to move any quicker the knight would come off." But there were a number of obsolete weapons and appliances hanging about the saddle that didn't seem of the least practical use.
>
> "You see, I had read a book," the Knight went on

> in a dreamy far-away tone, "written by someone to prove that warfare under modern conditions was impossible. You may imagine how disturbing that was to a man of my profession. Many men would have thrown up the whole thing and gone home. But I grappled with the situation. You will never guess what I did."
>
> Alice pondered. "You went to war, of course – "
>
> "Yes, *but not under modern conditions.*"

One writer, however, stands out as having gone beyond simply ridiculing the specific personalities and events of the day. Douglas Blackburn in *A Burgher Quixote* (1903) encompassed a broader vision of human folly and hypocrisy than his contemporaries. Instead of mocking particular individuals, Blackburn's satire had a wider focus. It was aimed at two of the dominant forces that shaped the 19th century: Laissez-faire capitalism and the resurgence of 'romantic medievalism' as expressed in the writings of the Pre-Raphaelites. He set about exposing the corrupting force of capitalist imperialism in conflict with a theocentric rural republic, and the inappropriateness of the chivalric (that is, a medieval European) code of honour in love and war, transplanted into the continent of Africa.

Although *A Burgher Quixote* has been largely forgotten and neglected, Blackburn's contemporaries recognised its worth. A contemporary reviewer in *Blackwood's Magazine* described it as:[3]

> … a model of irony, simple and sustained. Nowhere is there any faltering, nor any forgetfulness of the method employed. And how great this achievement is, will be understood if we consider the few ironists that our literature may boast. To the ironist one temptation is constant: he becomes so earnest in his desire to prove his point that he drops into argument, or even into morality. Of this cardinal sin Sarel Erasmus [the protagonist] is always guiltless. He never knows what is patent to the reader, that he is a sorry scamp. He preserves from beginning to end the beautiful

> appearance of simplicity, which makes the most dastardly of his actions seem respectable. It is true that Mr Blackburn had already shown how great is his power of satire. But his *Burgher Quixote* will manifestly increase his reputation, and we recommend this masterpiece of irony to our readers, not merely because it will teach them a profound lesson of South Africa … but because it is packed with amusement, and prompts a smile with every page.

And, *The Natal Witness* had the following opinion:[4]

> The author of *Prinsloo of Prinsloosdorp* has given us another work, which will be read with entertainment by all who appreciate the best of fiction with a firm basis in fact. Among the scores of novels written on the late war the *Burgher Quixote* will stand out foremost in its power of literary expression and striking humorous portraiture.

The Spectator, reviewing *Prinsloo of Prinsloosdorp*, the first novel in the Sarel Erasmus trilogy, described Blackburn as 'a true disciple of Swift'.[5]

Blackburn's mischievous title obviously invites a comparison with Cervantes' *Don Quixote*. In fact, Sarel Erasmus describes himself as 'A Don Quixote, fighting on behalf of Great Britain against the folly and ignorance that have caused so much loss and suffering.'[6] Like Cervantes' hero he is a pursuer of lost causes in a world he does not understand. Similarly, Sarel stands for an age that has passed. But, whereas Don Quixote's monomania leads him into a twilight world of chivalric 'romance' as he loses his grip on reality, Sarel, with an eye to the main chance, struggles to adapt to the demands of the present. In fact, Sarel's struggle is the Boer's struggle: to come to terms with the demands of the new century.

Blackburn lays bare the inconsistencies, contradictions and inadequacies of both old and new. Although the British and the Boers are the initial and most obvious butts of his ridicule, Blackburn's criticism has a much more general application. He exposes the false heroics of war, the dubious advantages of industrial capitalism, religious hypocrisy, the arguments people used to convince themselves of their own rectitude, indifference to suffering and, in the end, the limitations of 'romantic' love.

Blackburn's strength as a satirist lies in his ability to focus on the particular and the general at the same time. Sarel begins and ends his 'truthful story' while sitting in jail waiting to know what his fate will be. It is a story in which he has a large vested interest, and which he little realises reveals more of the truth than he would care to admit. Although Sarel conforms more to the picaresque hero or traditional trickster than does Don Quixote, Sarel is, like his literary predecessor, paradoxically spiritually superior to those characters in the novel who have a firm grip on reality. For, although Sarel is a rogue, he retains his naïveté. He never fully understands what is happening to him and, instead of adapting to the world, is more often its victim. The knaves in *A Burgher Quixote*, like those in Cervantes' novel are those who can deal with reality most successfully.

Blackburn's satire was never vicious. He never allows his indignation with human folly, greed or cowardice to overwhelm his sense of humour. Irony is the hallmark of Blackburn's style. If Sarel condemns anything in other people, he is likely to be found guilty of a similar offence fairly soon. For all his conniving and using his public position for private gain, Sarel remains a victim. He may be irredeemably corrupt, but his corruption remains at the level of the petty official. The world he inhabits is infinitely more self-seeking and more treacherous than he is.

Sarel persistently traps himself with his own disclaimers. 'I am not given to boasting, least of all of my forefathers,' he protests, and then follows a lengthy account documenting the deeds and achievements of his ancestors:[7]

> When I look back at the work that I have done – being yet only twenty-eight years of age – I can see that people who put importance on good breeding have much good cause, for all the Erasmuses, with a few exceptions, have been marked by great qualities above their fellows, and all of them have done something out

> of the common, even the bad ones being horribly and unusually clever in their wickedness. It would seem that the family was destined to be, even as the original Erasmus was, teachers and instructors of their fellow-men, for the stories told of my ancestors in the Cape Colony are largely made up of records showing their superiority. It was an Erasmus who first made up for a bad grape harvest by putting Cape gooseberries with the wine, which has since been a universal habit. Another Erasmus discovered the Dassie serpent – that great snake with the head of a rabbit and body of a reptile, only seen about the season of Nachtmaal; though there be those that say my ancestors came upon a puff-adder that was just swallowing a rock-rabbit. But those that said this did not stand well in the kerk, and were afterwards proved infidels.
>
> A third Erasmus discovered a way to make medicine for smallpox and scurvy out of a prickly pear of a particularly malignant and fast growing kind, that was making the best ground of his farm useless. There happened to be in Simon's Bay certain British ships visited badly with both these diseases. My ancestor offered to make large quantities of the medicine if the captains would let their sailors dig up all the prickly pear roots, which they did. But when some of those who took the medicine got worse, the captains said it was a trick planned by Erasmus to get his farm cleared cheaply, and they tried to make the Governor of the Cape Colony order that the work be paid for; but the ships being English, and the governor a Hollander who hated Englanders, he refused, and there was nearly war between the two countries.

Sarel's ancestors may not have been much better than petty crooks given to occasional bouts of the DTs, but they were still smart enough to get the English to clear their land for nothing, though, South Africa's wine industry deserves a better press. Sarel never gains from his roguery, nor does he complain about how fate has treated him. He muses that even jail has its advantages:[8]

> John Bunyan, Sir Walter Raleigh, and I are striking examples of the blessing that prison-life may become to those who know how to use and value it by thinking out, properly and fully, thoughts that have stayed but a short time in the heart during freedom; for when such finished thoughts are put upon paper, they become a value to our fellow-creatures.

Sarel cannot refrain from trying to turn his imprisonment to advantage. He is well aware of the British tradition of sympathy for the imprisoned underdog. Both Bunyan and Raleigh spent portions of their lives in jail unjustly where they wrote their masterpieces. Both were the victims of political forces beyond their control. The irony is compounded by the fact that for all his unctuous and patronising tone, he has been unjustly duped and jailed.

Above all he is anxious to impress his captors with his sincerity to become 'a loyal British subject, and to do all that lies [in him] to prevent Great Britain being again deceived by those who would perhaps form another corrupt Boer Government in some other part of South Africa'.[9] Incidentally he hopes to save his own skin and perchance return to his 'old profession of public prosecutor, but in a larger and better paying dorp',[10] that is, one with a greater potential for the misappropriation of public funds.

Sarel's description of his early achievements as a public prosecutor allow Blackburn to comment in passing on the corruption of Kruger's pre-war civil service. The question that is left hanging is: what were the political, economic and social conditions that promoted such widespread corruption?[11]

> Of my six years' experience as public prosecutor in the court of my father-in-law I will not occupy time in saying much, for if I once began saying all that I might, I should fill many chapters, as there is much in my career that needs explaining, especially to those

who know not the ways of the officials of the Transvaal. It is sufficient that I should say that being by nature honest and kind-hearted, I was never properly understood or appreciated. I confess that I now and then made mistakes, for having learnt my law as I went on from a landdrost who knew none himself, and having to fight clever advocates from Johannesburg who knew more law than all the landdrosts and public prosecutors of the land, it was not to be wondered at that my law was not always of the best quality. But it should not be forgotten that my salary was not large, and even then, I was more successful in getting convictions than my father-in-law was in having them upheld on appeal.

As is usual with public prosecutors, my most successful and profitable work was in breaking down my cases, which was done by purposely putting in a wrong date or name in the summons and not defending it when the lawyer for the defence objected; for I hold with the great English lawyers who say it is better that fifty guilty men escape than that one innocent man be convicted. Therefore I could never see wrong in taking a reward to see the weak and merciful side of my case for the prosecution. I am not wishful to take part in the great and long discussion on the morality of officials who take payment from the public, for I have long since agreed with that Transvaal judge and the later President Kruger, who declared that it is neither wrong nor is it bribery to give a reward to an official for paying special attention to your case, any more than it is unrighteous to give a policeman a few shillings for keeping an eye on your house while you and your family are at Nachtmaal. Such a reward is but an inducement to further vigilance; and I freely confess I have often been able to see the weakness in my summons when I have been promised a reward if the accused should be acquitted.

> Otherwise I might have been careless and got a conviction that would have been upset on appeal, causing unnecessary expense, and making both my father-in-law and myself appear ridiculous – a thing no man who values his professional reputation can afford.

When Sarel goes on to reveal how he and his father-in-law dealt with cases involving drunken miners, Blackburn was able to touch on an issue that was the cause of much controversy and concern at the time:[12]

> When prosecuting miners for drunkenness I always tried to find out how much money they had spent on drink in the dorp, which was often the whole of their monthly cheque; and in stating the case I would mention that the prisoners had spent so much, instead of doing as some did, go to Johannesburg and squander their money there, only coming back to finish their drunkenness in the dorp on credit. My father-in-law always favourably considered such cases and made the fine no more than the prisoner had left. Naturally this good nature was made matter for spiteful comment by the Rooinek papers, which went so far as to state that my father-in-law was interested in canteens in the dorp when as a matter of fact he was only partly owner of one; while the 'Critic' actually declared that he issued permits for drunkenness, an utterly false charge, seeing that there was no such printed form issued to landdrosts.

Prior to the 1899–1902 war, A.H. Nellmapius, I.A.B. Lewis and Sammy Marks held the monopoly for distilling alcohol in the Transvaal. It was the most notorious concession granted by Kruger's government, but certainly not the only one. The consumption of cheap alcohol by black miners worked in favour of the mining companies, for the more money the miners spent on drink, the less they saved, and the less they saved the longer they had to work for the mines to pay off their debts in the canteens and the mine concession stores. A large proportion of the shares in Sammy Marks's company was held by the mining houses. As Blackburn said in a letter to W.T. Stead:[13] 'Every canteen owner is a believer in Rhodes.' The capitalist financiers were certainly much more efficient in perusing their nefarious ends than Sarel and his father-in-law.

Blackburn was under no illusion about the motivation and morality of the Uitlanders in Johannesburg:[14]

> Here in Johannesburg the men who by act or word admitted that one had any duty higher than the consideration of his own interests could be regarded with suspicion and contempt … . Who are the supporters and admirers of Rhodes in South Africa? Almost to a man they belong to the class who declare their faith in the doctrine of might against right, who shout for the extension of an empire or anything else if they can share in the plunder … . If the enslavement of the workers, the crushing out of the poor man and the perpetuation of countless deeds of cruel injustice in the cause of capitalist ascendancy be a credible work then Cecil Rhodes is of all men entitled to praise.

By comparison, Sarel and his father-in-law's petty corruption pales into insignificance. But more importantly, Blackburn suggested that if it were not for what he called 'the grossest, most material, unscrupulous and sordid community that civilisation has produced'[15] there would have been nothing like the public corruption that existed at the time.

In a letter to the publisher William Blackwood, Blackburn spelled out his qualifications for writing with authority on the Boers:[16]

> Although I have followed up the new line I created in *Prinsloo*, and though the new work is strictly humorous, I have been very careful to keep as my objective throughout, my desire to interpret and convey to English readers that strange mental attitude of the Boer which is always so great a puzzle to the newcomer, and leads to so much misunderstanding.

> I think I am justified in saying that I am accepted by South Africans as the leading literary exponent of the Boer character. I have made a careful study of him for ten years, and have watched him in the Dorp, Veld, City and Battlefield, and I think I know him well, for he has been a delightful study. I have been on commando with him in two Kafir wars and had the specially good fortune to be the only English correspondent on the Boer side up to Elandslaagte, where I was at the request of certain Hollanders put under arrest and conveyed over the border to Delagoa Bay, and later I went to the front on the British side and was badly wounded at the Battle of Pieter's Hill. Since then I have been recuperating in Natal and writing the present book, which as an old journalist – I think I am senior acting pressman in the Transvaal – is a successful attempt to present the Boer as he is, with due regard to his good as well as bad points and his limitations.

How is such insight translated into fiction? In the following passage, old Piet Fourie is sold a bottle of foul sticky medicine, said to guarantee immunity from exploding lyddite shells by an English apothecary:[17]

> Piet, being foolish thought it must be good medicine because it had a dreadful smell, being what is called asafoetida. Piet took a very large quantity with him when he went with the commando to Sandspruit, and at first caused great trouble, for the Burghers would not have him in any tent because of the odour, until he told them it was a cure for lyddite, when they all begged some, and rubbed their heads so many times a day that the Kafir servants could only be got to come near them with the sjambok. But the cruel part of the business was that the stuff was no protection at all, as was proved very soon, for the very first Burgher killed by lyddite had not only rubbed his head, but his body,

> and had been living alone in the veld for a week, as the others would not have him with them.

This episode is of course amusing in its own right but the humour is touched by pathos. Sarel who spends most of the war trying to defect to the British to save his own skin, is intent on exposing the Boer's lack of sophistication and his gullibility. Unwittingly he reveals his own limitations as surely as he tries to ridicule his compatriots. For all Sarel's attempts to disclaim his people, he shares their attitudes and values as for example when he describes how he dispensed justice to the black population:[18]

> ... If we flogged all the guilty Kafirs, the landdrost got a name for cruelty with the Rooinek papers, and the Government would not pay all the fees of the jail doctor who examined the Kafirs for flogging; so there was nothing for it but to fine them what money they had, except when much labour was needed for the roads, when of course they were always sent to jail without the option of a fine.

As much as anything, what Blackburn was describing through Sarel was his own, and the generally held British prejudice about the way the Boers treated the African population. On the other hand, what the English-speaking writers saw as evidence of Boer religious hypocrisy and exclusivism was used generally in the fiction as a vehicle to express moral outrage and to re-enforce the negative stereotype of the bigoted and narrow-minded Boer. Blackburn, however, was able to balance his picture with that of the opportunistic Britisher who takes advantage of the unsophisticated Boer and cheats him out of almost all he owns. This view of the relationship between Boer and Brit has its own tradition in South African literature. Bonapart Blenkins in *The Story of an African Farm* is the literary model for a type for whom, for both Schreiner and Blackburn, 'Cecil John Rhodes is the embodiment of the unscrupulous plutocratic idea, a person utterly destitute of those humane considerations that should underlie the acts of a benefactor of his species.'[19]

> In many like ways [speaking of the apothecary] did many unworthy Rooineks take advantage of the faith of the trusting Burghers, thereby bringing the name of the Englander into evil repute, as in the early days in the Colony and the Transvaal.
>
> The predikant took the subject for his sermon one Sunday, and using words of wisdom when he made plain that while it was only right and godly to spoil an enemy, as did the Israelites the Egyptians, yet it was sinful to ride upon the ignorance of a Burgher; and he read the story of the hairy Esau stealing the birthright of his brother and deceiving his father, for which he was justly punished by being made the servant of servants, as the British would be to the Boers whom they had so greatly deceived. The sermon had a very comforting influence, being preached on the Sunday after the battle of Elandslaagte when the people were beginning to doubt all that had been said about the Lord being on the Boer side.[20]

Although Sarel represents the English as sophisticated confidence-tricksters, their relationship with the Boers is much more complex. The Biblical allusion to Jacob and Esau in the above passage suggests that they are linked by more than time or place. Far from being implacable enemies like the Israelites and the Egyptians, the British and Boers are bound to each other by bonds of blood. But there is a flaw in the predikant's sermon. There are two stories in Genesis about Jacob and Esau. In both of them it is Jacob not Esau who resorts to dishonest means to deprive his brother of his birthright, not the other way around. The sermon may have been intended to boost flagging morale, but Blackburn, by juxtaposing it with the account of the Rooinek apothecary, forces the conclusion that neither side can claim moral privilege. A further twist in this episode is the fact that it was Jacob who founded the people of Israel. The parable had to be twisted if it was to have any value in the predikant's sermon. It is a difficult thing to admit that the founding father of a people one has chosen to identify oneself with as the chosen people of God, is depicted in the Bible as a heartlessly materialistic confidence-trickster.

Writing for a sophisticated and largely British imperialist readership, Blackburn was assured of a sympathetic response to any parody he might make of the Boers and their attempts to govern themselves according to the precepts of the Old Testament. This was particularly so as the official Anglican response to the war was that it was a holy war that was being waged in the interests of the black population. The fact that President Kruger did not believe, on Biblical grounds, that the world was round, was seen as added evidence of Boer backwardness and stubbornness.

Like so many deeply held prejudices, the British view of the Boers as backward, bigoted and Bible-ridden, prevented the British from acknowledging very easily that there were other kinds of Boer. The fiction set in the Boer War certainly drew on the popular perception. However, in the character of Ben Viljoen whom he fictionalised in *A Burgher Quixote* Blackburn presented the complementary hard-headed, practical side of the Boer people. Viljoen is shown as no Bible-punching backvelder, but as a pragmatic Vechtgeneraal. In fact, Blackburn and Viljoen knew each other and had become good friends when they worked on *The Sentinel* newspaper in Krugersdorp in the late 1890s. Viljoen eventually succeeded Blackburn as the paper's last editor. Manfred Nathan, himself a Boer War novelist, records in his autobiography *Not Heaven Itself* (1944) that Viljoen was the prototype of Sarel Erasmus. If this is true, Blackburn certainly did not stick closely to his original in creating his narrator. In a letter to his publishers Blackburn says of *A Burgher Quixote* that he was 'expecting a review of it by Ben Viljoen who [had] returned to Johannesburg and [was] the man of the hour'.[21]

According to Sarel (and Blackburn may well have had privileged information), Ben Viljoen is credited with having persuaded General Piet Joubert to cross the border and invade Natal on 10 October 1899:[22]

> This success pleased him very much, for he was a young man who had much to do with the Rooineks, and did not care to read in his Bible how pride goeth before a fall. "Nay," said he, when an old Burgher named Paul du Plooy read him this, "I believe that

part which says the first shall be last and the last first, and the humble shall be exalted. That's me. So now go on horse-guard and take your Bible with you, and read it closer before you throw it at my head again."

This Paul du Plooy had been a Dopper, but did nothing but study the Bible and quarrel with the deacons. He next went over to the Dutch Reformed Church, where the predikants are more college-learned; and they confuted old Paul so often that he left them and had a Church of his own made up of his family, though he was always trying to get Burghers to join, and did not even mind having Rooineks and Germans and a Jew, who only pretended to agree because old Paul sold him tobacco cheaper than anyone else, whereby the old man lost money.

When I hear Ben use these jeering words, and saw how abased the old Burgher was, I felt sorry for him; but before long I learnt to mitigate my grief, for old Paul proved a great depression in the laager. He would come half-a-dozen times a-day to Ben or the General, carrying his Bible and pointing out some verse which showed that the Boers were either in the right and were going to smite the Rooineks hip and thigh, or if we got a reverse it was a punishment for not holding more prayer-meetings, at which Paul did all the praying. As Paul always had a verse to prove what he said, and could talk more persuasively than an auctioneer, much time was wasted in listening to his discourses, which gave many Burghers an excuse for not fighting.

At last Ben Viljoen made an order that no more verses were to be shown him or the Burghers unless they encouraged fighting, and then they were not to be discovered until they had worked out true, – an order that puzzled Paul deeply, and for a time checked the output of prophecies.

Encouraging the soldier to put his trust in God, or the gods, before battle has long been a favourite ploy of generals, but is seldom as effective as sound planning. Nonetheless, there is undeniable comfort to be drawn from believing that God is on one's side. Nevertheless, Blackburn's Viljoen is well aware of the dangers of committing all his military eggs to the Lord's basket. Here Blackburn is touching on a weakness that bedeviled the Boer command structure at the outset of the war. Initially, the Boer armies were dominated by cautious old men who, in many respects, were reminiscent of the patriarchs of the Old Testament. But after General Piet Joubert's death and General Cronje's defeat and capture at Paardeberg, it was Ben Viljoen and his contemporaries who took over: Louis Botha, De la Rey, De Wet and Smuts. As a comment on British prejudices though, when Ben Viljoen, G.G. Munnik and Louis Leipoldt wrote their novels after the war, none of them mentioned the Bible as playing a determining role in the conduct of the war. A new pragmatic generation was emerging.

It was common cause among writers at any rate that the Boers were cowards who took unfair advantage of cover, and fled as soon as there was any possibility of being shot. At first glance, Blackburn's Boers appear to conform to this stereotype.[23]

> [Sarel] got a certificate from the district surgeon that [he] was suffering from an internal complaint that might prove fatal, not merely if [he] got into fighting, but even, as the doctor told [him] privately, if [he] got near where the danger was.

However, for Sarel and his fellow burghers, acknowledging fear has nothing to do with their moral status. It is simply part of the practical business of staying alive:[24]

> I have noticed, among other great peculiarities of the English that make them so different to us Afrikanders, one thing very particularly, and that not only in their talk, but in their books and newspaper writings. It is their obstinate refusal to confess like men that they know fear. How often have I heard young Rooineks,

> fresh from the country, boasting of being in danger, such as crossing a river in flood, or going close to a smallpox ambulance, and even playing cards during a thunderstorm, and saying they were not frightened. Now all this is vain boasting and unseemly, for it is natural and religious for men to have fear, as the Bible often shows; and for a man to proclaim he knows not that godly feeling, which is given us that we may keep out of danger, is to confess himself a blasphemer. We Afrikanders are much more honest in this thing, for we are not ashamed to declare openly when we are afraid; and there is no phrase more often on our lips than, "I got a bad schrick," which means, "I got a bad fright," a thing no Rooinek would say, his vanity and ignorance of the Bible preventing him from being truthful in such matters. We have seen how dangerous such foolishness may be in war-time, for again and again, if the British had been more fearful, they would not have had so many of their soldiers killed.

Sarel's experience never equips him to cope successfully. He remains an amateur in a world increasingly dominated by professionals, be they soldiers or capitalist financiers.

It is difficult to reconcile the fact that although *A Burgher Quixote* was hailed as the Boer War novel of its day, (it went through three editions shortly after it was published), it disappeared from view, only to be recently rediscovered and recognised for its undoubted worth.

Blackburn's view of the world was at odds with the more generally accepted heroic picture at the turn-of-the century. The point is not that a satirical view was unusual because it clashed with prevailing modes, but that his satire took the particular slant it did. Blackburn's satire does not have the savage wit of Swift or Pope. Like H.C. Bosman of a later generation, his satire looks at the grotesque actions of men as almost whimsical attempts to come to terms with a bizarre and unpredictable universe; a universe that has more in common with that depicted by Ionesco or Beckett rather than the universe of static values and naïvety of Henty, Hemyng or even Kipling.

Endnotes

1 Lionel James, *Truth* (London: Christmas 1900).
2 Munro 1949: 306–7.
3 *Blackwood's Magazine* quoted in Stephen Gray's 'Douglas Blackburn' unpublished typescript, page 116.
4 Ibid: 116.
5 Blackburn 1903 quoted in Stephen Gray 'Douglas Blackburn: Journalist into Novelist' *English in Africa*, Grahamstown, Vol 5 No. 1 (March 1978) page 46.
6 Blackburn 1903: 15.
7 Ibid: 5–6.
8 Ibid: 244.
9 Ibid: 16.
10 Ibid: 16.
11 Ibid: 12–13.
12 Ibid: 14–15.
13 Blackburn, D., An Open Letter [To Mr W. T. Stead], 'The Sentinel', Krugersdorp (1 April 1896).
14 Ibid.
15 Blackburn, D., An Open Letter [To Mr Moneypenny, Editor of *The Star*], 'Life: A Sub-Tropical Journal', (Johannesburg, 4 March 1899).
16 Blackburn, D. Letter to publisher, William Blackwood, 29 September 1902.
17 Blackburn 1903: 25.
18 Ibid: 13–14.
19 Blackburn, D., op sit 'Open Letter [To Mr W. T. Stead], 1896.
20 Blackburn 1903: 25.
21 Blackburn, D., Letter to William Blackwood (4 July 1903).
22 Blackburn 1903: 33–34.
23 Blackburn 1903: 22.
24 Ibid: 290.

DURBAN, SUNDAY, JUNE 1, 1902.

E.  R.

Peace at Last.

TREATY SIGNED.

OFFICIAL TELEGRAM.

The Prime Minister telegraphed this morning as follows :—

June 1.—I am desired by His Excellency the Governor to inform you that PEACE was signed last night.

The "Natal Mercury" is printed and published by the Proprietors, ROBINSON AND CO., LTD., at their General Steam Printing Works, Mercury Buildings, Mercury Lane, Durban, Natal.

CONCLUSION

The Anglo-Boer War has been the focus of a considerable body of popular fiction. This fiction numbers over two hundred novels and at least fifty short stories, in English, Afrikaans, French, German, Dutch, Swedish, and even Urdu if we count the translation of Rider Haggard's *Jess* in 1923. In terms of quantity alone it has made a significant contribution to South African literature, but it has done more than that. For the social and literary historian it provides a hundred-year record of the subtle relationship between literature and history, of the transmission of ideas, values and the intricate modification of sensibilities. Nor is its value any the less for those interested in the interplay between history and the uses to which literature can be put, as the story of South Africa unfolded for the rest of the 20th century. Fiction, as much as any other literary form, can and has been used for its propaganda value. Writers of popular fiction, and certainly those who wrote about the Anglo-Boer War, tended to be less self-conscious than the supposedly serious writers. The writers of popular fiction could afford to be less guarded about revealing their own attitudes and ideological positions. After all, their success hinged on their ability to reflect and appeal to the widely held opinions of their times.

The response of British, European and American writers at the turn-of-the-19th century provided a unique window on social and political tensions at the birth of the modern era. For contemporaneous South African writers or those who had a stake in the country, it was a natural subject: the birth of a nation. The obligations and rights of Empire – socialism, democracy, women's rights, religion – were all being held up to view and were questioned. The war itself came as a curtain raiser to the 20th century. The Soviet gulags and Nazi stalags were anticipated in the concentration camps, while at Magersfontein, the combination of trench warfare and barbed wired was used with devastating effect for the first time. From an ideological point of view, the war gave voice to what was to become one of the major obsessions of the 20th century: anti-Semitism and racism generally. The Rand Lords or 'goldbugs' were identified with Hoggenheimer, the caricature of the rapacious Jewish finance capitalist. Even as late as 1982, in Peter Padfield's *Gold Chains of Empire*, there are still allusions to the German Jews' manipulation of Kruger for their own ends. The Treaty of Vereeniging, which brought the war to a close, specifically avoided dealing with the 'problem' of the indigenous black African population, setting up a store of suspicion, exploitation, bitterness, tragedy and waste, for which South Africa will continue to pay for many generations to come.

With the passage of time the subject of the Anglo-Boer War remains the same but the focus changes. Between the world wars, the fiction (almost entirely the preserve of South African writers) reflects the desire to build a white union of South Africa. In these second-wave stories and novels, the Anglo-Boer conflict is most often interpreted as a civil war. Boers and British are depicted as members of the same family who have quarrelled, and in whose interests it would be best to work together to heal the wounds of the past. The Afrikaners, though, were still struggling to come to terms with their defeat in 1902. Afrikaans-speaking writers used the war, by and large, as a means to remind the volk of their heritage and encourage them to preserve their identity.

After World War II, the picture is not as clear-cut, but certain ideological preoccupations concurrent with, and subsequent to, the Apartheid era have appeared. Chief among these is a concern with racial issues, though the call to union is still heard. The race issue is treated largely from a conservative and patronising point of view. There is little evidence in the later fiction that the black/white conflict and not the Boer/British conflict is the major area of tension in the South African experience; through novels like Daphne Rooke's *Mittee* (1951), and Henry Gibbs' *The Tumult and the Shouting* (1957) that have sex across the colour lines as a sub-theme, it could be argued, were in part a reflection of the tensions generated by the passing of the Mixed Marriages Act (1949) forbidding marriage and sex across the colour line. Peter Padfield's *Gold Chains of Empire* (1982) is as good an example as any of some of the directions Boer War fiction has taken in the last twenty years or so. The hero pointedly does not smoke, and contemplates attending a lecture on 'The fate of the numerous species of wild animals in southern Africa with particular reference to the ELEPHANT'.[1] Two markers of contemporary political correctness: a healthy life-style and sustainable development. With all the insight of hindsight Padfield had Lord Milner say:[2]

> "There are two great race questions in southern Africa. And if you had to ask me which I thought the most important for the future, … I should have to say 'the native question'. It's at its worst in the Transvaal. There the native has no rights at all and there is neither kindliness nor wisdom to restrain the brutality of that medieval race oligarchy."

Later, Milner says:[3] 'what we are fighting against [is] this damnable idea of one-race supremacy', but then goes on to propose an apartheid model as a solution:[4] 'Perfect equality of all races – one self-governing white community … supported by *well-treated, fairly governed* (sic) black labour.' Dr Verwoerd would have approved.

Whatever their ideological points of view, the fictional strategies writers have used to manipulate their readers are often of as much interest as the context in which they were writing. Style is often more revealing of a writer's preoccupations than many of them would care to admit. Julian Ralph (he of the love letter to Miss Bloemfontein) and Wilbur Smith, the quintessential popular novelist of the last thirty years or so, illustrate this point vividly.

Whereas the experience of living through the war was traumatic for those in it (and provided the major part of the material for the fiction), those who stayed at home were not untouched. Of course, for people in England, six thousand miles away, the even tenor of their lives was only minimally disrupted. However, English public interest and involvement in South Africa was high. In his second volume of *The Forsyte Saga: In Chancery* (1920), John Galsworthy uses the war as a dominant theme. It is not only an ever-present reality for the Forsytes, who respond to it solely in terms of their financial interests, but the marital conflict – between Soames Forsyte and his wife, Irene – is depicted in terms of the conflict between the British and Kruger.

It is in his description of *Mafeking Night* that Galsworthy drives home the point of what democracy meant to the upper middle classes:[5]

> Soames wandered … one May night into Regent Street and the most amazing crowd he had ever seen; a shrieking, whistling, dancing, jostling, grotesque and formidably jovial crowd, with false noses and mouth-organs, penny whistles and long feathers, every appendage of idiocy, as it seemed to him. Mafeking! Of course, it had been relieved! Good! But was that an excuse? Who were these people, what were they, where had they come from into the West End? His face was tickled, his ears whistled into. Girls cried: "Keep your hair on, stucco!" A youth so knocked off his top-hat that he recovered it with difficulty. Crackers were exploding beneath his nose, between his feet. He was bewildered, exasperated, offended. This stream of people came from every quarter, as if impulse had unlocked floodgates, let flow waters of whose existence he had heard, perhaps, but believed in never. This then, was the populace, the innumerable living negation of gentility and Forsyteism. This was – egad – Democracy! It stank, yelled, was hideous. In the East End, or even Soho, perhaps – but here in Regent Street, in Piccadilly! What were the police about! In 1900, Soames, with his Forsyte thousands, had never seen the cauldron with the lid off; and now looking into it, could hardly believe his scorching eyes. The whole thing was unspeakable! These people had no restraint, they seemed to think him funny, such swarms of them, rude, cross, laughing – and what laughter! Nothing sacred to them! He shouldn't be surprised if they began to break windows … . From the Club windows, his own kind was looking out on them with regulated amusement. They didn't realise! Why, this was serious – might come to anything! The crowd was cheerful, but some day they might come in

> a different mood … . But more than dread, he felt a deep surprise. They were hysterical – it wasn't English! And all about the relief of a little town as big as – Watford, six thousand miles away. Restraint, reserve! Those qualities to him more dear almost than life, those indispensable tributes of property, where were they? … . It was as if he had suddenly caught sight of someone cutting the covenant "for quiet possession" out of his legal documents; or a monster lurking and stalking out in the future, casting its shadow before … . It was like discovering that nine-tenths of the people of England were foreigners. And if that were so – then anything might happen!

Soames and Lord Salisbury felt the same about democracy. Separate power from those who pay the taxes and 'anything might happen'. Soames manages to comfort himself, but such comfort is an illusion. *Mafeking Night* marks the passing of an era.

In *The Threepenny Opera*, Bertolt Brecht used the Second Anglo-Boer War to launch a vehement attack on capitalism and war in general. For Brecht there was little or nothing to choose between war and murder:[6]

> In the consciousness of the average Londoner, no very great role was played by such figures as 'Jack the Ripper' or that unknown murderer popularly called the 'Knife'. Even though they bobbed up now and again, they could not hope, in those uncertain times, to compete for notoriety with the generals conducting the war in the Transvaal; besides, these latter were a menace to incomparably more people than the most active knife hero. But in Limehouse and Whitechapel the fame of the 'Knife' far exceeded that of the generals who were fighting the Boers. The people in the great stone tenements of Whitechapel were excellent judges of the difference between the accomplishments of a fancy general and those of their

> own heroes. To them it was plain that the 'Knife' carried out his crimes at a far greater personal risk than the official picture-book heroes did theirs.

The centenary of the Second Anglo-Boer War has just been celebrated, and the conflict continues to intrigue writers of fiction and history alike. Not only did the war mark the failure of biblical pastoralism to adapt to the modern era, it was a harbinger of 20th-century cynicism and 'romantic' nationalism. More specifically, the war created more conflicts than it resolved. The rise of Afrikaner nationalism, which institutionalised race separation was to a large degree a consequence of misguided British imperialist idealism and greed. Rhodes' messianic ambition to spread what he and many of his contemporaries saw as the God-ordained benefits of British 'civilisation' was no less and no more a factor than the lure of the richest gold fields in the world. Everything was in place for an epic drama: high idealism, untold wealth and two diametrically opposed cultures.

Afrikaner nationalism rose from the ashes of defeat and with it an obsession never to be subjugated again. The tragedy is that Afrikaner nationalists did not learn from their own bitter experience. It is of such strife that history and literature are made, for both are concerned with telling the story of human conflict. As for the 'truth', Pilate posed the question two thousand years ago. Events, times, and dates provide merely the barest of bare bones. Understanding is necessarily speculative and is always shaped by the times and circumstances in which we find ourselves. The historian and novelist simply approach the problem from different points of view. Neither has a monopoly on understanding human motivation. The writings of historians no less than those of novelists are suffused with speculative imagination; that indefinable territory between slippery fact and palpable fiction. As far as the social and literary historian is concerned, what popular novelists lack in imagination they make up in their largely unselfconscious reflection of their times. Therein lies their value as recorders of the generally held attitudes and values of a particular time. They are popular because they reflect widely held views.

The potpourri of cultures, languages, conflicting ideologies, values, religions, competing economic systems, together with the usual human capacity for, on one hand, ambition, self-aggrandisement, and avarice, and on the other, self-sacrifice, and selflessness – to say nothing of the pseudo-philosophies of race superiority that have bedevilled the 20th century – combined in the sub-continent to provide a particularly rich, resource for novelists and historians alike.

Endnotes

1 Padfield 1982: 18.
2 Ibid: 76.
3 Ibid: 77.
4 Op cit.
5 Galsworthy 1967: 216–7.
6 Brecht 1937: 125.

BIBLIOGRAPHY

Primary sources and references

Abbott, J.H.M., *Tommy Cornstalk* (London: Longman, 1902)
— *Plain and Veldt* (London, Methuen, 1903)
Adams, Rev. H.C., *Perils in the Transvaal and Zululand* (London: Griffith, Farren, 1887)
Adcock, Arthur St John, *The Luck of Private Foster* (London: Hodder & Stoughton, 1910)
Allen, Phoebe, *Mafeking Day* (London: London Society for the promotion of Christian knowledge, 1901)
Allison, Thomas J., *Della Dorn* or *Struggles of the Boers* (n.p: J.S. Hyland, 1908)
Ames, Ernest, *The Tremendous Twins* or *How the Boers were Beaten* (London: Grant Richards, 1900)
Anon, *Mr Dooley's Philosophy* (London: Heinemann, 1900)
— *Observations by Mr Dooley* (London: Heinemann, 1903)
— *From the Front: Stories from the Seat of War* (London: Sands, 1900)
Balfour, Andrew, *Cashiered and Other War Tales* (London: Nisbet, 1902)
Bancroft, F., *The Veldt Dwellers* (London: Hutchinson, 1912)
— *Thane Brandon* (London: Hutchinson, 1913)
— *The Brandons* (London: Stanley Paul, 1923)
Beddoes, Captain Willoughby, *Under One Flag* (London: Drane, 1902)
Beith, Janet, *Sand Castle* (New York: Hodder & Stoughton, 1936, 1974)
Belloc, Hilaire, *Mr Clutterbuck's Election* (London: Everleigh Nash, 1908)
Bernstein, Birch, *Tomorrow is Another Day* (Cape Town: Juta, 1951)

Bevan, Tom, *Dick Dale, the Colonial Scout: A Tale of the Transvaal War 1899–1900* (London: S.W. Partridge, 1900)
Black, Stephen, *Love and the Hypen* (Cape Town: Maskew Miller, 1908)
Blackburn, Douglas, *Kruger's Secret Service* (London: John McQueen, 1900)
— *A Burgher Quixote* (Edinburgh: Blackwood, 1903)
Blignaut, A.J., *Dead End Road* ('Magersfontein', 'The Hottentots' God') (Johannesburg: A.D. Donker, 1980)
Blore, Harold, *An Imperial Light Horseman* (London: C. Arthur Pearson, 1900)
Boileau, Ethel (Young) Lady, *The Arches of the Years* (London: Hutchinson, 1930)
Bosman, Herman Charles, *Mafeking Road* ('Mafeking Road', 'The Rooinek') (Cape Town: Human & Rousseau, 1969)
— *Unto Dust* ('Peaches Ripening in the Sun', 'The Traitor's Wife', 'The Affair at Ysterspruit', 'A Boer Rip van Winkel') (Cape Town: Human & Rousseau, 1963)
Brandt, Johanna, *The Petticoat Commando* or *Boer Women in Secret Service* (London: Mills & Boon, 1913)
Brecht, Bertolt, *Threepenny Novel* (New York: Grove, 1937)
Brereton, Captain F.S., *One of the Fighting Scouts: A Tale of Guerrilla Warfare in South Africa* (London: Blackie, 1903)
— *With Rifle and Bayonet: A Story of the Boer War* (London: Blackie, n.d.)
Brooks, Elbridge S., *With Lawton and Roberts* (Boston: Lothrop, Lee & Shepard, 1900)
Bucholz, Johannes, *The Saga of Frank Dover*, trans. from Danish by Eugene Gay-Tifft (New York: Putman, 1938)
Burrage, Edwin Harcourt, *Carbineer and Scout* (London: Blackie, n.d.)
Burrow, S., *Friend or Foe?* (London: Pickering & Inglis, n.d.)
Butler, Maynard, *The Little Afrikander and the Great Queen* (London: Swan Sonnenschein, 1904)
Campion, Sarah, *The Pommy Cow* (London: Peter Davies, 1944)
Carolin, Emily Olivia, *Standerton under Martial Law* (London: Henry J. Drane, 1902)
Carsens, Netta, *Nor Pride, nor Pity* (London: Robert Hale, 1972)

Cary, Joyce, *A Fearful Joy* (London: Michael Joseph, 1949)
— *A Prisoner of Grace* (London: Michael Joseph, 1952)
Cathcart, Vera, *Men for Pieces* (London: John Long, 1927)
Chesterton, G. K., *The Napoleon of Notting Hill* (London: John Lane, 1904)
Chinon, S., *Luck's Way* (London: Henry Walker, 1930)
Cios, *Life in Afrikanderland, as reviewed by an Afrikander: A Story in South Africa Based on Truth* (London: Digby, Long, 1897)
Cloete, Stuart, *The Hill of Doves* (London: Collins, 1942)
— *Rags of Glory* (New York: Collins, 1963)
— *The Soldiers' Peaches and Other African Stories* ('The Soldiers' Peaches') (London: Collins, 1959)
— *The Silver Trumpet* ('Always Light') (London: Collins, 1961)
Collins, Ronin, *The Four-coloured Flag* (London: Jarrolds, 1958)
Cossins, George, *A Boer of To-day: A Story of the Transvaal* (London: Allen, 1900)
Crisp, Robert, *The Outlanders* (St. Albans: Mayflowr Books Ltd., 1904)
Crocker, Mrs B M., *Johanna* (Philadelphia: J.B. Lippincott, 1903)
Dallas, Oswald *Private Smith* (London: Jenkins, 1913)
Dashwood, Winifred, *That Looks on Tempests* (unpublished ms. in the possession of the author)
Denton, Kit, *The Breaker* (Sydney: Angus & Robertson, 1973)
De Wet, Sampie, *Nine Stories* ('Concentration Camp') (Cape Town: Balkema, 1956)
Dixon, J. Qallan, *Genevieve de Brabant* (n.p., 1904)
Dodsworth, F., *Gilbert Logan, V.C.: A Tale of the Boer War* (1899–1900) (London: R.E. King, 1900)
Doyle, C., 'Captain John Adams, Missing' (190? probably an excerpt from *Harper's New Monthly Magazine*)
Drummond, Edna, *The Burning Land* (Cape Town: Parnell, 1979)
Eden, Dorothy, *Siege in the Sun* (London: Hodder & Stoughton, 1967)
Edgar, Josephine, *Time of Dreaming* (London: Collins, 1968)
Emmanuel, Victor Rousseau, *Derwent's Horse* (London: Metheun, 1901)
Faidy, Rene, *The Fight for Independence* (Dublin: Dollard, 1901)

Fenn, George Manville, *A Dash for Diamond City* (London: Ernest Nistor, 1901)

— *Charge! A Story of Briton and Boer* (London: W & R. Chambers, 1900)

— *The Kopje Garrison* (London: W & R Chambers, 1901)

Finnemore, John, *Two Boys in War-time* (London: A & C Black, 1928)

Fitchett, William Henry, *Ithurial's Spear* (London: Charles H Kelly, 1903)

Foden, Giles, *Ladysmith* (London: Faber & Faber, 1999)

Fourie, Pierre Johan, *The Cavaliers: the Story of a Hundred Horsemen* (trans. from Afrikaans, Carlos Pienaar) (Cape Town: Nasionale Boekhandel, 1963)

Galsworthy, John, *In Chancery* (Harmondsworth: Penguin, 1967)

Gibbs, Henry, *The Splendour and the Dust* (London: Jarrolds, 1955)

— *The Winds of Time* (London: Jarrolds, 1956)

— *Thunder at Dawn* (London: Jarrolds, 1957)

— *The Tumult and the Shouting* (London: Jarrolds, 1957)

Glanville, Ernest, *The Dispatch Rider* (London: Metheun, 1900)

— *The Beautiful Rebel* (London: John Long, 1902)

— *The Commandant* (London: Digby, Long, 1902)

Gratus, Jack, *The Redneck Rebel* (London: Corgi, 1980)

Graves, Clothilde Inez Augusta Mary (pseud. Richard Dehan) *The Dop Doctor* (London: Heinemann, 1910)

Gray, Stephen, *Caltrop's Desire* (Cape Town: Philip, 1981)

Grayton, William Murray, *With Boer and Britisher in the Transvaal* (New York: Street & Smith, 1900)

Griffith, George, *Briton or Boer? A Tale of the Fight for Africa* (London: F.V. White, 1897)

Grit and Go, stories told by G.A. Henty and others (including Boothby, Guy 'Whitledge's Revenge', Bryden H.H. 'Hendrick Swanepoel's Promised Land', O'Niel, Francis, R., 'De Wet's First and Worst Repulse') (London: W. & R. Chambers, 1902)

Haggard, Henry Rider, *Jess: A Tale of the Transvaal* (London: Smith Elder, 1887)

Hales A G., Driscoll, *King of Scouts: A Romance of the South African War* (Bristol: J.W. Arrowsmith, 1901)

— *Campfire Sketches* (London: R.A. Everett, 1902)

— *McGlusky, being a Compilation from the Diary of Trooper McWiddy of Remington's Scouts* (London: Anthony Treherne, 1904)
Hallowes, Francis S., *The Wedge of War* (London: Elliot Stock, 1900)
Hansen, Brooks, *The Chess Garden* (Sceptre, 1996)
Harris, Frank, *How to Beat the Boer: A Conversation in Hades* (London: Heinemann, 1900)
Harris, John, *Smiling Willie and the Tiger* (London: Hutchinson, 1974)
Haskins, Caryl Davis, *For the Queen in South Africa* (London: Putnam, 1900)
Hayens, Herbert, *Scouting for Buller* (London: Nelson, 1904)
Hemyng, Samuel Bracebridge, *Jack Harkaway in the Transvaal*, or *Fighting for the Flag* (London: E.J. Brett, 1902)
— *Jack Harkaway's War Scouts among Boer Guerrillas* (London: E.J. Brett, 1902)
Henty G. A., *With Buller in Natal or A Born Leader* (London: Blackie, 1901)
— *With Roberts to Pretoria: A Tale of the South African War* (London: Blackie, 1902)
Holt, Victoria, *Snare of Serpents* (London: Collins, 1990)
Hornung, E.W., *Raffels the Amateur Cracksman* (London: Chatto & Windus, 1972)
Hough, Richard, *Buller's Guns* (London: Widenfield & Nicolson, 1981)
Janson, Gustaf, *Abraham's Sacrifice* (London: Methuen, 1903)
Johnston, Sir Harry, *The Veneerings: A Novel* (London: Chatto & Windus, 1922)
Johnston, William, *The Kopje Farm* (London: Collins, n.d.)
Kelly, Sheilagh, *My Father, My Son* (London: Arrow Books, 1989)
Kipling, Rudyard, *Land and Sea Tales for Scouts and Guides* ('The Way that He Took') (London: Macmillan, 1923)
— *Traffics and Discoveries* ('The Captive', 'A Sahib's War', 'The Comprehension of Private Copper') (London: Macmillan, 1904)
— *Fables for the Staff* ('King Log and King Stork' (24 March 1900), 'The Elephant and the Lark's Nest' (26 March 1900), 'The Persuasive Pom-Pom' (28 March 1900), 'Vain Horses' (29 March

1900), 'Untitled' (30 March 1900), 'Untitled' 31 March 1900) (Bloemfontein: *The Friend*)
Kuhn, Christoffel Hermanus (pseud. Mikro), *The Nightrider* (trans. W. Golightly) (Bloemfontein: Nasionale Boekhandel, 1950)
Lamont, Archibald, *South Africa in Mars* (London: Grant Richards, 1923)
Laycock, Arthur, *Steve, the Outlander: A Romance of South Africa* (London: Digby Long, 1900)
Leipoldt, C. Louis, *Stormwrack* (Cape Town: Philip, 1980)
Le Roux, Etienne, *Magersfontein, O Magersfontein!* (trans. Ninon Roets) (Wynberg: Hutchinson, 1983)
Lowth, Alys, *A Daughter of the Transvaal* (London: Hutchinson, 1899)
Lyall, Edna, *The Hinderers* (London: Longmans, Green, 1902)
MacKenzie, Kenneth, *The Deserter* (London: Eyre & Spottiswoode, 1965)
MacNiel, Duncan, *Halfhyde Goes to War* (London: Weidenfeld & Nicolson, 1986)
— *The Red Daniel* (London: Hodder & Stoughton, 1972)
Marchant, Bessie, *Tommy's Trek* (London: Blackie, 1902)
Manion, S., *The Great Hunger* (Ilfracombe: Arthur H. Stockwell, 1964)
Mason, A.E.W., 'How Barrington returned to Johannesburg', *For Britain's Soldiers*, comp. W. L. Allen (London: Methuen, 1900)
Maydon, Major H C., *The Other Side of the Picture* (unpublished ms., National English Literary Museum and Documentation Centre, Grahamstown)
McKoen, Norman (pseud. Norman Giles), *The Ridge of White Waters* (London: Collins, 1934)
Meade L.T., *A Sister of the Red Cross: A Tale of the South African War* (London: Nelson, 1900)
Meyler, Desiree, *The Gods are Just* (London: Hurst & Blackett, 1973)
Michener, James A., *The Covenant* (London: Secker & Warburg, 1980)
Miles, Alfred Henry, ed. *Fifty-two Stories of Great Britain* (including 'How Buller won the Victoria Cross', Anon., 'One of Jameson's Troopers' Nellie Holderness, 'Christmas on the Kopjes', Robert Overton, 'The Honourable's Honour', Mary Dicken, 'One of the C.I.V.s', Robert Overton) (London: Hutchinson, 1901)

Millin, Sarah Gertrude, *Adam's Rest* (London: Collins, 1922)
Milner, James, *The Epistles of Atkins* (London: Dent, n.d.)
Mitford, Bertram, *Aletta: A Tale of the Boer Invasion* (London: F.V. White: 1900)
Molyneux, J., *Fall in* (London: Hust & Blackett, 1915)
Moor, Charlotte, *Marina de la Rey* (London: Digby, Long, 1903)
Moray, Helga, *Beacon of Gold* (London: Hale, 1980)
Muir, Daphne, *A Virtuous Woman* (London: Chatto & Windus, 1929)
Munnik, G.G., *Major Greville, V.C.: A Tale of the Great Boer War* (Cape Town: Maskew Miller, 1913)
Munro, H. H., *The Novels and Plays of Saki* ('Alice in Pall Mall') (London: John Lane, 1949)
Nash, James Everleigh ed., *The Ladysmith Treasury* (London: Sands, 1900)
Nash, Thirza, *The Geyer Brood* (London: Cassell, 1946)
Nathan, Manfred, *Sarie Marais: A Romance of the Anglo-Boer War* (Johannesburg: Central News Agency, 1938)
Nicole, Christopher, *The Regiment* (London: Century, 1988)
Niemann, August, *The Boer Boy of the Transvaal*, trans. Kate Milner (Philadelphia: Penn, 1900)
Nisbet, Hume, *For Right and England: A Story of the South African War (1899–1900)* (London: F.V. White, 1900)
— *The Empire Makers: A Romance of Adventure and War in South Africa* (London: F.V. White, 1900)
Onions, Oliver, *Whom God Hath Sundered: A Trilogy: In accordance with the Evidence, The Debit Account, The Story of Louie* (London: Seker & Warburg, 1947)
Padfield, Peter, *Gold Chains of Empire* (London: Hutchinson, 1982)
Parker, Gilbert, *The Judgement House* (London: Methuen, 1913)
Pearsall, Ronald, *Tides of War* (London: Joseph, 1978)
Pearson, Diane, *The Marigold Field* (London: Corgi, 1976)
Prance, C.R., *Tante Rebella's Saga* ('Tante Rebella's Saga', 'Between Two Stools', 'A Transvaal Ulysses') (London: Witherby, 1937)
— *Under the Blue Roof* ('Dead Man's Corner') (Bloemfontein: White, 1944)
– *Dead Yesterdays* ('The Lone Grave in the Veld') (Port St Johns: Prance, 1943)

Rice, Michael, 'The Black Cat' in *A Century of Anglo-Boer War Stories* Van der Merwe, Chris and Rice, Michael (Johannesburg: Jonathan Ball, 1999)
Roberts, Marley Charles, *The Fugitives* (New York: McClure, Phillips, 1900)
Rodd, Ralph, *A Fighter in Khaki* (London: John Long, 1900)
Ronan, Barry, *The Passing of the Boer: A Stirring and Sensational Story of the Boer War of 1899* (Port Elizabeth: W.L. Chandler, 1899)
Rooke, Daphne, *Mittee* (London: Gollancz, 1951)
Roodt, A., *Kaapse Rebel* (Johanneburg: Afrikaans Pers, 1945)
Rose, F. Horace, *Haidee* (London: Hodder & Stoughton, 1917)
— *Kruger's Waggon* (London: Duckworth, 1943)
Russell, Fox, *The Boer's Blunder: A Veldt Adventure* (London: Wells, Gardiner, Darton, 1900)
Russell, George Hansby, *On Commando* (London: Hutchinson, 1902)
Sachs, Bernard, *The Utmost Sail* (Johannesburg: Kayor, 1955)
Schreiner, Olive, 'Eighteen-Ninety-Nine' in *A Century of South African Short Stories*, Jean Marquard, ed. (Johannesburg: Donker, 1978)
— *Trooper Peter Halket of Mashonaland* (Johannesburg: Donker, 1974)
Scully, W.C., *The Harrow* (Cape Town: Nasionale Pers, 1921)
Seed, Jenny, *The Red Dust Soldiers* (London: Heinemann, 1972)
— *Place Among the Stones* (Cape Town: Tafelberg, 1987)
Sinclair, Kathleen, (pseud. Brigid Knight) *Walking the Whirlwind* (London: Cassell, 1940)
— *The Sun Climbs Slowly* (London: Cassell, 1942)
— *The Covenant* (London: Cassell, 1944)
— *Southern Cross* (London: Cassell, 1949)
Skelton, Clement Lister, *The Regiment* (New York: Dialpress, 1979)
— *Sweethearts and wives* (London: Granda, 1979)
Skelton, Mrs Gladys (pseud. John Presland) *Dominion* (London: Phillip Allan, 1925)
Smith, Wilbur A., *The Sound of Thunder* (London: Heinemann, 1966)
Stables, Gordon, *On War's Red Tide: A Tale of the Boer War* (London: James Nisbet, 1900)
Steenkamp, Willem, *The Blockhouse* (Pretoria: Folio, 1987)
Stevenson, Nora, *So Much Has Happened* (London: Cape, 1939)

Stratemeyer, Edward, *Between Boer and Briton* (Boston: Lee & Shepard, 1900)
Swinton, Major-General Sir Ernest Dunlop (pseud. Backsight Forethought), *The Defence of Duffer's Drift* (London: William Clowes, 1904)
— *The Green Curve and Other Stories* ('Cuvee Reservee; pr. the Widow's Curse', 'One Night', (Edinburgh: Blackwood, 1916)
— *The Great Tab Dope and Other Stories* (Edinburgh: Blackwood, 1915)
Tessier, Ernest Maurice (pseud. Maurice Dekobra), *Diamond Queen*, trans. Peter J. Sinclair (London: Allen, 1965)
Thompson, E.V., *The Stricken Land* (London: Macmillan, 1986)
Trelawney, George, *In a Cottage Hospital* (London: T. Werner Laurie, n.d.)
Trollope, Joanna, *The Steps of the Sun* (London: Hutchinson, 1983)
Vachell, Horace Annesley, *The Hill: A Romance of Friendship* (London: John Murray, 1905)
Valour and Victory: Stories by Gordon Stables and others (London: John F. Shaw, 1900)
Van Bergen, Susan, *My Country is a Sad Story* (Pretoria: Nebotrust, 1975)
Van Bruggen, J.R.L., *Bittereinders* (Potchefstroom: Huyser, 1935)
Van Straten, Maria, J., *Saam Verbind* (Stellenbosch: Pro-Ecclesia, 1940)
Van der Merwe, Chris and Rice, Michael *A Century of Anglo-Boer War Stories* (Johannesburg: Jonathan Ball, 1999)
Van der Post, Laurens, *In a Province* (Penguin: Harmonsworth, 1984)
Vaughan, Owen, *Old Fireproof: Being the Chaplain's Story* (London: Duckworth, 1906)
Visser, Sannie, *Via Dolorosa* (Johannesburg: Voortrekkerpers, 1942)
Viljoen, General Ben, *Under the Vierkleur: A Romance of a Lost Cause* (Boston: Small, Maynard, 1904)
Walpole, Hugh, *The Duchess of Wrexe* (London: Martin Seeker, 1914)
— *Vanessa* (London: Macmillan, 1933)
Webster, F.A.M., *African Cavalcade* (London: Hutchinson, 1936)
Webster, Paul, *Kruger's Gold* (London: Constable, 1984)

Wells, Herbert George, *The Passionate Friends* (London: Macmillan, 1913)
Whishaw, Fred, *The Three Scouts* (London: Griffith, Farran, Browne & Co. n.d.)
Wilhelm, Peter, *L. M. and Other Stories* ('Homecoming') (Johannesburg: Ravan, 1975)
Wyllarde, Dolf, *The Story of Eden* (London: Heinemann, 1903)
Young, Francis Brett, *Second Mercury Story Book* ('A Message') (London: Longman, 1931)
— *The City of Gold* (London: Heinemann, 1939)

Other literary sources and references

Arnold, Matthew, *The Poems of Matthew Arnold* (London: Oxford University Press, 1913)
Austen, Jane, *Northanger Abbey* (London: Nelson, n.d.)
Blackburn, Douglas, *Prinsloo of Prinsloosdorp* (Edinburgh: Blackwood, 1905)
— *Richard Hartley, Prospector* (Edinburgh: Blackwood, 1905)
Buchan, John, *Prester John* (London: Nelson, 1961)
Bidwell, Maude, *Pen Pictures of the Past* ed Karl Schoeman (Cape Town: Human and Rousseau, 1986)
— *Breath of the Veld* (Cape Town: Juta, 1923)
Cervantes, Miguel de, *Don Quixote*, trans. Peter Motteux (New York: Random House, 1930)
Chapman, Michael, *A Century of South African Poetry* (Johannesburg: Donker, 1981)
Coetzee, J.M., *Dusklands* (Johannesburg: Ravan, 1974)
— *Waiting for the Barbarians* (Johannesburg: Ravan, 1981)
Conrad, Joseph, *Heart of Darkness* (Ed. Robert Kimbrough, New York: 1971 W. W. Northon & Co. Inc.)
Crane, Stephen, *The Red Badge of Courage* (New York: New American Library, 1960)
Davis, Alexander, *Umbandine* (London: Unwin, 1898)
Fischer, Ella, *Die Loutering van Petrus* (published by the author, n.d.)

Fitzpatrick, Sir J. Percy, *Jock of the Bushveld* (London: Longmans, 1954)
Forster, E.M., *A Passage to India* (Harmondsworth: Penguin, 1967)
Gibbon, Percival, *Souls in Bondage* (Edinburgh: Blackwood, 1904)
— *Margaret Harding* (London: Methuen, 1911)
Glanville, Ernest, *The Last Heiress* (London: Chatto & Windus, 1891)
Gordimer, Nadine, *A World of Strangers* (London: Gollancz, 1958)
Grover, M., 'I killed a man at Graspan' *A Century of South African Poetry* (Johannesburg: Michael Chapman, 1981)
Heller, Joseph, *Catch 22* (New York: Reprint Society, 1963)
Hemingway, Ernest, *A Farewell to Arms* (Harmondsworth: Penguin, 1966)
Holm, Anne, *I am David* (Harmondsworth: Penguin, 1969)
Howarth, Anna, *Jan: An Afrikander* (London: Smith, Elder, 1898)
— *Sword and Assegai* (London: Smith, 1899)
Hughes, Thomas, *Tom Brown's School* Days (London: Dent, 1875)
Ibsen, Henrik, *A Doll's House* (London: Dent, 1960)
Kipling, Rudyard, *Rudyard Kipling's Verse* (London: Hodder 1912)
Krige, Uys, *The Dream and the Desert* (London: Collins, 1953)
Meij, Trienie, *Diep Waters* (Johannesburg: Nasionale Pers, 1935)
Melville, Herman, *Billy Budd, Sailor and Other Stories* (Harmondsworth: Penguin, 1976)
Millin, Sarah Gertrude, *God's Stepchildren* (London: Constable, 1924)
Mitford, Bertram, *The King's Assegai* (London: Chatto & Windus, 1894)
— *The White Shield* (London: Cassell, 1895)
— *The Induna's Wife* (London: F.V. White, 1898)
Monsarrat, Nicholas, *The Cruel Sea* (Cadet ed.) (London: Cassell, 1953)
Newbolt, Arthur, *The Book of the Long Trail* (London: Longmans, 1922)
Ouida, *Under Two Flags* (reprint of 1867 ed.) (New York: AMS Press, n.d.)
Paton, Alan, *Towards the Mountain* (Oxford: Oxford University Press, 1981)
— *Cry, the Beloved Country* (Penguin: Hornsworth, 1966)

Pienaar, Talitha C., *'n Merk vir die Eeue* (Bloemfontein: Nasionale Pers, 1939)
Plomer, William, *Turbott Wolfe* (Johannesburg: Donker, 1980)
Reid, Mayne, *The Bush Boys* (London: Routledge, n.d.)
Reitz, F. W., 'Gods of the Jingo' in *A Century of South African Poetry* (Johannesburg: Donker, 1981)
Schreiner, Olive, *The Story of an African Farm* (London: Collins, 1965)
— *Undine* (London: Benn, 1929)
Scully, W.C., *Kafir Stories* (London: Unwin, 1896)
Shakespeare, W., *Henry IV Part I William Shakespeare Complete Works* (London: Odams Press, 1953)
Sherriff, R.C., *Journey's End* (London: Samuel French, 1929)
Smith, Pauline, *The Beadle* (Cape Town: Balkema, 1981)
Steenkamp, E., *Helkampe* (Johannesburg: Voortrekkerpers, 1941)
Tennyson, Alfred Lord, *The Complete Works of Alfred, Lord Tennyson* (London: Macmillan, 1900)
Vonnegut, Kurt, *Slaughterhouse 5* (London: Jonathan Cape, 1970)
Wilde, Oscar, *The Importance of Being Earnest* (Harmondsworth: Penguin, 1963)

Literary criticism

Anderson, Rachel, *The Purple Heart Throbs: The Sub-literature of Love* (London: Hodder & Stoughton, 1974)
Angelo, Michael, *Penny Dreadfuls and Other Victorian Horrors* (London: Jupiter, 1977)
Baker, Ernest A., *History in Fiction: A Guide to the Best Historical Romances, Sagas, Novels and Tales* (London: Routledge, 1904)
Beeton, Ridley, *Olive Schreiner: A Short Guide to Her Writings* (Cape Town: Howard Timmins, 1974)
Benson, Frederick, R., *Writers in Arms: The Literary Impact of the Spanish Civil War* (London: University of London Press, 1968)
Bigland, Eileen, *Marie Corelli: The Woman and the Legend* (London: Harrolds, 1953)
Buchanan-Gould, Vera, *Not Without Honour: The Life and Writings of Olive Schreiner* (London: Hutchinson, 1948)

Cadogan, Mary and Craig, Patricia, *Women and Children First: The Fiction of the Two World Wars* (London: Gollancz, 1978)
Carrington, Charles, *Rudyard Kipling: His Life and Works* (London: Gollamez, 1955)
Clayton, Cherry, 'Feminism and Popular Literature', *Lip from Southern African Women*, Susan Brown, Isobel Hofmeyr, Susan Rosenberg (eds.) (Johannesburg: Ravan, 1983)
Clingman, Stephen, 'History from the Inside: The Novels of Nadine Gordimer' in *Journal of Southern African Studies*, London:, Vol. 7, No. 2 (1981)
Coates, Thomas F.G., and Warren Bell, E.S., *Marie Corelli* (London: Hutchinson, 1903)
Cohen, Morton, *Rudyard Kipling to Rider Haggard* (London: Hutchinson, 1960)
— *Rider Haggard: His Life and Works* (London: Hutchinson, 1960)
Coleridge, Samuel, *Biographia Literaria* (London: J. M. Dent & Co, 1906)
Daiches, David, *A Study of Literature* (London: Deutsch, 1968)
Dalziel, Margaret, *Popular Fiction One Hundred Years Ago* (London: Cohen & West, 1957)
Dickinson, A.T., *American Historical Fiction* (New York: Scarecrow, 1958)
Dickson, V.M., *The Fiction of Herman Charles Bosman: A Critical Examination*, Ph.D. thesis (unpublished), University of Texas at Austen, 1975
Eagleton, Terry, *Marxism and Literary Criticism* (London: Methuen, 1976)
English in Africa, Grahamstown: Vol. 5 No. 1 (March 1978)
— Vol. 6 No. 1 (March 1979)
FAK-Volksbundel vir Suid-Afrika, saamgestel deur Dr Hugo Gutsche, W.J. du P. Erlank, S.H. Eyssen, (Pretoria: De Bussey, 1938)
Feuchwanger, Lion, *The House of Desdamona*, or *The Laurels and Limitations of Historical Fiction* (Detroit: Wayne University Press, 1963)
Fiedler, Leslie, A., *Waiting for the End* (Harmondsworth: Pelican, 1964)

First, Ruth and Scott, Ann, *Olive Schreiner* (New Brunswick: New Jersey: Rutgers University Press, 1990)
Friedman, Marion V., *Olive Schreiner: A Study of Latent Meanings* (Johannesburg: University of the Witwatersrand Press, 1955)
Fussell, Paul, *The Great War and Modern Memory* (London: Oxford University Press, 1975)
Gardner, Susan, 'From Murder to Martyr: The Legend of Breaker Morant' *Critical Arts Monograph*, No. 1 (Johannesburg: July 1981)
Gorman, G.E., *The South African Novel in English since 1950: An Information and Resource Guide* (Boston: G.K. Hall, 1978)
Gould, Gerald, *The English Novel of To-day* (London: John Castle, 1924)
Gray, Stephen, *Southern African Literature: An Introduction* (Cape Town: Philip, 1979)
Green, R.L., (ed) *Rudyard Kipling: The Critical Heritage* (London: Routledge & Kegan Paul, 1971)
Grylls, David, *Guardians and Angels: Parents and Children in Nineteenth Century Literature* (London: Faber & Faber, 1978)
Haining, Peter, *Mystery: An Illustrated History of Crime and Detective Fiction* (London: Souvenir, 1977)
Hammond, Dorothy and Jablow, Alta, *The Africa That Never Was* (New York: Twayne, 1970)
Hewitt, Douglas, *The Approach to Fiction* (London: Longman, 1972)
Hollindale, Peter, *Choosing Books for Children* (London: Paul Elek, 1975)
Howarth, Patrick, *Play Up and Play the Game: The Heroes of Popular Fiction* (London: Eyre Methuen, 1973)
James, Louis, *Fiction for the Working Man* (1830–1850) (Harmondsworth: Penguin, 1974)
Jan, Isabelle, *On Children's Literature* (London: Allen Lane, 1973)
Kennedy, Alan, *Meaning and Signs in Fiction* (London: Macmillan, 1979)
Killam, G.D., *Africa in English Fiction* (1874–1939) (Ibadan: Ibdan University Press, 1968)
Leavis, Q.D., *Fiction and the Reading Public* (London: Chatto & Windus, 1968)

Lindenberger, Herbert, *Historical Drama* (Chicago: University of Chicago Press, 1975)
Linnemann, Russell J., *The British Literary Image of Africa in the Nineteenth and Twentieth Centuries* Ph.D. thesis (unpublished), University of Michigan, 1972
Lodge, David, *Language of Fiction* (New York: Columbia University Press, 1966)
Lubbock, Percy, *The Craft of Fiction* (London: Cape, 1921)
Lukacs, Georg, *The Historical Novel* (Harmondsworth: Penguin, 1962)
Marriot, Sir John, *English History in English Fiction* (London: Blackie, 1944)
Marshall, William H., *The World of the Victorian Novel* (South Brunswick: A.S. Barnes, 1967)
Matthews, Brander, *The Historical Novel* (Freeport: Books for Libraries Press, 1968)
Mendelssohn, Sidney, *South African Bibliography* (London: Holland Press, 1910)
Meyers, Jeffery, *Fiction and the Colonial Experience* (Ipswich: Boydell, 1972)
More, Margaret and Percival, Alicia C., *The Victorian Best-seller: The World of Charlotte M. Yonge* (Port Washington: Kennikat Press, 1970)
McDonald, Jane, *The Boer War in English Fiction* (M.A. dissertation (unpublished) Columbia University, New York, 1940)
Nathan, Manfred, *South African Literature* (Cape Town: Juta, 1925)
Nield, Jonathan, *A Guide to the Best Historical Novels and Tales* (London: Putnam, 1904)
Perspectives on South African Fiction, Sarah Christie, Geoffrey Hutchings, Don Maclennan (Johannesburg: Donker, 1980)
Rabkin, David, 'Ways of Looking: Origins of the Novel in South Africa', *Journal of Commonwealth Literature*, Vol.12 No.1 (Leeds: August 1978)
Rockwell, Joan, *Fact in Fiction* (London: Routledge & Kegan Paul, 1974)
Rutherford, Andrew, *The Literature of War* (London: Macmillan, 1978)

Saintsbury, George, *The Historical Novel* (London: Dent, 1895)
Sands, Raymond, 'The South African Novel in English: Some Observations', *English Studies in Africa*, Vol. 13 No. 1 (Johannesburg: March 1970)
Scholes, Robert, *Structuralism in Literature: An Introduction* (New Haven: Yale University Press, 1978)
Schreiner, S. C. Cronwright (ed) *The Letters of Olive Schreiner* (London: Fisher Unwin, 1924)
Simmons, James C., *The Novelist as Historian* (The Hague: Mouton, 1973)
Snyman, J.P.L., *The South African Novel in English* (1880–1930) (Potchefstroom: Potchefstroom University Press, 1953)
— *The Works of Sarah Gertrude Millin* (Johannesburg: CNA, 1955)
Stemmet F.J., *Gepubliseerde Outobiografiese Bronne oor die Tweede Vryheidsoorlog* (M.A. dissertation (unpublished) University of Potchefstroom, 1972)
Sutherland, John, *Best Sellers: Popular Fiction of the 1970s* (London: Routledge and Keagan Paul, 1981)
Trench, H., *New Poems* (London: Methuem, 1907)
Tucker, Martin, *Africa in Modern Literature* (New York: Unger, 1967)
Van Wyk Smith, M., *Drummer Hodge: The Poetry of the Anglo-Boer War (1899–1902)* (Oxford: Clarendon Press, 1978)
— 'The Origins of Some Victorian Images of Africa', *English in Africa*, Vol. 6 No. 1 (Grahamstown: March 1978)
Warner, Philip, (ed) *The Best of British Pluck: The Boys' Own Paper* (London: Macdonald James, 1976)
Weinstock, Donald J., *The Boer War in the Novel in English* (1884–1966): *A Descriptive and Critical Bibliography*, Ph.D. thesis (unpublished) University of California, Los Angeles, 1969
Wessels, J.H., *From Olive Schreiner to Nadine Gordimer: A Study of the Development of the South African Short Story in English* (M.A. dissertation (unpublished), University of the Orange Free State, n. d.)
Young, Francis Brett, 'South African Literature', *The London Mercury* Vol. 19 No. 113 (March 1929)

Historical background

Baker, Ernest A., *History in Fiction: A Guide to the Best Historical Romances, Sagas, Novels and Tales* (London: Routledge, 1904)

Ballyfrench, Morton, *The Lighter Side of War* (London: Century, 1902)

Bidwell, Maude, 'Sulk or Duty' (pamphlet), *Pen Pictures of the Past*, ed. Karel Schoeman (Cape Town: Human & Rousseau, 1986)

Brady Rev. J.E., *Trekking for Souls* (Cedra Missionary Association of Mary Immaculate, St Joseph's Scholasticate, 1952)

Buchan, John, *Memory Holds the Door* (London: Hodder & Stoughton, 1941)

Cantor, Norman F., and Werthman, Michael S., *The History of Popular Culture since 1815* (New York: Macmillan, 1968)

Carr, E. H., *What is History?* (Harmonsworth: Penguin, 1967)

Chiaromonte, Nicola, *The Paradox of History* (London: Weidenfield & Nicolson, n.d.)

Chisholm, Ruari, *Ladysmith* (Johannesburg: Jonathan Ball, 1979)

Cox, C.B. and Dyson, A.E. (eds.) *The Twentieth Century Mind Vol. 1 (1900–1918)* (London: Oxford University Press, 1974)

Creswicke, Louis, *South Africa and the Transvaal War*, 8 vols. (London: Caxton, 1900–3)

Cullinan, Patrick, *Robert Jacob Gordon 1743–1795* (Cape Town: Struik Winchester, 1992)

Davey, Arthur, *The British Pro-Boers* (1877–1902) (Cape Town: Tafelberg, 1978)

Doyle, A. Conan, *The War in South Africa* (London: Smith, Elder, 1902)

Farwell, Byron, *Queen Victoria's Little Wars* (London: Allen Lane, 1973)

— *The Great Boer War* (London: Allen Lane, 1977)

Fisher, John, *The Afrikaners* (London: Cassell, 1969)

Fitzpatrick, J.P., *The Transvaal from Within* (London: Heinemann, 1899)

Greenwall, Ryno, *Artists and Illustrators of the Anglo-Boer War* (Vlaeberg: Fernwood Press, 1992)

Haggard, Henry Rider, *The Last Boer War* (London: Kegan Paul, 1900)

Harris, W. Cornwallis, *Portraits of the Game and Wild Animals of*

Southern Africa (Cape Town: Balkema, 1969)
Koss, Stephen (ed.), *The Pro-Boers* (Chicago: University of Chicago Press, 1973)
Kruger, Rayne, *Goodbye, Dolly Gray* (London: Mentor, 1967)
Langer, William, L., *The Diplomacy of Imperialism* (1890–1902) (New York: Knopf, 1962)
Lee, Emanel, *To the Bitter End* (London: Guild Publishing, 1985)
Livingstone, David, *Missionary Travels and Researches in South Africa* (London: John Murray, 1857)
Magnus, Philip, *Kitchener: Portrait of an Imperialist* (London: John Murray, 1964)
Marais, Eugene, N., unpublished letter dated 22 February, 1897 (National English Literary Museum and Documentation Centre, Grahamstown)
Meintjies, Johannes, *De la Rey: Lion of the West* (Johannesburg: Keartland, 1966)
— *General Louis Botha* (London: Cassell, 1970)
— *President Kruger* (London: Cassell, 1974)
— *The Anglo-Boer War: A Pictorial History 1899–1902* (Cape Town: Struik, 1976)
Midgely, J.F., *Petticoat in Mafeking: The letters of Ada Cook* (Kommetjie: J.F. Midgely, 1974)
Morris, James, *Pax Britannica* (London: Faber & Faber, 1968)
— *Farewell the Trumpets* (London: Faber & Faber, 1978)
Nathan, Manfred, *Not Heaven Itself* (Durban: Knox, 1944)
Nimcocks, Walter, *Milner's Young Men* (London: Hodder & Stoughton, 1968)
Pakenham, Thomas, *The Boer War* (Johannesburg: Jonathan Ball, 1979)
— *The Scramble for Africa* (Johannesburg: Jonathan Ball, 1991)
Pearsall, Ronald, *The Worm in the Bud* (Harmondsworth: Pelican, 1971)
Plaatjie, Sol T., *The Boer War Diary of Sol T. Plaatjie* (Johannesburg: Macmillan, 1973)
Ralph, Julian, *War's Brighter Side* (London: Pearson, 1901)
— *At Pretoria* (London: Pearson, 1901)
Reckett, B.N., *The Lindley Affair* (Hull: A. Brown, 1972)

Reitz, Deneys, *Commando* (London: Faber & Faber, 1935)
Rhoodie, Denys, *Conspirators in Conflict* (Cape Town: Tafelberg, 1967)
Sandison, Alan, *The Wheel of Empire* (New York: Macmillan, 1967)
Sandys, Celia, *Wanted, Dead or Alive* (London: Harper Collins, 1999)
— *My Early Life* (London: Harper Collins, 1999)
Sassoon, Siegfried, *Memoirs of a Fox-Hunting Man* (London: Faber & Faber, 1924)
Schikkerling, R.W., *Commando Courageous: A Boer's Diary* (Johannesburg: Keartland, 1964)
Schreiner, Olive, *Thoughts on South Africa* (London: Allen & Unwin, 1923)
Spies, S.B., *Methods of Barbarism?* (Cape Town: Human & Rousseau, 1977)
Stead, W.T., 'Shall I Slay My Brother Boer?' Pamphlet (London: *Review of Reviews*, 1897)
Streak, Michael, *The Afrikaner as Viewed by the English (1795–1854)* (Cape Town: Struik, 1974)
Thornton, A.F., *The Imperial Idea and its Enemies* (London: Macmillan, 1959)
Todd, Pamela and Fordham, David (eds.), *Private Tucker's Boer War Diary* (London: Elm Tree, 1980)
Trevelyan, G.M., *English Social History* (London: Longman, 1946)
Tuchman, Barbara, *The Proud Tower* (London: Hamilton, 1966)
Uys, Ian, *Heidelbergers of the Boer War* (Cape Town: Ian Uys, 1981)
Van Onselen, Charles, *Randlords and Rotgut* (1886–1903) (Oxford: History Workshop No.2, 1976)
Warwick, Peter (ed.), *The South African War* (Harlow: Longman, 1980)
Williams, Raymond, *The Long Revolution* (Harmondsworth: Pelican, 1965)
Wilson, Monica and Thompson, Leonard, *The Oxford History of South Africa Vol. 2 (1870–1966)* (Oxford: Clarendon Press, 1971)

INDEX

E

F

G

H

I

J

K

P

R

S

T